JOSÉ MARTÍ

"Not only was Martí one of the most brilliant literary figures in the history of Latin American letters, but also—as the relevance of his observations more than a century later shows—he was one of the most underrated political thinkers of modern times."

John Kirk
José Martí: Mentor of the Cuban Nation

"[Martí] added a social agenda to the historic program of national liberation and instantly converted a movement devoted to the establishment of a new nation into a force dedicated to shaping a new society. Martí transformed rebellion into revolution.... Like a master weaver, Martí pulled together all the separate threads of Cuban discontent—social, economic, political, racial, historical—and wove them into a radical movement of enormous force."

Louis A. Pérez, Jr.
José Martí in the United States: The Florida Experience

"Oh Cuba! ... the blood of Martí was not yours alone; it belonged to an entire race, to an entire continent; it belonged to the powerful youth who have lost probably the best of teachers; he belonged to the future!"

Rubén Darío

"From 1898 to the present day the validity of the admonitory words of Martí has retained its force. The main problems confronting *nuestra América* since the 1880s ... are those foreseen by Martí."

Roberto Fernández Retamar

José Martí READER

A special series published by Ocean Press
40 years of the Cuban Revolution: 1959-99

Series editors:
David Deutschmann and Mirta Muñiz

Cuban Revolution Reader 1959-98
Key documents, writings and speeches
edited by Julio García Luis

Fidel Castro Reader
Volume 1: Speeches
Volume 2: Writings, interviews and letters
edited by Mirta Muñiz and Pedro Alvarez Tabío

Che Guevara Reader
Writings on Guerrilla Strategy, Politics & Revolution
edited by David Deutschmann

José Martí Reader: Writings on the Americas
edited by Deborah Shnookal and Mirta Muñiz

Cuba and the United States: A Chronological History
by Jane Franklin

Psywar on Cuba
The Declassified History of U.S. Anti-Castro Propaganda
by Jon Elliston

A New Society: The Cuba Years 1959-65
A selection of speeches and essays by Che Guevara

José Martí READER

Writings on the Americas

edited by Deborah Shnookal and Mirta Muñiz

OCEAN PRESS
Melbourne • New York

Riverside Community College
Library
APR '99
4800 Magnolia Avenue
Riverside, CA 92506

F 1783 .M38 J68 1999

Jos e Mart i Reader

Cover graphic: Raul Martinez courtesy of Centro de Estudios Martianos

Copyright © 1999 Ocean Press
Copyright © 1999 Editorial José Martí and Centro de Estudios Martianos

All rights reserved. No part of this publication may be reproduced, stored in a retrieval system or transmitted in any form or by any means, electronic, mechanical, photocopying, recording or otherwise, without the prior permission of the publisher.

ISBN 1-875284-12-5

First printed 1999

Printed in Australia

Published by Ocean Press
Australia: GPO Box 3279, Melbourne, Victoria 3001, Australia
• Fax: (61-3) 9372 1765 • E-mail: ocean_press@msn.com.au
USA: PO Box 834, Hoboken, NJ 07030 • Fax: 201-617 0203

Library of Congress Catalog Card No: 98-65908

OCEAN PRESS DISTRIBUTORS
United States: LPC/InBook,
1436 West Randolph St, Chicago, IL 60607, USA
Canada: Marginal Distributors,
277 George St. N., Unit 102, Peterborough, Ontario K9J 3G9
Britain and Europe: Global Book Marketing,
38 King Street, London, WC2E 8JT, UK
Australia and New Zealand: Astam Books,
57-61 John Street, Leichhardt, NSW 2040, Australia
Cuba and Latin America: Ocean Press,
Calle 21 #406, Vedado, Havana, Cuba
Southern Africa: Phambili Agencies,
PO Box 28680, Kensington 2101, Johannesburg, South Africa

Contents

PART 2: LETTERS 193

PART 3: VERSE 239

PART 3: VERSE *continued*

Preface

Why publish a new collection of the writings, letters and verse of José Martí more than 100 years after his death in the Cuban War of Independence?

"Martí was the guide of his time but also stands as the anticipator of ours, " wrote Cuban revolutionary leader Carlos Rafael Rodríguez. Martí was an outstanding teacher, journalist, poet and revolutionary of his time, able to interweave the threads of Latin American culture and history. In his brilliant writings and impassioned speeches, he was able to capture and ignite the spirit of the Americas.

Committed to the task of completing "the poem of 1810"— the independence of Latin America from Spanish rule— Martí also saw a specter haunting the continent: the North American "monster." He feared that the growing economic predominance of the United States would soon lead to political domination. He insisted that "Cuba must be free of the United States, as well as Spain."

"I have lived inside the monster and I know its entrails," Martí wrote to his old friend Manuel Mercado, the day before his death fighting for Cuba's independence in 1895.

A fierce Cuban patriot, Martí also felt himself to be a citizen of all nations, as expressed in the first poem in *Simple Verses* which has become known as the words of Cuba's most popular song: "Guantánamera,"

> I am a traveler to all parts,
> And a newcomer to none.

It could be said that this sense of Cuba's place in the world and its spirit of international solidarity, evident in Martí, has also been a feature of revolutionary Cuba in the 20th century.

The 1959 Cuban revolution took place in a very different world from Martí's, yet Fidel Castro always insisted on the continuity of the Cuban struggle for sovereignty from the first declaration of independence at Yara, October 10, 1868. A reading of Martí sheds much light on the roots and ideology of the Cuban revolution of 1959, as well as the political and moral inspiration guiding Fidel Castro and the other young Cubans who, calling themselves the Centennial Youth, launched the bold attack on the Moncada Barracks on July 26, 1953, the year of the 100th anniversary of Martí's birth. This was no whim or artifice.

In particular, Martí writings make clear that the tumultuous U.S.-Cuba relationship cannot be explained simply as a Cold War construct, but has a much longer and more complex history.

Martí's vision went beyond simply an independent Cuban republic, involving a "fundamental transformation of Cuban society," which meant "a radical restructuring of the economic, social and political spheres, based not on ideology but on a moral transformation of what can be termed the human dimension of *patria* [homeland]."[1] Martí himself observed: "It is a case of changing a nation's soul, their entire way of thinking and acting, and not just their external clothes."

It has been said that the complexity of Martí's thought can mean many things to many people. Yet there are obvious, constant ideas running through all his writings: his egalitarian spirit, his profound belief in the human dignity of all peoples, his sincere rejection of racism, his absolute humility and denial of self, and his deep commitment to "the poor of the earth" with whom he wished to "throw [his] luck."

Above all, Martí's pleas on behalf of the peoples of Latin America, in this age of globalization and new forms of colonization, give his voice a remarkably modern resonance and an obvious relevance to the political and philosophical debates of the late 20th century.

On the 100th anniversary of Martí's death, Fidel Castro summed up the man who has often been referred to as the "Apostle": "Martí was a universal man with extraordinary ideas."

* * * * * *

Martí's complex literary style is difficult to translate satisfactorily into English. As one biographer remarked, "the romantic exhuberance of his prose seems rather heady to readers brought up in a more sober

---

[1] John Kirk, *José Martí: Mentor of the Cuban Nation.*

tradition."[2] The publishers wish to acknowledge the valiant efforts of the team of translators who worked on this project.

The collaboration of both the Centro de Estudios Martianos and Editorial José Martí in Havana was essential to the initiation and completion of this new selection of Martí's writings. Our thanks also to Iván Pérez Carrión, José Amieva Dalboys, Jorge Fernández Paz and Jim Shnookal; to Elinor Randall, Mary Todd and Carmen González Díaz de Villegas for their translations; and Ivan Schulman for his introduction.

Finally, my co-editor Mirta Muñiz must be acknowledged for the considerable amount of work she did in order to bring this project to fruition.

Deborah Shnookal

---

[2] Peter Turton, *José Martí: Architect of Cuba's Freedom.*

Chronology of events in José Martí's life

1853

January 28: José Julián Martí y Pérez is born in Havana. His parents, Mariano Martí and Leonor Pérez, were Spaniards; his father came from Valencia, and his mother, from the Canary Islands.

1865

Martí begins studying at the Havana Municipal Boys School with Rafael María de Mendive, a teacher who greatly influences his sense of patriotism.

1868

October 10: The Ten Years War begins against the Spanish colonial power in Cuba.

1869

January 19: Martí has his first political essay published in the single-edition *El Diablo Cojuelo* (*The Crippled Devil*), followed shortly by his own newspaper *La Patria Libre (Free Homeland)*, which made only one appearance, publishing his dramatic poem "Abdala."

October 21: Martí is arrested and sent to the National Prison, accused of treason. A few days earlier, a group of Spanish Volunteer troops had searched the house of a friend (Fermín Valdés Domínguez) and had found a compromising letter, accusing a former fellow student for "apostasy" for enlisting in the Spanish armed forces. The letter was signed by Martí and Valdés Domínguez, who is subsequently imprisoned for six months.

1870

March 4: Martí is condemned to six years' hard labor and sent to work in a prison quarry.

August–December: His parents manage to get his sentence commuted to exile—which he began on the Isle of Pines—and then obtain permission for him to live in Spain.

1871

February: Martí arrives in Madrid, after spending a few days in Cádiz. He publishes his short work, *El presidio político en Cuba* (*Political Prison in Cuba).*

May 31: He enrolls in several courses at Madrid's Central University.

November 27: Eight medical students in Havana are shot for protesting against Spanish colonial rule. This has a profound effect on Martí's view of Spain and Cuba's struggle for independence. He writes an ode about the event.

1873

February 15: Martí's short essay "La República española ante de la Revolución cubana" ("The Spanish Republic and the Cuban Revolution") is published as a pamphlet in Madrid.

May: He moves to Zaragoza and enrolls in the Literary University while continuing his other studies.

1874

June–October: During this period, Martí obtains a Bachelor of Civil and Canon Law and Doctoral Degree of Philosophy and Humanities with exceptional grades.

December 1874–February 1875: He travels from Spain to Mexico, stopping over in Paris, Le Havre, Liverpool, New York (where he stays 11 days), Havana, Progreso, Campeche and Veracruz.

1875

February: Martí arrives in Mexico City, where he is reunited with his parents and sisters and meets Manuel Mercado.

May: He becomes a member of the editorial staff of the *Revista Universal*, a newspaper on which he has worked since March.

December 19: His short play *Amor con amor se paga* (*Love Must Be Repaid with Love*) has its first performance.

1876

February 20: Martí begins to work on *El Socialista*, organ of the Great Workers' Circle of Mexico (GCOM).

June: The Workers' Hope (EE) society, whose headquarters were in the capital, names him a representative to the first workers' congress ever held in Mexico, although there is no documentation on his participation.

December 29: He leaves Mexico shortly after General Porfirio Díaz takes power through a bloody civil war.

1877

January-April: Martí arrives in Havana clandestinely, then goes on to Progreso and to Guatemala.

April: He begins teaching at the Normal School in Guatemala.

May 29: He is appointed as a professor at the university of French, English, Italian and German literature.

December 20: Martí returns to Mexico City, where he marries Carmen Zayas Bazán. He also publishes his pamphlet *Guatemala* there.

1878

February 10: The Zanjón Pact is signed in Cuba, ending the Ten Years War and allowing exiles to return to the island.

April 6: Martí resigns from the Normal School in protest against the arbitrary removal of its principal José María Izaguirre. This is his last public opposition to the policies of Guatemalan President Justo Rufino Barrios.

July-August: He travels to Honduras and then to Havana.

October: He immerses himself in the conspiracies of the clubs in Havana attached to the Cuban Revolutionary Committee (CRC), which is based in New York.

November 22: His only son, José Francisco, is born.

1879

March 18: The Central Revolutionary Club (CCR) is founded in a meeting of conspirators in Havana, and Martí is elected Vice-President.

June: The Cuban Revolutionary Committee names Martí as its deputy delegate on the island.

August 24-25: The so-called Little War of Independence begins in Santiago de Cuba.

September 17: Martí is arrested and accused (without process of law) of being linked to the insurrectional movement.

September-December: He is deported to Spain, from where he leaves clandestinely for France and then New York.

1880

January 9: A few days after his arrival in New York, the Cuban Revolutionary Committee resolves to make Martí one of its directors.

March 26: He becomes acting Chairman of the Committee when General Calixto García, its Chairman, leaves for Cuba. General García is taken prisoner in August, and the war ends unsuccessfully.

1881

January: Martí travels from New York to Caracas, Venezuela.

February-March: He works as a teacher in the Santa María and Villegas schools.

June: He contributes to *La Opinión Nacional* in Caracas.

July 1: The first issue of *Revista Venezolana* (*Venezuelan Magazine*), which Martí finances and edits, is published. After the second issue of the publication is distributed, General Antonio Guzmán Blanco, President of Venezuela, accuses Martí of interfering in the internal affairs of the country and orders him to leave Venezuela.

August 20: From New York, he writes what is considered to be his first feature article for *La Opinión Nacional*.

1882

April: Martí's book of poems *Ismaelillo,* written in Caracas, is published in New York.

July 15: He writes his first feature article for *La Nación* of Buenos Aires.

July 20: Martí asks Generals Máximo Gómez and Antonio Maceo to help organize the pro-independence forces and oppose those who seek Cuba's annexation to the United States.

1883

March: Martí begins to work on *La América* magazine. The following year, he becomes its editor.

1884

October 10: Martí's first public speech in New York commemorating the beginning of Cuba's first War of Independence in 1868.

October 20: Martí writes to General Máximo Gómez explaining that he is withdrawing his support for the revolutionary activities of Generals Gómez and Maceo— whom he had joined as soon as they reached New York— because he is concerned that they are putting personal aims ahead of the interests of the movement.

1885

His novel *Amistad funesta* (*Ill-Fated Friendship*) is published (as Adelaida Ral) as a serial in *El Latino Americano* of New York.

1886

May 15: Martí sends in his first feature article to *El Partido Liberal* of Mexico.

1887

April 16: Martí is appointed Uruguay's Consul in New York.

October 10: He gives a speech to pro-independence emigrés, one of many on this anniversary of the "Cry of Yara" in 1868.

November 30: He is elected Chairman of the Executive Committee that was set up to organize revolutionary activities by emigrés and Cubans on the island. (Five months later, he acknowledges that no significant advances had been made.)

1889

March 25: The daily New York *Evening Post* publishes Martí's "Vindication of Cuba," a letter replying to two anti-Cuban articles that had appeared in the U.S. press. He includes both of those articles and his reply in a pamphlet, *Cuba y los Estados Unidos* (*Cuba and the United States*), which he translated and for which he wrote the introduction.

July: The first issue of *La Edad de Oro* (*The Golden Age*), a magazine for children of the Americas, appears. In the following months, he put out three more issues.

September 28: He writes his first feature article about the Pan American Congress, which is to begin in Washington on October 2. He warns of the expansionist designs of the United States in Latin America— a theme he develops in his address to the Latin American literary society ("Mother America") in December.

1890

January: Along with Rafael Serra, Martí founds *La Liga* (The League) in New York for the education and advancement of black Cuban workers in that city.

July 24: Martí is named Consul of the Argentine Republic in New York. A week later, he also becomes Paraguay's Consul.

1891

January 1: Martí publishes his important essay "Nuestra América" ("Our America") in *La Revista Ilustrada* of New York.

February–April: As Uruguay's delegate, Martí attends the sessions of the American International Monetary Commission and actively defends the rights of Latin America.

October 11: He resigns as the Consul of the Republics of Argentina, Uruguay and Paraguay.

October: His *Versos sencillos* (*Simple Verses*) is published.

November 26 and 27: Martí travels to Florida and gives important speeches at meetings of Cuban exiles. He joins the Patriotic Cuban League.

November 28: In the farewell that the exiles in Tampa give him, the resolutions drafted by Martí, which seek to unify the Cubans revolutionary movement, are approved.

1892

January 5: The Cuban Revolutionary Party is formed with aims and statutes which Martí had written and discussed with the leaders of the main organizations in Key West.

March 14: The first issue of *Patria*, which Martí financed and edited, appears. As the voice of the Cuban Revolutionary Party, its goal is to promote the cause of Cuban independence.

April 8: Martí is elected a delegate of the Cuban Revolutionary Party. He is reelected in each of the next three years.

April 10: The Cuban Revolutionary Party is proclaimed in Key West, Tampa and New York.

July 3: Martí begins the first of many trips to places where the Cuban emigrés live, doing intensive organizational work.

September 11: In La Reforma, Santo Domingo, Martí meets with General Máximo Gómez, who will be commander-in-chief of the war for independence.

1893

May: Martí clarifies the Cuban Revolutionary Party's position on the armed uprising in Cuba, which the Party had not ordered.

July: He meets General Antonio Maceo in Costa Rica after having conferred with Gómez in Montecristi, Santo Domingo, some days earlier.

1894

April 8: Martí meets with Gómez in New York.

June: He visits Costa Rica and exchanges views with Generals Antonio and José Maceo concerning war preparations.

July-August: He goes to Mexico seeking political and financial support.

December 8: Martí writes and cosigns— with Commander Enrique Collazo, representative of the conspirators on the island, and Colonel José María Rodríguez, on behalf of General Gómez— the *Fernandina* Plan for an uprising, which he sends to Cuba.

1895

January: A traitor alerts U.S. authorities, who seize both the ships that were to have taken the expeditionaries to Cuba and their supplies and equipment, thus frustrating the *Fernandina* Plan.

January 29: From New York Martí sends the order for the uprising to the island.

February 7: He arrives in Montecristi, Santo Domingo, where he meets with General Gómez.

February 24: Cuba's War of Independence begins.

March 25: Martí and Gómez sign the Manifesto of Montecristi.

April 9: Martí and a small group of revolutionaries set out by boat for Cuba.

April 11: After many vicissitudes, Martí manages to land at Playita, in the eastern part of the island, together with Generals Máximo Gómez and Francisco Borrero, Colonel Angel Guerra, César Salas and Marcos del Rosario.

April 15: General Gómez informs Martí that the Chiefs of Staff have resolved to recognize him as Cuban Revolutionary Party Delegate and to give him the rank of Major-General in the Liberation Army.

May 2: Martí writes a manifesto in the form of a letter to the editor of the *New York Herald*, which he and Gómez sign.

May 18: He writes his last letter (to Manuel Mercado) which he never completes.

May 19: Martí is fatally wounded in his first armed combat against enemy troops at Dos Ríos, Oriente Province.

Introduction

José Martí (1853–1895) was a revolutionary writer in every sense of the word. Born of Spanish parents in colonial Cuba, he witnessed the oppressive measures imposed on the island by the Spanish colonial administration. Early in his life he made the decision to fight for the liberation of his country and similarly oppressed Antillean peoples. But Martí was not merely a political revolutionary: he was a revolutionary in literature who gave expression to the emerging ideas and emotions of a modernizing world in a language and style that perplexed and fascinated many of his contemporaries. Manuel Gutiérrez Nájera (1859–1895), for example, wrote of the Cuban that at times he could not follow his ideas, "because his ideas have sturdy wings, strong lungs, and rise inordinately ... [in his] magical style we lose ourselves from time to time, like Reynaldo in the garden of Armida..."

Martí's conscious resolve to devote himself to revolutionary political and literary ideals became clear shortly after the first Cuban war against Spain (1868). During this period he participated in the publication of clandestine newspapers and circulars, including *El Diablo Cojuelo (The Crippled Devil)*, and later, *La Patria Libre (Free Homeland)*. In the latter, in 1869, he published a dramatic poem, "Abdala," in which the main character sacrifices his life to defend his country against its oppressors. For a while the colonial regime took no action against Martí; but in 1869, when he and a friend, Fermín Valdés Domínguez, signed a letter questioning the political behavior of one of their classmates, Martí was accused of treason against the Spanish colonial regime. He was tried and condemned to six years' hard labor in the quarries of San Lázaro in Havana.

The San Lázaro experience is recorded in a political essay "Political Prison in Cuba," published in 1871, that is both moving and revealing: moving, because it records an adolescent's reaction to the harsh, sometimes nightmarish conditions of a forced labor camp; revealing, because it foreshadows the expressive force of a mature writer. "Political Prison in Cuba" is directed to the Spanish authorities; it is a plea for humanity and reform in the administration of the island. It is also a milestone in the evolution of the prose in a period of metamorphic change called *Modernismo* in Latin American literature and culture. "Political Prison in Cuba" was followed by a companion piece entitled "The Spanish Republic and the Cuban Revolution," written in Spain in 1873, where the young Martí was exiled following the commutation of his sentence.

Martí's Spanish exile marks the initiation of a lengthy period of peregrination: Spain, Mexico, Venezuela, and, finally, the United States, a productive period during which he wrote, spoke to Cuban and Hispanic revolutionary and cultural societies, and organized the invasion of colonial Cuba in 1895.

Spain is where Martí received his formal education: at the universities of Zaragoza and Madrid he earned degrees in philosophy and law. Late in 1874 he left Spain for Mexico, with a brief stay in France. After Europe, Martí found Mexico to be a hospitable environment. He participated widely in the country's cultural life, wrote for the *Revista Universal*, helped found the Sociedad Alarcón, debated the merits of spiritualism and materialism in a national forum, wrote a play entitled *Amor con amor se paga (Love is Repaid with Love)*, which premiered in 1875. It was in Mexico where Martí met Carmen Zayas Bazán, who was to become his wife and, subsequently, the symbol of a painful, frustrated domestic life. The rise of the dictator, Porfirio Díaz, signaled the end of Martí's Mexican residence and the renewal of his wanderings in search of a place where he could work with personal freedom. He returned briefly to Cuba, responding to the pull of family and a desire to resettle in his homeland.

Guatemala was Martí's next resting place. His stay there also proved to be brief. He was appointed to the faculty of the Escuela Central de Guatemala where he taught French, English, German and Italian literature as well as the History of Philosophy. For a while life seemed prosperous and serene; he married Carmen

Zayas Bazán, contributed to Guatemala's developing cultural life, and wrote of his gratitude to Guatemala in a slender volume entitled *Guatemala* (1878). A shift in political factions made life there untenable for him. Once again Havana drew him; but while working in the Havana law offices of Miguel Viondi, his revolutionary activities resulted in his second deportation to Spain in 1879.

Instead of staying there, he left almost immediately for France, and then to the United States. While in New York, he met Charles A. Dana who invited him to write for the *New York Sun*; but New York was not to become Martí's home until he attempted life in Venezuela. In 1881 he went to Caracas with the hope of finding refuge and solace in "Our America," as he called the Hispanic countries of the New World. Things went well in Venezuela, but again, for an extremely short period. Nevertheless, in that time he succeeded in founding an important Modernist magazine, the *Revista Venezolana*. In its second issue of July 15, 1881, he defended his magazine's style, and in the course of this defense, developed one of Modernism's early manifestos:

> Some of the "simple" pieces that appeared in our last issue have been tagged and polished exquisite. What follows is not a defense, but a clarification. Private speech is one thing; passionate, public discourse, another. Bitter polemics speak one language; quite another, serene biography .... Thus, the same man will speak in a different language when he turns his searching eyes to past epochs, and, when with the anguish and ire of a soldier in battle, he wields a new arm in the angry struggle of the present age .... The sky of Egypt ought not be painted with London fogs, nor the youthful verdure of our valleys with the pale green of Arcadia, or the mournful green of Erin. A sentence has its adornments, like a dress, and some dress in wool, some in silk, and some become angry because their dress is wool and are displeased to see another's is silk. Since when has it become a defect to write in polished form? .... It is essential that notice be taken of the following truth about style: writers should paint just

as the painter does. There is no reason for one to use different colors from the other.

When Martí left Venezuela for New York, he renewed his writing for the *Sun*. New York was to be Martí's permanent home until he returned to Cuba, just prior to his untimely death fighting for Cuba's liberation on May 19, 1895. In New York, which both attracted and repelled Martí, he wrote his best prose and poetry. Amidst the din and clatter of an industrializing society, plagued by labor strikes, anarchist terrorist attacks, racial and religious conflicts, Martí peered into the fortune of a capitalist society, and from this vantage point drew conclusions he described in his prose pieces about life in the United States written for Latin America's major newspaper, *La Nación* (Buenos Aires). His association during 1883 with this newspaper was followed by invitations from others, among them, *La República* (Honduras), *La Opinión Pública* (Uruguay), and *El Partido Liberal* (Mexico).

To earn enough for survival, this extraordinary writer became a versatile professional: a translator for Appleton, a clerk for Lyon and Company, a consul for Uruguay (1887) and Argentina (1890). Writing and political organization took up the rest of his energy and time. Martí immersed himself in the careful planning of the Cuban revolutionary process. He organized patriotic clubs not merely in the New York area, but all along the Eastern seaboard, especially in Florida among the tobacco workers of Tampa and Key West. Addressing these working class groups he displayed a passion and fervor that transfixed his audiences. Unfortunately, many of these speeches have been lost. A few that have survived, such as "Los pinos nuevos" ("The New Pines") show the hand of a writer of learning, passion, rhythmic prose and an accomplished political tactician who skillfully swayed his audience.

With the generals of the revolutionary forces, Máximo Gómez and Antonio Maceo, Martí organized and monitored the emigré groups. In 1884 he had a falling out with the generals, especially Gómez; but later he worked with them again to raise the funds and provide the organization and arms for the 1895 invasion of Cuba. Martí's was a Herculean task, superior to his dwindling physical strength, vitiated years before by lesions and diseases contracted in the quarries of San Lázaro. Yet such was his determination to see the liberation of his homeland, that will and desire sustained a calendar of activities which would have sent more robust souls to an early grave.

Patriotism and martyrdom in the cause of Cuba and Puerto Rico consumed his being. Writing and his faith in the revolution kept him alive. To be sure, there were frequent moments of despair. His experiences with human cruelty were such that at one point he wrote: "It is with horror that one looks within many intelligent and attractive men. One leaves in fight, as from a lion's den (30:106)." This modern Machiavellian analyst wrote: "Men like to be guided by those who abound in their own shortcomings (30:18)." Cognizant of human foibles, but committed to social redemption, he noted: "Man is ugly, but humanity is beautiful." Martí's was an 18th century faith in the perfectability of humankind, in social progress and in the feasibility of socio-economic reform. Like the thinkers of the Enlightenment, he needed to be persuaded of the inevitability of violent change, which he espoused only when all other viable channels were exhausted.

Martí found temporary release from anguish in poetic creation. Poetry had a double interface for him: "To create beautiful poetry one has only to turn one's eyes outward: to Nature; and inward: to the soul (19:76)." Nature was an enchantress, who consoled, fortified and soothed. By contrast, internal suffering purified inspirations and provided release from the oppressive realities of everyday existence. Pain, said Martí, "matures poetry.... Man needs to suffer. When he lacks real pain, he creates it. Pain purifies and prepares (27:217)." Convinced that suffering engenders art, the poet poured his personal anguish into his verses.

Martí wrote three major books of poetry: *Ismaelillo* (1882), *Versos sencillos* (*Simple Verses*, 1891), and *Versos libres* (*Free Verse*, 1913). A fourth volume, entitled *Flores del destierro* (*Flowers of*

Exile, 1933), somewhat loosely organized by Gonzalo de Quesada y Miranda, and some other poems have been traditionally included in other volumes. *Ismaelillo* and *Simple Verses* were published in New York during the poet's lifetime; he read the proof for both works. *Free Verse* was first published posthumously, transcribed inaccurately from complex manuscripts and corrected by the present writer.

All of the volumes have one element in common: one which Karl Vossler described as the characteristic of all poets of intense fantasy: a capacity for liberating themselves from the norms of the linguistic community; by passing under or over words, such poets create works by means of notes, melodies, rhythms, images, gestures and dances. This is the case with Martí and that of other Modernist poets of his generation: they were subjective creators, attentive to internal flux. In this connection, Fina García Marruz finds syllabic groupings of suffering in *Free Verse*, and Cintio Vitier senses the voice of a poet of light and movements, who creates a baroque, obscure, foaming, volcanic, abrupt and strange world. Martí's is a highly original verse, in which there is both innovation and tradition, a paradoxical admixture common to the poets of the Age of Modernity, intent upon recasting the past to express an unstable present.

Of Martí's three principal poetic works, *Ismaelillo* is a free, luminous volume, written largely in Caracas, and published in New York. Its imagery is so singular that the poet felt compelled to comment on its oneiric quality in a letter to Diego Jugo Ramírez on May 23, 1882:

> I've seen those wings, those jackals, those empty goblets, those armies. My mind was the stage, and on it all those visions were actors. My work, Jugo, consisted of copying. There isn't one single mental line there. And, how should I be responsible for the images which come to me without calling them? I have done nothing more than put my visions into verse.

The volume is dedicated to the poet's absent son. The poet occupies the center of a visionary space in which the perils of modern life assault the poet/narrator. "Alarmed by everything, I take refuge in you," he writes to his son in the brief introduction. The absent son is ever-present in verses whose levels of reality and dreams reach beyond the limits of 19th century positivism and reason. "I dream with open eyes," reads the first line of "Sueño despierto" ("I Dream Awake"). The visionary quality is sometimes surrealistic: "And on the backs/Of giant birds/Endless kisses/Awaken/." Though a process of inversion, a metamorphosis is effected by filial love; the father conjures up the vision of the son, and in this vision is reborn through the son: "I am the son of my son!/He remakes me!" This identification of father and son orchestrates and unifies the metaphoric eruptions of a volume, which, at bottom, is a musical concert centering around three motifs, filled with chaotic, tender and troubled leaps to a loosely associated poetic space. *Ismaelillo*'s motifs are the poet, the son, the world; the leaps are executed in the form of voyages in which traditional time and space concepts are unhinged so that the poet–son can move freely outside the limitations of a traditional Logos. In "Musa traviesa" ("Mischievous Muse") he writes: "Often, a rider/In momentous dreams,/I ride long hours,/Through the air./I pierce rosy clouds/I fathom deep seas,/And in the eternal bowels/I travel."

In these travels the poet/son/seer comes upon battles, visions of martyrdom, caves, dances, erotic scenes, heights of idealism and depths of materialism; it is a confusing world the narrator captures: reflecting the frightening realities of modern life. We witness torments, confused scenes, temptations, moments of disarray, and spirited battle. It is a spectacle of "splendid transformations" that boils, creaks, bites and assaults the agonists of modern life. In keeping with these decentered, fragmented visions, the son is Ismael, Jacob, the object of pleasure, love, tenderness, the heart, the soul of the father and, finally, not merely his reflection but his very being. Thus, this volume, more than the lyric prayer book Rubén Darío found it to be, more than the "Art of Being a Father" which the latter saw in it, is rather a *voyage* that incarnates a modern mythic sense of experience and existence.

Equally personal, and equally anguished are the poems of *Free Verse*. Darío said of them that they were free verse, produced by a free man. Martí called them "my irritated Free Verses," "my rough hendecasyllables, borne of great fears, or of great hopes, or of an unbridled love of liberty, or of a painful love of liberty... ." In his preface, Martí insisted, once again, as in his *Ismaelillo*, upon the visionary quality of his verses, visions that he "copied" and for whose strangeness, singularity and passion he alone was accountable. These are verses written, "not in academic ink, but rather in my own blood," an image used by the poet to refer to their personal quality as well as the aura of sacrifice and martyrdom that pervades so many of the poems. Their key words are *love*, *liberty*, *unconquered*, *passionate*, *natural*, *vigorous*. To this linguistic base, José Olivio Jiménez adds another that centers around the terms *circumstance*, *nature*, *transcendence*, and three concepts: *love*, *suffering*, *duty*. The originality of these poems consists in their anguish. It is a poetry of existence in which the poet/narrator confronts the imperative to transmit an authentic, sincere, necessary reality. "What matters in poetry," he wrote, "is to feel, regardless of whether it resembles what others have felt; and what is felt anew, is new (12:222)."

Images of nature, often traditional in origin, appear in this volume as in others by the Cuban, but it is man, not nature, that occupies the center of his poetic discourse. It is a poetry that speaks of daily cares, experiences, existences; it radiates in circular patterns, reaching toward the upper spheres, that is, toward a quality of transcendence noted by Jiménez, and which in spatial form points to the fundamentally realistic; it is based upon specific, concrete circumstances: those of his life, and of the emotions of his existence. Unamuno called Martí's words "acts"; but when the Cuban poet harnessed his words to his thoughts he created novel structures which even today surprise us by dint of their modernity.

The visionary quality of his first volume persists in *Free Verse*; present also are the dualities of experience, the antithetical images that constitute Martí's assumption of the contradictions of modern life and the aspirations of perfection and idealistic placement of his visionary poetics. The dualities sometimes represent a world truncated, or the poet's simple vision of life: "I have lived: I have died." The poet, in his anguish wishes to sacrifice himself to his fellow man, for that is his mission in life. At times, he feels useless, unable to realize the martyrdom that will release him from his terrestrial struggle and allow him, finally, to seek an undefined solace in a vaguely expressed afterlife.

Less anguished, at least at first glance, are the poems of *Simple Verses*. Their apparent serenity is linked to their traditional, popular metrics, and to the poet's insistence upon more direct and unencumbered forms of expression in comparison with the volcanic "eruptions" of the previous volumes. In this volume there is an emphasis upon the harmony of life and philosophy, or at least upon a system of transformation from crass, material forms to noble, ideal objects. And this search for and belief in idealism and harmony lends the volume a placid quality which has disquieting moments, for the *Simple Verses* are poems born of pain and anguish: "My friends know how these verses were born in my heart. It was in that winter of anguish, in which out of ignorance, or due to fanatic faith, or fear, or courtesy, that the Spanish American republics met in Washington, in the shadow of the dreaded eagle," wrote Martí in the introduction. Martí represented Uruguay at the International Monetary Conference in Washington, D.C., called by the United States to standardize currency in Latin America. Martí lead the opposition of the Latin American countries to the plans of the United States to impose a silver standard.

Elsewhere, the poet explained that "To suffer is a duty. With what does one write well in prose or verse, but with blood?" The poet's anguish is personalized. The verses speak of his individual view of the world, as the poet/seer turns his eyes upon the universe internalized, and describes its external and internal structures. The poet has assumed the universe, and from a symbiotic stance he offers new insights into its meaning. Martí's experience is broad: it includes the divine spirit, the terrestrial clamor of voices, envy, hate, human ugliness, materialism, idealism, the metamorphosis of reality. The nature of writing poetry is also present here as in previous volumes. But, unlike these, experience is expressed from the viewpoint of a compendium, seen, to be sure, from the interior world ("I know," "I've seen," "I hear," "I am,") of the creator in search of harmony:

> All is beautiful and constant,
> All is melody and reason,
> And all, like a diamond,
> Is dark before light.

In *Simple Verses* one finds the most frequently cited Martí verses: IX is devoted to "La niña de Guatemala" ("The Girl From Guatemala"), and X to "La bailarina española" ("The Spanish Dancer"). Other sections may be less musical and more anguished, but all point to the future in modern poetry. In VIII and XI the poet carries on a dialogue with his doubles: a page/skeleton; a dead friend. In the end, in XLVI a conversation is established between the poet and his verse in which he declares, "Verse, as one our fates are sealed:/We are damned or saved together!"

Both Martí and his poetry have survived; but not merely Martí the poet. Martí is one of Spanish America's most original prose writers. "Verses," he said, "can be improvised, but not prose; prose style comes with maturity (22:84)." His early prose works, mentioned above, were followed by a voluminous opus of imaginative, rhythmic, chromatic pieces that found their way into the cultural and literary life of his period through a network of contemporary artists and the columns of the most prestigious newspapers of both North and South America. It is perhaps as a *cronista*, a chronicler of contemporary events—political, social and literary—that Martí is best known. He read accounts of current events voraciously. Such was his imagination that he was capable of creating visions of them as they occurred, even when he was not a witness to them.

His 1889 account of the opening of the Oklahoma frontier, for example, appears to have been written by a journalist astride a horse, who observed the excitement and violence of the events.

His moving account of the 1886 earthquake in Charleston, South Carolina, contained the shrill cries and the emotional despair, the fervent, frightened prayers of the residents, as if the chronicler himself had experienced the tragedy. Martí wrote with vision, compassion, uncanny perception and a highly developed concept of innovative style on subjects as diverse as European monarchs, American anarchists, New York elevated railways, urban tenements, violent crimes, St. Valentine's Day, Buffalo Bill, the Cody Brothers, Walt Whitman, Ralph Waldo Emerson, American technology and agricultural and floral exhibitions. On all of these, and others too numerous to mention, Martí informed his Latin American readers. He was especially careful to show them the advantages as well as the dangers of life in a modernizing, capitalist society such as the United States, hoping to interest his fellow men in technical innovations while avoiding the social, racial, and political strife he observed in New York. For his American readers of the *New York Sun* he wrote mainly of life in Europe, signing with a pseudonym, M. de S.

Another of Martí's major undertakings while in New York was *La Edad de Oro: Publicación mensual de recreo e instrucción dedicada a los niños de América* (*The Golden Age: A Monthly Magazine of Instruction Dedicated to the Children of Spanish America*). He contributed his own writing to the magazine as well as selecting artists for translations. *La Edad de Oro* became a milestone in Spanish children's literature.

Freedom from Spanish rule for his native Cuba, the liberation of Puerto Rico, and economie and political independence for the Antilles and Latin America, were constantly on Martí's mind. In essays, speeches and poems, this liberating discourse— a hallmark of Modernism— is a recurring mark. Though he suffered physically and emotionally at the hands of the Spanish colonial authorities in Cuba, Martí never expressed a sense of animosity toward Spain. Instead, he espoused a doctrine of love and brotherhood; he hoped that the war with Spain, if unavoidable, would be brief and swift. In his writings on Cuba he argued for political unity, economic modernization (without the pitfalls of U.S. capitalism), respect for human rights, and a broad, democratic, participatory social compact. When it was clear there was no other road but revolution to achieve Cuba's freedom from colonial rule, he organized a political party among exiled Cubans residing in the United States—the Cuban Revolutionary Party—and almost single-handedly planned the 1895 invasion of Cuba. As a political strategist his sights were set on achieving independence for his native island, hence, like so many other Latin American essayists, his political writings are fundamentally instrumental or programmatic. His grasp of the present and future social and economic institutions was stunning, so much so, that critics such as Cintio Vitier perceive in his essays on Cuba a futurity that guided not merely Martí's generation, but generations of writers and thinkers since. Martí wrote no single, organic political treatise on Cuba. However, he left a rich legacy of conceptualizations—perceptive and "necessary"—in separate, substantive essays such as "Con todos y para el bien de todos" ("With All and For the Good of All"), "El Partido Revolucionario Cubano" ("The Cuban Political Party"), or "El manifiesto de Montecristi" ("The Montecristi Manifesto").

Less known, and less studied, are Martí's letters. His epistolary art fascinated Unamuno and continues to attract devoted readers. Next to his poetry, the medium in which Martí expressed his most intimate thoughts are his letters, especially those to his closest friends and confidants. The letters to his friend Manuel A. Mercado, to María Mantilla, to his mother, are filled with the tenderness and anguish of *Free Verse*. In his letters Martí dared to bare his soul and allowed the solitude and suffering of a mission-driven artist and revolutionary to surface. The prose of these epistolary pieces, baroque at times, at others, limpid; sometimes convoluted, sometimes succinct; at others is telegraphic. He once complained: "Words I cannot." The reader at such moments is placed in the role of having to add, interpret, complete.

One other prose genre merits special comment: the novel, a single narrative written by Martí without great enthusiasm as a favor to a friend. She had accepted to write the work for a New York magazine but could not. Under the pseudonym of Adelaida Ral, the Cuban agreed to compose a novel in her place in seven days; its format followed the prescriptions laid down by the editor: lots of love, a death, many young girls, no sinful passions, and nothing that might offend fathers of families or priests. And, it had to have a Spanish American setting. The narrative was not Martí's favorite genre because, as he put it, one had to feign the existence of people, scenes and dialogues.

In this narrative, in his other prose pieces, his poetry, letters, and in his journals, Martí understood that man stood at the crossroads of an entirely new world order, the Age of Modernity. He understood its metamorphic qualities, he often felt anguished about their influence over man, the socioeconomic progress of Latin America, the liberation of Cuba and Puerto Rico, always uppermost in his mind. He saw and understood the falling away of traditional institutions—religious, social and economic—and the accompanying cultural and ideological void. This visionary writer was thus able to write as early as 1882: "There are no permanent works, because those which are the product of reframing and recasting are by their very essence mutable and restless; there are no constant roads; the new altars, great and open as the woods, are barely visible (20:51)." Though they were invisible to most people, Martí was able to see and foresee, to write and speak the signs of both his age and the future, scanning the past and linking its universal values to an unstable chaotic present.

Ivan A. Schulman

PART 1

Writings

Political Prison in Cuba

At the age of 16, José Martí was arrested and charged with treason on the basis of a letter signed by him and his friend Fermin Valdés Domínguez, accusing a fellow student of selling out to Spain. After serving several months of his sentence of six years' hard labor, Martí was deported to Spain in January 1871. Soon after his arrival in Madrid, Martí published the pamphlet Political Prison in Cuba, *excerpted here.*

I

These pages should be known by no other name but infinite pain.

Infinite pain, for the pain of prison is the harshest, the most devastating of afflictions, that which kills the intelligence and withers the soul, leaving effects that will never be erased.

It begins with a length of iron chain; it drags with it this mysterious world that troubles the heart; it grows, nourished upon every somber sorrow, and finally wanders about magnified by every scalding tear.

Dante was never in prison.

If he had felt the dark cavern of that living torture topple upon his head, he would have stopped depicting his inferno. He would have set down those experiences and thus created a better description.

If a provident God had existed and he had seen him, he would have covered his face with one hand and with the other tossed such a denial of God into the abyss.

Yet God does exist in the idea of good, which watches over the birth of every being and leaves in the soul embodied in that being one pure tear. Good is God, and the tear the source of eternal feeling.

God does exist, and I come in his name to break in Spanish hearts the cold and indifferent glass that contains their tears.

God does exist, and if you people make me move away from here without having torn out of you your cowardly, unfortunate indifference, let me despise you, since I am unable to hate anyone; let me pity you in the name of my God.

I will not hate you, nor will I curse you.

If I were to hate anyone, I would hate myself for so doing.

If my God were to curse, I would deny him for so doing.

IV

You who have never had a thought of justice in your heads, or a word of truth upon your lips for the most grievously sacrificed, most cruelly crushed race upon this earth.

You who have sacrificed some people upon the altar of enticing words, and have gladly listened to others, to the most elemental principles of righteousness, to the commonest notions of feeling—cry out for your honor, cry out at such sacrifice, cover your heads with dust, fall to your bare knees and begin picking up the pieces of your reputation which are scattering over the ground in all directions.

What were you beginning to do so many years ago?

What have you done?

There was a time when sunlight was not hidden from your lands. And today there is scarcely a ray of it shining upon them from here, as if the sun itself were ashamed of giving light to your possessions.

Mexico, Peru, Chile, Venezuela, Bolivia, New Granada, the Antilles all came in festive attire, kissed your feet, and carpeted with gold the wide wake left by your ships upon the Atlantic. You crushed the freedom of all those countries; they all joined hands in placing one more sphere, one more world in your kingly crown.

Spain was reminiscent of Rome.

Caesar had returned to the world and had divided himself into pieces, each piece lodging in one of your men with their thirst for glory and their delirious ambition.

Centuries passed.

The subjugated nations had laid a golden highway across the North Atlantic for your ships. And across the South Atlantic our captains laid a path of clotted blood in whose swampy pools floated heads black as ebony; and threatening arms rose up like thunder paving the way for a storm.

And finally the storm broke; and just as it was slowly prepared, so it was furiously and inexorably unleashed upon us.

Venezuela, Bolivia, New Granada, Mexico, Peru and Chile bit your hands that were convulsively holding fast the reins of their freedom, opening deep wounds in them. And since your courage was flagging and weary and buffeted about, an *ay!* escaped from your lips, blow after blow resounded dismally in the bloody sea path, and the head of Spanish domination rolled over the American continent, traversing its plains, tramping its mountains, crossing its rivers, and falling at last to the bottom of a deep canyon, never again to rise from it.

The Antilles, the Antilles alone, especially Cuba, groveled at your feet, put her lips to your wounds, licked your hands, and carefully and affectionately made a new head for your mistreated shoulders.

And while she carefully restored your strength, you folded your arms beneath her arms, reached into her heart, tore it out, and ruptured its arteries of learning and morality.

And when she demanded of you a niggardly pittance in recompense for the hardships she had suffered, you held out your hands and showed her the shapeless mass of her shattered heart, and laughingly threw it in her face.

She felt her chest, found another new heart beating vigorously, and blushing with shame she stilled its beating, bowed her head, and waited.

But this time she waited on guard, and the treacherous claw was able to draw blood only from the iron wrist of the hand that covered her heart.

And when she again held out her hands pleading for more help, you once again showed her the mass of flesh and blood, once again laughed, and once again threw it in her face. And she felt the blood rise to her throat, choke her, and mount to her brain. It needed to flow, for it was compressed in her vigorous heart, and boiling throughout her body in the heat of mockery and outrage. At last it did flow. It did because you yourselves drove it to do so, because your cruelty caused her veins to burst, because you have so many times broken her heart to pieces and she did not want you to break it again.

And if this was your desire, why are you surprised?

And if you think it is a question of honor to continue writing your colonial history with such pages, why do you not even sweeten with some justice your supreme effort to establish the shreds of your conqueror's cloak in Cuba forever?

And if you know and recognize this, because you cannot help knowing and recognizing it; if you understand this, then why in your comprehension do you not even begin to practice those unavoidable precepts of honor whose avoidance makes you suffer so much?

When all is forgotten, when all is lost, when in the turbulent sea of human misery the God of Ages sometimes stirs the waves and finds a nation's disgrace, he never finds compassion or feelings in them.

Honor can be stained. Justice can be sold.

Everything can be torn apart.

But the notion of righteousness floats over all and never sinks.

Preserve that notion in your land if in the history of this world you do not want the first ones to sink to be yourselves.

Preserve it, for that land can yet be a Nation in which, even where all feelings have vanished, there might finally remain the feelings of sorrow and of its own dignity.

XII

And so many have died!

And so many sons are going to the quarries in the dark of night to weep upon the stone under which they assume rests the spirit of their forefathers!

And so many mothers have lost their reason!

Mother, mother! How I feel you living in my soul! How your memory inspires me! How the bitterest tears of your memory burn my cheeks!

Mother, mother! So many are weeping as you have wept! So many mothers are losing the sparkle in their eyes as you have lost it!

Mother, mother!

In the meantime, the nation's deputies are applauding.

Look, look.

There before me parade in a heartrending and silent procession the specters that resemble living men, and the living men that resemble specters.

Look, look!

Here goes happy, satisfied, joyful cholera laughing with horrible laughter. It has exchanged its scythe for the prison whip. It carries a bundle of chains upon its back. From time to time a drop of blood falls from that shapeless group of men that raises an infernal noise. Always blood! This time the cholera is loading its back in the political prison of Cuba.

Look, look!

Here comes a head embellished with snow. It bends upon a neck that groans because it cannot support it. Purulent matter runs down its wretched clothing. A heavy chain clanks with a dull thud at its feet. And yet it smiles. Always that smile! The martyr is truly something of God. And how hapless the people when they murder God!

Look, look!

Here comes loathsome, filthy smallpox, a scarlet tear out of hell that laughs with frightful laughter. It has one eye like Quasimodo. It carries a living body on its hideous humped back. It throws the body upon the ground, leaps around it, tramples upon it, tosses it into the air, picks it up and replaces it upon its back, throws it down again, dances around it and cries: "Lino, Lino!" And the body moves, and it fastens shackles to the body and pushes it a long way, a very long way, down, far down to the mound over there known as the quarry. "Lino! Lino!" it repeats as it moves away. And the body rises to its feet, and the lash is brandished, and Lino works. Always that work! It is true that his spirit is God himself. How far astray do people go when they apply the lash to God!

Look, look!

Here it comes, laughing—a wide Negro mouth laughing. The world depends upon it. Memory folded the wings in its brain and flew farther. The curly wool is already white. It laughs and laughs.

"Master, why am I living?"

"Master, master, how ugly it sounds!" And he shakes the leg irons and laughs and laughs.

God is weeping.

And how the people weep when they make God weep!

Look, look!

Here comes the quarry. It is an immense mass. Many arms covered with gold braid are pushing it. And it rolls, rolls along, and at every revolution a mother's despairing eyes shine forth within a black disc and disappear. And the men with the arms keep laughing and pushing, and the mass keeps rolling, and at every revolution a body is crushed and the chains clang together and a tear wells out of the stone and alights upon the neck of one of the laughing, pushing men. And the eyes shine and the bones break and the tears weigh heavily upon the necks, and the mass rolls along. *Ay*! When the mass finishes rolling, such a gross body will weigh upon your heads that you never will be able to lift them again. Never!

In the name of compassion, in the name of honor, in the name of God, stop that mass; stop it, lest it turn toward you men and drag you down with its horrible weight. Stop it, for it is scattering many tears upon the earth, and the tears of the martyrs are ascending to the sky in the mists, and then condensing; and if you fail to stop it, the sky will tumble down upon you.

The terrible cholera, the snowy head, the frightful smallpox, the wide Negro mouth, the mass of stone. And everything—like the corpse looming out of the coffin, like the white face looming out of the black robe—everything passes by enveloped in a heavy, spreading, reddish, suffocating atmosphere. Blood, always blood!

Oh, look, look!

Spain cannot be free.

Spain still has too much blood upon her head.

Now approve the Spanish government's conduct in Cuba.

Now, fathers of the country, declare in the country's name that you sanction the most iniquitous violation of morality, and the most complete obliviousness to every sentiment of justice.

Declare it, sanction it, approve it—if you can.

The Spanish Republic and the Cuban Revolution

When the first Spanish Republic was proclaimed in February 1873, Martí published this booklet in Madrid. Sent to Don Estanislao Figueras, head of the new republican government, Martí sought to shift Spanish republican opinion in favor of Cuba.

Glory and triumph are no more than incentives to the fulfillment of duty. In the practical life of ideas, power is simply respect for all the manifestations of justice, firm determination in the face of the prompting of cruelty or pride. When respect for justice disappears and there is no fulfillment of duty, triumph and glory are enveloped in infamy, and power has a senseless, hateful existence.

As a man of good will, I salute the triumphant Republic— salute it now, as I will curse it in the future if it strangles another Republic, if a free people constricts the freedoms of another people, if a nation that says it is a nation subjugates another nation which is asserting itself, too. If the freedom of the tyranny is tremendous, the tyranny of freedom is repugnant to it and shocks and frightens it.

Freedom cannot be fruitful for peoples whose foreheads are stained with blood. The Spanish Republic is opening the way to an era of happiness for its homeland; it should take care to cleanse its forehead of all the stains that becloud it, so it will not go calmly and confidently along paths that lead to remorse and oppression, along paths that involve even the merest violation or hinder understanding of the people's will.

No will that represses the will of another should be respected. The Spanish Republic is built on universal suffrage, on conscientious and informed suffrage, on the spirit that gives life to the most sacred body of law, on the words that beget freedoms. How can it impose its will on one who expresses its own will by means of suffrage? How can it reject the unanimous will of a people, when it itself is built on the free, unanimous will of the people?

I neither prejudge acts of the Spanish Republic nor think that the Republic should be timid or cowardly. But I do warn it that actions are always prone to injustice. I remind it that injustice is a death knell to the respect of others; I warn it that being unjust means being wicked; and I implore it never to betray the universal conscience of honor— which does not rule out patriotic honor but which demands that patriotic honor exist within universal honor.

Basing themselves on republican ideas, the Cuban people considered that their honor was threatened by the government that denied them this right. And, since they had no honor and felt a strong need for it, they sought it in sacrifice and martyrdom— where Spanish republicans have been wont to find it. I look angrily away from the niggardly and suicidal republicans who deny the right of insurrection to that ill-treated, oppressed, impoverished, sold-out people whose hands are tied— because the Spanish Republic has sanctioned so many insurrections of its own. Cuba had been sold out to further the ambitions of its rulers, sold out to be exploited by its tyrants. The proclaimed Republic has said so many times. The triumphant Republic has often accused them of being tyrants. That Republic hears and will defend me.

For Cuba, the struggle has meant the death of its most beloved sons, the loss of its prosperity, which it cursed as dishonorable because it was based on slavery; the government permitted it to grow wealthy in exchange for infamy, and Cuba preferred poverty to that evil concession of the government. What profound grief for those who denounce the sudden acknowledgment of slaves' honor and Cuba's energetic determination!

It asked, begged, groaned and hoped. How can one who replied to its entreaties with sneers and fresh ridicule of its hopes have the right to denounce it?

Let the pride of those whose honor is besmirched speak out opportunely; those who do not understand that there is honor only in the satisfaction of justice are sad, indeed. Let the merchant defend the source of wealth that is escaping from him. Some say that the separation of the Antilles is not in Spain's interests, but love of material possessions upsets the spirit; unreasonableness abides in men's brains; and excessive pride condemns what you can achieve, seek and acquire. I cannot understand that there should be a mire where a heart should be.

The wealthy Cubans blessed their misery, the battlefield was nourished by the blood of martyrs; and Spain knows that those who live have not been affrighted by the dead, that the insurrection was the consequence of a revolution, that freedom had found another homeland, that it would have been Spanish if Spain had so wished, but that it was free in spite of Spain's will.

The insurgents do not yield. Just as Spain burned Sagunto, Cuba burned Bayamo; the struggle that Cuba wanted to make more human continues dreadful through Spain's will, for it refused to make it more human. For four years— without respite, without any sign of ceding in their effort— the insurgents have been requesting their independence from oppression, their honorable freedom, and requesting it dying, just as the Spanish republicans have for their freedom so many times. How can any honorable republican dare to deny a people a right which he has claimed for himself?

My homeland is writing its irrevocable resolution with blood. On the dead bodies of its sons, it is rising up to say that it firmly wants its independence. They are fighting and dying. Both the sons of Spain and the sons of my homeland are dying. Does it not shock the Spanish Republic to learn that Spaniards are dying in combat against other republicans?

Cuba wanted Spain to respect its will, which is the will of honored spirits; it should respect Cuba's will, for my homeland wants the same thing Spain wants, but wants it alone, because it has been alone in asking for it, because, alone, it has lost its much-loved sons, because nobody else has had the courage to defend it, because it understands how far its vitality reaches, because it knows that a war filled with horror must always be a bloody bond, because it cannot love those who have treated it without compassion, because cordiality and peace are not built on foundations of the recent dead and smoking ruins. Those who have trampled upon it should not invoke it. Those who know what must be do not want a bloody peace.

The Republic denies the right of conquest. Cuba became Spain's through right of conquest.

The Republic condemns those who oppress. Spain has perpetually employed the right of oppression and of shameful exploitation and cruel persecution against Cuba.

The Republic, therefore, cannot retain what was acquired by means of a right it denies and kept by a series of violations of the right it condemns.

The Republic is raised on the shoulders of universal suffrage, of the people's unanimous will.

And Cuba is raising itself that same way. Its plebiscite is its martyrology. Its suffrage is its revolution. When does a people express its desires more firmly than when it rises up in arms to obtain them?

Cuba proclaims its independence through the same right by which the Republic was proclaimed; how, then, can the Republic deny Cuba its right to be free, which is the same it claimed to become free itself? How can the Republic deny itself? How can it determine the fate of a people by imposing a way of life on it that does not include its complete, free and very evident will?

The President of the Republican Government has said that, if the Constituent Cortes did not vote for the Republic, the republicans would leave power, become the opposition again and respect the people's will. How can the one who thus gives all-embracing power to the will of one people fail to hear and respect the will of another? Under the Republic, it is no longer a crime to be a Cuban—that tremendous original sin of my much-loved homeland, of which it bore only the baptism of degradation and infamy.

"Long live Spanish Cuba!" said the one who had to be President of the Assembly, and the Assembly said the same with him. Those who were carried to power by suffrage denied the right of suffrage as soon as they had ascended to power; those who, with Mr. Martos, said "No!" and abused reason, justice and gratitude. In the name of liberty, respect for the will of others, the sovereign will of the peoples, right, conscience and the Republic: No! "Long live Spanish Cuba!" if that is what she wants, and "Long live free Cuba!" if such is her desire.

Cuba has decided on her emancipation; she has always wanted

emancipation so she could rise as a Republic; she ventured to achieve her rights before Spain achieved her own; and she has sacrificed herself to gain her freedom. Will the Spanish Republic, then, be willing to use force to subdue those who are risking martyrdom to create a sister, Cuban Republic? Will the Republic be willing to rule her against her will?

People will say that, since Spain is giving Cuba the rights she requested, there is no longer any reason for her insurrection. I cannot think of that poor argument without bitterness, and I must truly blame those who provoke me for the harshness of my argument. Spain now wants to do good for Cuba. What right does Spain have to be beneficent after having been so cruel? And if it is to recover its honor, what right does it have to pay for that honor, which it did not gain in time, with another people's freedom, granting benefits which that people did not request, for it had already won them? Why does it want them to be accepted now when it failed to grant them so many times? Why should the Cuban revolution agree to having Spain concede—as if they were within its competence to grant—the rights which cost Cuba so much blood and grief to defend? Spain is now atoning terribly for its colonial sins, which place it in such extremity that it no longer has any right to remedy them. The law of its errors condemns it to not appear kind. It would have the right to be kind if it had avoided that immense series of very great wrongs. It would have the right to be kind if it had even been humane in the continuation of that war that it has made barbarous and ungodly.

I am not referring now to the fact that Cuba has firmly resolved not to belong to Spain; I mean only that Cuba cannot belong to it any more. The chasm that divided Spain and Cuba has been filled, by Spain's will, with corpses. Neither love nor harmony thrives on corpses; he who failed to pardon deserves no pardon. Cuba knows that the Republic is not clothed in death, but she cannot forget those many days of executions and of grief. Spain has come too late; the law of time condemns it.

The Republic knows that it is separated from the island by a broad space filled with the dead. The Republic hears, as I do, their terrifying voices. The Republic knows that to preserve Cuba new corpses must be heaped and much blood be spilled. It knows that to subjugate, subdue and do violence to the will of that people its own sons must die. Will it consent to have them die for what, if it were not the death of legality, would be the self-destruction of its honor? How ghastly if it consents! Wretched are those who dare to spill the blood of others who seek the same freedoms they themselves have sought. Wretched are those who thus abjure their right to happiness, honor and the esteem of humanity.

There is talk of the territory's integrity. The Atlantic Ocean destroys that ridiculous argument. Enemy hands could show those who thus abuse the people's patriotism, those who drag them down and deceive them, an English Rock; harsh hands could show them Florida; injudicious hands could show them vast Lusitania.

It is not the land that constitutes what is called the homeland's integrity. A homeland is something more than oppression, something more than bits of land without freedom or life, something more than the right of possession by force. A homeland is a community of interests, the unity of traditions, a singleness of goals, the sweet and consoling fusion of love and hope.

Cubans do not live as Spaniards do; Cuban history is not that of Spaniards; what was imperishable glory for Spain, Spain itself has sought to be the deepest disgrace for Cubans. They thrive on different trade, have links with different countries and rejoice with different customs. They have no shared aspirations or identical goals, nor do they have cherished memories to unite them. The Cuban spirit thinks with bitterness of the grief the Spanish spirit has brought it; it struggles vigorously against Spanish domination. And then, since all the communities and all the identities that constitute the whole homeland are lacking, they invoke an illusion which will not serve; they invoke a deceitful lie when they invoke the integrity of the homeland. Peoples are joined only by bonds of fraternity and love.

Spain has never wanted to be Cuba's sister; why should it pretend now that Cuba should be its sister? To secure Cuba to the Spanish Nation would be to exercise a right of conquest over her— more abusive and repugnant now than ever before. The Republic cannot exercise it without bringing the curses of the honored peoples upon its guilty head.

Many times, Cuba asked Spain for the rights which Spain now

wants to grant it. Many times, Spain refused to grant those rights; how then, can it be surprised that Cuba refuses, in its turn, to accept as a tardy gift, an honor which it has purchased with the generous blood of its sons, an honor which it still seeks now with unbreakable determination and a firmness which no one should seek to destroy?

Because of different pressing needs, endowed with opposite characters, surrounded by different countries and deeply divided by past cruelties, without Cuba's having any reason for loving Spain or any will to belong to it and in view of the grief that Spain has amassed over Cuba, is it not crazy to pretend that two peoples which are separated by character, customs, needs, traditions and lack of love should be joined as one simply because of their memories of bereavement and pain?

They say that Cuba's separation would mean the crumbling of the homeland. It would be so if the homeland were equivalent to that selfish, sordid idea of domination and avarice. But even if it were, the retention of Cuba for Spain against its extremely explicit and powerful will—the will of a people that is struggling for its independence is always powerful—would mean the crumbling of the honor of the homeland they invoke. Imposition is the mark of tyrants. Oppression, that of the infamous. May the Spanish Republic never want to be tyrannical and cowardly. The good of the homeland, which is being achieved nobly after so many difficulties, should not be thus sacrificed. Honor won at such great cost should not be so stained.

Cuba's unanimous, persistent struggle shows its firm determination to obtain its emancipation. The memories that link it to Spain are of bitterness and grief. It thinks that it has paid a high price for the sonorousness of the Spanish tongue, with the illustrious lives which Spain has caused to be lost. Does this new, regenerated Spain called the Spanish Republic wish to become involved in the disgrace of imposing oppression that is, above all, unfair, ungodly and irrational? This would be such a mistake that I hope it will never engage in anything so filled with misery.

The revolutionaries in Cuba declared its 400,000 Negro slaves free before Spain did any such thing. The government's political prisons are filled with 10- and 11-year-old Negroes who have just been shipped in, venerable 80-year-olds and idiot Negroes of 100, and they are whipped through the streets and mutilated— and killed— by the blows. In Cuba, the authorities shoot those who seem suspicious— even members of the government— and the women are raped and dragged through the streets. Those who are fighting for their homeland are killed, either immediately or, if their immediate deaths cannot be excused, slowly. Some leaders have been sentenced to imprisonment for having beaten captured rebels to death and for having continued to vent their rage on their dead bodies, yet others, who have presented parts of the bodies of mutilated rebels as trophies, have been pardoned. Such horrors have taken place that I don't want to remind the Republic of them, nor do I want to tell you, lest I upset you, but they are so terrible that merely to say that they must be corrected is to offend your honor.

This shows that any union between Cuba and Spain is quite impossible. If there is to be a fruitful, loyal and affectionate union, as a fair and patriotic resolution is needed, the fate of the peoples must be decided by working with perfect reason, and the homeland— disfigured by the arrogant, debased by the ambitious, discredited by fools and deserving of so little fortune because of its actions in Cuba— must be honored by strictly upholding justice.

Cuba calls for the independence to which it is entitled by life itself, which it knows it has; by the energetic steadfastness of its sons; by the richness of its territory; by the natural independence of that territory; and, more than anything else, because this is the firm, unanimous will of the Cuban people.

Spain feels that it must hold on to Cuba and cannot do so except— I've forgotten why— by trampling on its rights, imposing its will and staining its honor. Whoever wanted to retain Cuba's wealth at such a cost would be unworthy, as would anyone who let other nations think he was sacrificing his honor for material benefit.

Virtue now is simply the performance of duty, no longer its heroic exaggeration, and the Republic does not consent to its diminution. Its government knows how to build a foundation on wise and generous justice and does not govern a people against its will— for justice brings forth all powers from the will of the people. That government does not struggle against itself; is not dishonored; does not fear; and does not cede to demands of ridiculous arrogance, exaggerated pride or disguised ambition. Because the law, the needs of republics and sublime republican ideas recognize Cuba's independence, it recognizes it, too. Thus, if it should end its domination over Cuba, which would be simply the legitimate consequence of its principles, the strict observance of the tenets of justice, it would bring imperishable glory to Spain. For too long, Spain has been beset by indecision and fear; let Spain at last have the courage to be glorious.

Does the government of the Republic fear that the people would not respect such a noble solution? This would be to confess that the Spanish people are not republicans.

Does it not dare persuade the people that this is what true honor demands? This would mean that it prefers power to heeding the prompting of conscience.

Won't the Republican government think as I do? This would mean that the Spanish Republic neither respects the will of the sovereign people nor has managed to understand the republican ideal.

I do not think that it will give way to fear. But, if it should, that transferal of its rights would be the first sign of the loss of all.

If it does not do as I think it should, because it fails to understand things as I do, this means that it pays more attention to its past errors than to the extension of new ideas— sublime because they are limitless and pure— and that irrational pride over very painful glories still disturbs its spirit and makes it want to hold fast to things it never should have possessed, because it never knew how to possess them.

If it thinks as I do, meets with resistance, defies it (even though its effort is not crowned with victory) and accepts Cuba's independence— because Cuba's sons declare that only force can make them belong to Spain— it will lose nothing, because Cuba is already lost to Spain. It will wrest nothing from its territory, for Cuba has already torn itself away. It will be complying with the republican ideal in its legitimate purity. It will be opting for life, because failure to accept is tantamount to suicide. It will be confirming its own freedoms, because anyone who denies the right to govern itself to a people that has already freed itself does not deserve to have freedoms himself. It will avoid the shedding of republican blood and will not be oppressive and fratricidal. It will acknowledge that it is losing— in fact, it has already lost— possession of a people that does not want to belong to it and has shown that it does not need its protection or its government to live in glory and firmness. In short, by sanctioning a right, it will be renouncing the shedding of blood and giving up a territory it has already lost in exchange for the respect of humankind; the admiration of peoples; and ineffable, eternal glory in the future.

If the Spanish Republic's ideal is the universe and believes that it must live as a single people, as a province of God, what right does it have to take the lives of others who seek the same goal? More than unfair, more than cruel, shedding the blood of its brothers is infamous. When faced with the rights of the world, what weight do Spain's rights have? When compared with future divinity, what value does the violent wish for domination have? What value do rights acquired by means of conquest and bloodied by never interrupted but always sanctified oppression have?

Cuba wants to be free. That is what it says with incalculable hardships, with its struggle for the cherished Republic, with the blood of heroic American young men. Anyone who is too afraid to listen to his conscience must be a coward. Any republic that strangles another republic must be fratricidal.

Cuba wants to be free. And, since the peoples of South America obtained their freedom from the reactionary governments— Spain, from the French; Italy, from Austria; Mexico, from Napoleon's ambitions; the United States, from England; and all the other peoples, from their oppressors— so, under the law of its irrevocable will and the law of historic necessity, Cuba, too, must achieve its independence.

It will be said that the Republic will not oppress Cuba any more, and perhaps it will not, but Cuba became a Republic before Spain did. Why should those who have taken to the field of battle as free men and martyrs to make their country a republic accept that condition from someone who, posing as a master, offers it as a gift?

Let the Spanish Republic not be dishonored; let its triumphant ideal not be halted. Let it not murder its brothers or have its sons shed the blood of its other sons. Let it not oppose Cuba's independence. Otherwise, the Republic of Spain will be a Republic of injustice and ignominy, and the government of freedom will, in this case, be liberticidal.

Madrid, February 15, 1873

The Memorial Meeting in Honor of Karl Marx

Following the death of Karl Marx in London on March 14, 1883, a memorial meeting was held in the Cooper Union hall in New York City, March 20, 1883. The walls were hung with banners proclaiming "Workers of all lands, unite!" José Martí's account of the meeting was published in La Nación, *Buenos Aires, May 13 and 16, 1883.*

Look at this large hall. Karl Marx is dead. He deserves to be honored for declaring himself on the side of the weak. But the virtuous man is not the one who points out the damage and burns with generous anxiety to put it right; he is the one who teaches a gentle amendment of the injury.

The task of setting men in opposition against men is frightening. The compulsory brutalization of men for the profit of others stirs anger. But an outlet must be found for this anger, so that the brutality might cease before it overflows and terrifies. Look at this hall: dominating the room, surrounded by green leaves, is the picture of that ardent reformer, uniter of men of different peoples, and tireless, powerful organizer. The International was his creation: men of all nations come to honor him. The crowd, made up of valiant workers, the sight of whom affects and comforts, shows more muscles than jewels, and more honest faces than silk underwear. Labor beautifies: it is rejuvenating to see a farm worker, a blacksmith or a seaman. By manipulating the forces of Nature, they become as beautiful as Nature is.

New York goes on being a kind of vortex: what boils up in the rest of the world, in New York drops down. Here they smile at one who flees; out there, they make him flee. As a result of this kindness, a strength has come to this people. Karl Marx studied the methods of setting the world on new foundations, and wakened those who were asleep, and showed them how to cast down the broken props. But being in a hurry, with his understanding somewhat clouded, he did not see that children who do not have a natural, slow and painful gestation are not born viable, whether they come from the bosom of the people in history, or from the wombs of women in the home. Here are the good friends of Karl Marx, who was not only a titanic stimulator of the wrath of European workers, but also showed great insight into the causes of human misery and the destiny of men, a man driven by a burning desire to do good. He saw in everyone what he carried in himself: rebellion, the highest ideals, struggle.

Here is Schevitsch, a journalist: see how he speaks: reflections of the sensitive, radiant Bakunin reach him: he begins to speak in English; he addresses others in German. *Dah! Dah*! his compatriots reply enthusiastically from their seats when he speaks to them in Russian. The Russians are the whip of the Reform— no more! These impatient and generous men, tarnished with anger, are not the ones to cement the New World: they are the spur, and prick like the voice of a conscience which might be falling asleep: but the steel of the spur cannot be used as a construction hammer.

Here is Swinton, an old man inflamed by injustice, who saw in Karl Marx the grandeur of mountains and the light of Socrates. Here is the German Johann Most, persistent and unlovable shouter, lighter of bonfires, who does not carry in his right hand the balm to heal the wounds inflicted by his left. So many people have come to hear them that the hall overflows and they spill out into the street. Choral societies are singing. Among so many men, there are many women. With applause, they repeat in chorus quotations from Karl Marx on posters hanging on the walls. Millot, a Frenchman, says something lovely: "Liberty has fallen many times in France, but it has risen more beautiful from each descent." Johann Most speaks fanatic words: "From the time that I read Marx's book in a Saxon prison, I took up the sword against human vampires." Says McGuire: "Rejoice to see united, without hatred, so many men of all countries. All the workers of the world belong to a single nation, and do not quarrel among themselves but are united against those who oppress them. Rejoice to have seen 6,000 French and English workers meeting together near what had been the ominous Paris Bastille." A

Bohemian speaks. A letter of Henry George's[1] is read— the famous economist, friend to the distressed, loved by the people, famous here and in England. And with salvos of thunderous applause and frenzied hurrahs, the fervent assembly rises in one unanimous movement, while from the platform two men with open countenance and glance of Toledo steel read out in German and English the resolutions with which the whole meeting ends— in which Karl Marx is named the most noble hero and most powerful thinker of the world of labor. Music sounds; choirs resound; but note that these are not the sounds of peace.

New York, March 29, 1883

[1] Henry George (1839–97): American economist and reformer who argued that poverty could be overcome through a single tax on land.

Wandering Teachers

This article, published in La América, *New York, in May 1894, presents Martí's view that education in rural areas should combine work and study.*

"But how would you establish that system of wandering teachers that we have not seen mentioned in any book on education and you recommended in the last year's number of *La América*, which I have before me?" An enthusiastic gentleman from Santo Domingo respectfully asks us this question.

We will tell him briefly that it is an important matter, but not how to accomplish it.

There is a heap of essential truths that can fit upon the wings of a hummingbird, and yet they are the key to national peace, to spiritual advancement, and to the greatness of one's country.

Men must be kept in the knowledge of the land, and of the durability and transcendence of life.

Men must live in the peaceful natural and inevitable enjoyment of freedom, the way they live enjoying air and light.

A nation in which a taste for wealth and a knowledge of the sweetness, needs and pleasures of life do not develop equally is condemned to death.

Men must know the composition, enrichment, changes and applications of the material elements from whose development they derive the healthful pride of one who works directly with Nature, the bodily strength derived from contact with the forces of the land, and the honest and secure wealth produced by its cultivation.

Men need someone to stir their compassion often, to make their tears flow, and to give their souls the supreme benefit of generous feelings; for through the wonderful compensation of Nature whoever gives of himself, grows; and whoever withdraws within himself, living for small pleasures and afraid to share them with others, thinking only of greedily satisfying one's own appetites, will gradually change from a man into pure solitude, carrying in his heart all the gray hair of winter time. He becomes within— and appears to others— an insect.

Men grow, they grow physically and visibly, when they learn something, when they begin to possess something, and when they have done some good.

Only fools or egoists talk about misfortune. Happiness exists on earth, and it can be won by means of the prudent exercise of reason, the knowledge of universal harmony, and the constant practice of generosity. He who seeks it elsewhere will not find it, for after having drained all the cups life has to offer, only in this way will he find flavor. A legend of the Spanish American lands tells that at the bottom of ancient cups there was a picture of Christ, so that when one of them was drained, people said: "Until we meet, my Lord!" At the bottom of those cups a heaven unfolded— serene and fragrant, endless and overflowing with tenderness!

Being good is the only way to be free.

Being cultured is the only way to be free.

With human nature in general, however, to be good, one has to be prosperous.

And the only open road to a constant and facile prosperity is that of knowing, cultivating and benefiting from the inexhaustible and indefatigable elements of Nature. Nature, unlike men, is not jealous. Unlike men, she has no hates or fears. She does not bar the way to anyone. Men will always need the products of Nature. And since every region produces only certain products, active trade will always assure wealth and freedom from want for all peoples.

So now there is no need to engage in a crusade to reconquer the Holy Sepulcher. Jesus did not die in Palestine; he is alive in every man. Most men have gone through life half asleep; they ate and drank, but learned nothing about themselves. Now one must go on a crusade to reveal to men their own natures, and give them, with plain and practical scientific knowledge, the personal independence that fortifies a man's kindliness and gives rise to the pride and decency of being an amiable creature living in the great universe.

This, then, is what the teachers must take to the rural areas. Not merely explanations in the field of agriculture and mechanical implements, but the tenderness which is so lacking in men and does them so much good.

The farmer cannot leave his work to go many miles to see some incomprehensible geometric figures, to learn the names of capes and rivers and peninsulas in Africa, and to be provided with empty didactic lessons. The farmer's children cannot leave the paternal farm and day after day, go mile after mile, to learn Latin declensions and short division. And yet the farmers comprise the most valuable, healthful, and red-blooded segment of the population, because they receive directly and in full measure the emanations of the soil from whose friendly intercourse they live. Cities are the minds of nations; but their hearts, from where the mass of blood is sent in all directions, are in the countryside. Men are still mechanical eaters and the shrines of worry. We must make every man a torch.

For we are proposing, therefore, nothing less than a new religion with its new priests! We are describing nothing less than the missions by which the new era will soon begin to spread its religion! The world is changing; the regal priestly vestments, so necessary in the mystical ages of man, are lying upon their deathbed. Religion has not disappeared, it has been transformed. Above the affliction into which a study of the details and slow evolution of human history plunges observers, one can see that men are growing, and that they have already climbed halfway up Jacob's ladder; what beautiful poems are in the Bible! If huddled upon a mountain peak one suddenly glances at human progress, one will see that people have never loved each other as they do now, that in spite of the painful disorder and abominable selfishness to which a momentary absence of ultimate beliefs and faith in Eternal Truth is leading the inhabitants of this transitory age, the benevolence and impetus to expand, now burning in everyone, has never been of greater concern to human beings than they are today. They have stood up like friends eager to meet and move forward to a mutually happy encounter.

We walk upon the waves and are tossed about and caught in their swirling motion; perturbed by their action, we fail to see—and do not stop to examine—the forces that move them. But when the sea is calm, we can rest assured that the stars will be nearer to the earth. Man will finally sheathe his sword of battle in the sun!

All this is what we could call the spirit of wandering teachers.

How happy the peasants would be if some good man arrived now and then to teach them things they did not know, and with the warmth of a communicative manner leave in their spirits the quietude and dignity that always remain after seeing an honest and loving man! Instead of talking about cattle breeding and crops, there would be an occasional discussion—until the subject could be covered thoroughly—of what the teacher taught, of the curious implements he brought them, of a simple way to cultivate the particular plant they have been working so hard to develop, of what a fine teacher he is. Because he makes them impatient, they would talk about when he would come again so they might ask him what has been occurring to them ever since they began to acquire knowledge; for their minds have been expanding incessantly, and they have started to think. How happy all of them would be to leave their hoes and shovels, and filled with curiosity, take refuge in the teacher's campaign tent!

Extensive courses obviously could not be given, but if their propagators made a thorough study, they could certainly sow and cultivate the seeds of their ideas. They could awaken the appetite for knowledge.

And this would be a sweet intrusion, carried out in agreement with what is a common concern of the human soul; since the teacher would instruct the peasants in practical and beneficial things in a gentle manner, those peasants would gradually and effortlessly absorb a body of knowledge which begins by flattering and satisfying their interests. For whoever attempts to make men better must not disregard their evil passions; he must consider these as an extremely important factor and see to it that he does not work against them, but rather for them.

Instead of sending pedagogues through the rural areas, we would send conversationalists; instead of pompous schoolmasters, educated people responsive to the doubts presented to them by the ignorant, able to respond to the questions prepared for their arrival. They would observe when the farmers made mistakes in agricultural procedure, or when they overlooked some sort of wealth that could be developed, so they could be informed of these things and at the same time told how to remedy them.

In short, it is necessary to engage in a campaign of gentleness and knowledge, and give the farmers a corps— not yet in existence— of missionary teachers.

The itinerant school is the only kind that can eliminate peasant ignorance.

And in the rural areas, as well as in the cities, it is urgent to replace sterile and indirect book learning with the direct and fruitful knowledge of Nature.

It is urgent to open normal schools for practical teachers, to then scatter them over the valleys, mountains and outlying regions, much as the Amazonian Indians tell us that to create men and women Father Almalivaca scattered the seeds of *moriche* palm over all the earth!

Time is wasted upon elementary literary education, for it creates people aspiring to pernicious and fruitless values. The establishment of a fundamental scientific education is as necessary as the sun.

Indians in the United States

This article, describing the annual meeting of the Mohonk Convention on the Indian question, was published in La Nación, *Buenos Aires, December 4, 1885.*

Lake Mohonk is a lovely place in New York State. The forests of the adjacent Adirondacks beckon to grandeur, unsystematically cutting down crude speculators; with forests as with politics, it is unlawful to cut down unless one plants new trees. The lake invites serenity, and the nearby river quietly enriches the land and flows onward to the sea. Rivers go to the sea, men to the future. When the leaves turned yellow and red this autumn, the friends of the Indians foregathered in that picturesque retreat to calmly discuss some way of attracting them to a peaceful and intelligent life in which they could rise above their present condition of rights mocked, faith betrayed, character corrupted, and frequent, justified revolts. In that conference of benevolent men and women there was a notable absence of the spirit of theory which deforms and makes sterile, or at least retards, the well-meaning efforts of so many reformers— efforts which generally alienate them, because of the repulsion which a lack of empathy and harmony inspires in a healthy mind, from the solicitous support of those modest souls who otherwise would be efficient aids in the reformation process. Genius, which explodes and dazzles, need not be divested of the good sense that makes its life on earth so productive. Senators, attorneys and supervisors shared their generous task there with enthusiastic journalists and Protestant ministers. In the United States a woman opened men's hearts to compassion for the Negroes, and nobody did more to set them free than she. Harriet Beecher Stowe was her name, a woman passionately devoted to justice and therefore not afraid to sully her reputation, with tremendous revelations befitting a Byron, by the prolific success of her *Uncle Tom's Cabin*— a tear that has something to say!

It was also a woman who, with much good sense and sympathy, has worked year after year to alleviate the plight of the Indians. The recently deceased Helen Hunt Jackson, strong-minded and with a loving heart, wrote a letter of thanks to President Cleveland for his determination to recognize the Indian's right to manhood and justice. And at the Lake Mohonk Convention there were people with an apostolic sense of oratory, subsidized by the state. But the inflexible statistics, the exact accounts, the inexorable ciphers did not belong to the supervisors or attorneys or senators, but to a woman named Alice Fletcher, a lively speaker, sure in her reasoning and skilled in debate.

So the Lake Mohonk Convention was not composed of discouraged philanthropists who look at Indians only because they are Indians— seraphic creatures, so to speak— and it was not composed of those butterfly politicians who alight only upon the surface of things, and pass judgment on the basis of mere appearances and results, blind to the fact that the one way to right wrongs is to eradicate their causes.

This was a meeting of men and women of action. One of them, and surely among the most impassioned, "shuddered on recalling the sad scenes on the Indian reservations where they would divide the year's food rations, clothing, and money like wild animals fighting over raw meat." Anyone who has seen these signs of degradation, since he is human, must have experienced some shame and a desire to lift those unfortunate creatures out of their misery. For it is he who is responsible for all the wrongs he knows about but does nothing to correct. It is a criminal laziness, a passive guilt that is merely a matter of degree in the scale of crime; apostleship is a constant, daily duty. Another person at the convention has seen the Indians huddled in a circle, gambling their year's salary, betting nine out of every 10 dollars, like Chinese workers in the cigar factory of a Spanish prison, the moment they receive on a Saturday afternoon the overtime pay that they have to hand over to the establishment. The convention knows that they are not fond of working, because a bad system of government has accustomed them to being detestably apathetic. The convention is well aware that, since the government gives them a yearly stipend, and food and clothing, they will resist any reform that tends to improve their character by compelling them to earn their living from their own efforts; that, deprived of the social aspirations and civil pleasures of white people, they will view with indifference the public school system available to them as not proceeding from the tribe's savage existence, or seeming to be necessary to it. The convention knows this. But it also knows that the Indian is not like that by nature; he has been conditioned to it by the system of vilification and easy living imposed upon him for the last hundred years.

Where the Indian has been able to defend himself more successfully and stay as he was, it can be seen that he is by race strong-minded and strong-willed, courageous, hospitable and worthy. Even fierce, like any man or any people close to Nature. Those same noble conditions of personal pride and attachment to territory make him spring around like a wild animal when he is despoiled of his age-old grain fields, when his sacred trees are felled, when the hot winds from his burning homes scorch the manes of his fleeing horses. The one who is burned, burns; the one who is hunted, gives chase; the one who is despoiled of property, despoils in turn. And the one who is exterminated, exterminates.

Thus reduced to a poor nation of 300,000 scattered savages tirelessly fighting a nation of 50 million, the Indian does not enter the cities of his conquerors, does not sit in their schools, is not taught by their industries, is not recognized as a human soul. By means of onerous treaties he is obliged to give up his land. He is taken away from his birthplace, which is like robbing a tree of its roots, and so loses the greatest objective in life. On the pretext of farming, he is forced to buy animals to work the land he does not own. On the pretext of schooling, he is compelled to learn in a strange language, the hated language of his masters, out of textbooks that teach him vague notions of a literature and science whose utility is never explained and whose application he never sees. He is imprisoned in a small space where he moves back and forth among his intimidated companions, his entire horizon filled with the traders who sell him glittering junk and guns and liquor in exchange for the money which, because of the treaties, the government distributes among the reservations every year. Even if he should be possessed by a desire to see the world, he cannot leave that human cattle ranch. He has no land of his own to till, and no incentive to cultivate it carefully so that he may honorably leave it to his children. Nor does he have to in many of the tribes, because the government, by means of a degrading system of protection that began a century ago, gives him a communal place of land for his livelihood, and furnishes him with food, clothes, medicines, schools, with whatever is a man's natural objective when he works for a wage. If he has no property to improve or trip to take or material needs to satisfy, he spends this money on colored trinkets that cater to his rudimentary artistic taste, or on liquor and gambling that excite and further the brutal pleasures to which he is condemned. With this vile system that snuffs out his personality, the Indian is dead. Man grows by exercising his selfhood, just as a wheel gains velocity as it rolls along. And like the wheel, when a man does not work, he rusts and decays. A sense of disheartened ferocity never entirely extinguished in the enslaved races, the memory of lost homes, the council of old men who have seen freer times in their native forests, the presence of themselves imprisoned, vilified and idle—all these things burst forth in periodic waves each time the harshness or greed of the government agents is closefisted in supplying the Indians with the benefits stipulated in the treaties. And since by virtue of these treaties, and by them alone, a man is robbed of whatever nobility he has, and is permitted only his bestial qualities, it is only natural that what predominates in these revolts, disfiguring the justice producing them, is the beast developed by the system.

All enslaved peoples respond in like manner, not the Indians alone. That is why revolutions following long periods of tyranny are so cruel. What white man in his right mind fails to understand that he cannot throw in the Indian's face a being such as the white man has made of him? "He is graceful and handsome," said the venerable Erastus Brooks at the convention. "His speech is loving and meaningful. We have in American history tens, hundreds of examples to show that the Indian, under the same conditions as the white man, is as mentally, morally and physically capable as he." But we have turned him into a vagabond, a tavern post, a professional beggar. We do not give him work for himself, work that gladdens and uplifts; at best we force him to earn, with work affording him no direct profit, the cost of the rations and medicines we promise him in exchange for his land, and this in violation of the treaties. We accustom him not to depend upon himself; we habituate him to a life of indolence with only the needs and pleasures of a primitive, naked being. We deprive him of the means of obtaining his necessities through his own efforts, and with hat in hand and bowed head he is obliged to ask the government agent for everything: bread, quinine, clothes for his wife and child. The white men he knows are the tavern keeper who corrupts him, the peddler who cheats him, the distributor of rations who finds a way of withholding a part of them, the unqualified teacher who drills him in a language of which he can speak but a few words, unwillingly and without meaning, and the agent who laughs and shouts at him and bids him be off when he appeals to him for justice. Without work or property or hope, deprived of his native land and with no family pleasures other than the purely physical, what can be expected of these reservation Indians but grim, lazy and sensual men born of parents who saw their own parents crouched in circles on the ground, both pipe and soul snuffed out, weeping for their lost nation in the shade of the great tree that had witnessed their marriages, their pleas for justice, their councils and their rejoicing for a century? A slave is very sad to see, but sadder still is the son of a slave. Even their color is the reflection of mud! Great hotbeds of men are these Indian reservations. Pulling these Indians up by the roots would have been better than vilifying them.

The first treaty was in 1783, and in it the United States government reserved the right to administer the tribes and regulate their trade. And now the 300,000 Indians, subdued after a war in which theirs was not the greatest cruelty, are divided among 50 reservations whose only law is the presidential will, and another 69 known as treaty reservations because of an agreement between the tribes and the government. Thirty-nine of these have treaties stipulating the division of reservation lands into individual properties, an ennobling measure that has scarcely been attempted with 12 of the tribes. "The Indians are given the food that Congress orders for them," said Alice Fletcher, "and because this passes through many hands, there remains in each pair of them some part of it. But the allotment for schools is not distributed, because the employees can obtain from it the paltry teacher's salary, which is then passed along to their wives or daughters for augmenting household supplies. Thus, out of the $2 million that must have been spent from the years 1871 to 1881, including the obligations of all the agreements, only $200,000 have been spent on schools." Many of the tribes have been offered even more than the private property which they are denied, and the schools which have not been established for them: they have been offered citizenship.

All this was heard without contradiction; on the contrary, the Deputy Inspector of Indian Schools, the authors of the House and Senate reservation reform plans, and the members of the Indian Council supported and corroborated it. High government officials supported and corroborated it, too, and applauded the inspired defense of the Indian's character delivered by that fine man, Erastus Brooks. "There is not one of their vices for which we are not responsible! There is no Indian brutality that is not our fault! The agents interested in keeping the Indian brutalized under their control are lying!"

The government defiles the Indian with its system of treaties that condemn him to vice and inertia. And the government agent's greed keeps the government under a false concept of the Indian, or hides the causes of his corruption and rebellions in order to continue whittling away to his heart's content at the funds Congress sets aside for the Indian's maintenance.

Let the governor keep a wary eye on those rapacious employees!

Give President Cleveland high praise; with neither fanatical vanity nor prudery he has made efforts to investigate the Indians' sufferings, and instead of throwing in their faces the ignominy in which they are kept, Cleveland decided to shoulder the blame himself, and raise them by means of a just government to the status of men. This president wants no drunken insects; he wants human beings. "They are drunkards and thieves because we have made them so; therefore we must beg their pardon for having made them drunkards and thieves, and instead of exploiting them and disowning them, let us give them work on *their* lands and encourage them in a desire to live, for they are good people in spite of our having given them the right not to be."

Without a dissenting vote, then, in the shade of the Adirondacks, which beckon greatness, the convention recommended those practical reforms of simple justice that can change a grievous crowd of oppressed and restless men and women into a useful and picturesque element of American civilization.

Since they have already been robbed of their rights as freed peoples, for reasons of state, let us not rob the Indians of their rights as men. Since the despoiling of their lands, even when rational and necessary, continues to be a violent act resented by every civilized nation with hatred and with secular wars, it must not be aggravated by further repression and inhuman trading. The unfair and corrupting reservation system must be quickly abolished, and we must gradually make national lands available to the Indians, fusing them with the white population so they may promptly own state lands, enjoying the rights and sharing the responsibilities of the rest of the citizenry. The payment of yearly stipends must be abolished, for this encourages begging and vagrancy, and accustoms the Indians to neglect making use of their own resources. We must train the Indians in accord with their needs and potentialities, and they must be convinced—and when necessary compelled—to learn and to work, even if because of the present life of laziness in learning they may resist. The Indians will have to return to their unblemished souls and rise to citizenship.

To thus convert them into useful men and women, and change the regions which today are no more than extremely costly prisons into a peaceful and prosperous country, says the convention, the entire stupid, present-day teaching system will have to be changed. We must substitute the working of common lands, which neither stimulates nor permits the worker to see any profit, for the distributing of land into plots of ground for every family, inalienable for 25 years, in relation to the kind of terrain and the size of each house. The government should pay a good price for the lands not apportioned, and since these monies are to go right back into its own pocket, because the government is the guardian of the Indians who sell them, the government should retain the funds received from these lands for the industrial education and betterment of the Indians, and open the purchased lands to colonization. Let the tribes themselves revoke those treaties responsible for their wretched condition. Admit to citizenship all tribes which accept individual distribution of their lands, and all Indians who abandon the tribes that refuse to accept them, to comply with the uses of civilization. Stop taking the Indians away from the land of their forefathers and herding them into crowded centers under the self-seeking vigilance of offensive and avaricious government employees "Spread schools," said the Deputy Inspector of Indian Schools at last, but they must be useful and living schools, for every effort to disseminate instruction is futile if it does not apply to the needs, nature and future of the one receiving it. Engage no halfhearted teachers who know nothing of what they teach, and are appointed only to augment the family pittance of some employee, or to please the political bigwigs. Competent teachers will be hired and will compel the Indians to envy their children for the schooling they receive, even if the parents have to curtail their household rations for as long as the ominous rationing system persists. No textbook education, which is merely a storehouse of words weighing heavily upon the head to then tell the hands how to work well. Indians should be taught the nature of the fields they are to cultivate, and the nature of their true selves and the village in which they live; in this way they will understand and admire. Teach them something about practical politics so they may reach a suitable state of mutual respect.

Let them know how the country is run, and what are their human rights to possess it and think about it, and how they may exercise those rights. The school should instruct them in making their life a satisfying one: a country school for country people.

No details or fancy theories; only how to raise animals and plant fields, all the tasks that make them useful and self-possessed members of a community of workers. We should not send the Indians or country people teachers of literature alone. Living literature is the teacher. Let us send them teachers of crafts and agriculture.

That convention held by the friends of the Indians went well and ended well, there by the quiet waters of Lake Mohonk where the mountains are close at hand and where the beautiful square fields, cultivated with scrupulous care, look like colossal green flowers opening to the eyes of men worthy of contemplating them.

New York, October 25, 1885

Dedication of the Statue of Liberty

In this article, published in the daily La Nación, *Buenos Aires, January 1, 1887, Martí narrates in great detail the celebrations held on October 28, 1886, in New York, for the inauguration of the famous statue donated to the United States by the French people in recognition of the support given during the American War of Independence.*

For him who enjoys thee not, Liberty, it is difficult to speak of thee. His anger is as great as that of a wild beast forced to bend his knees before his tamer. He knows the depths of hell while glancing up toward the man who lives arrogantly in the sun. He bites the air as a hyena bites the bars of his cage. Spirit writhes within his body as though it were poisoned.

The wretched man who lives without liberty feels that only a garment made of mud from the streets would benefit him. Those who have thee, oh Liberty! know thee not. Those who have thee not should not speak of thee but conquer thee.

But rise, oh insect, for the city swarms with eagles! Walk or at least crawl: look around, even if your eyes fill with shame. Like a smitten lackey, squirm among the hosts of brilliant lords. Walk, though you feel the flesh stripped off your body! Ah! If they only knew how you wept, they would pick you up, and you too, dying, would know how to lift your arms toward eternity!

Arise, oh insect, for the city is like an ode! Souls ring out like well-tuned instruments. If it is dark and there is no sun in the sky, it is because all light is in the souls; it flowers within men's breasts.

Liberty, it is thine hour of arrival! The whole world, pulling the victorious chariot, has brought thee to these shores. Here thou art like the poet's dream, as great as space, spanning heaven and earth!

That noise we hear— it is triumph resting.

That darkness we see— it is not the rainy day, nor gloomy October; it is the dust, tinted by death, thy chariot has raised up in its wake.

I can see them with drawn swords, holding their heads in their hands, their limbs a formless pile of bones, their bodies girded with flames, the stream of life oozing out of their broken foreheads like wings. Tunics, armor, scrolls of parchment, shields, books gather resplendently at thy feet, and thou commandest at last over the cities of interests and the phalanxes of war, oh aroma of the world! Oh goddess, daughter of man!

Man grows. Behold how he has outgrown churches and chosen the sky as the only temple worthy of sheltering his deity! But thou, oh marvelous one! growest with man; and armies, the whole city, the emblazoned ships about to exalt thee approach thy mist-veiled feet, like variegated shells dashed on the rocks by the somber sea when the fiend of tempest, wrapped in lightning, rides across the sky on a black cloud.

Thou hast done well, Liberty, in revealing thyself to the world on a dark day, for thou canst not yet be satisfied with thyself! Now you, my feastless heart, sing of the feast!

It was yesterday, October 28, that the United States solemnly accepted the Statue of Liberty which the people of France have donated to them in memory of July 4, 1776, when they declared their independence from England, won with the help of French blood. It was a raw day: the air was ashy, the streets muddy, the rain relentless; but seldom was man's rejoicing so great.

One felt a peaceful joy as though a balm soothed one's soul. From brows to which light is not lacking, light seemed to shine more brightly, and that fair instinct of human decency which illumines the dullest faces emerged even from opaque spirits, like a wave's surge.

The emotion was immense. The movement resembled a mountain chain. Not an empty spot remained on the streets. The two rivers seemed like solid land. The steamers, pearly in the fog, maneuvered crowded from wheel to wheel. Brooklyn Bridge groaned under its load of people. New York and its suburbs, as though invited to a wedding, had risen early. Among the happy crowds that filled the streets there were none as beautiful— not the workmen forgetful of their troubles, nor the women, nor the children—as those old men who had come from the country with their flying cravats and greatcoats to salute, in the commemorative statue the heroic spirit of the Marquis de Lafayette,[1] whom they as children had greeted with waving hands and boughs, because he loved Washington and helped him make this country free.

A grain of poetry suffices to season a century. Who can forget that beautiful friendship? Washington was the graver and older of the two. There was scarcely a down on Lafayette's upper lip. But they shared, under different appearances, the same blind determination and capacity of ascent common to all great personalities. That noble child had left wife and king to help the humble troops that in America were pushing the English king to the sea and phrasing, in sublime words, the teachings of the Encyclopedists, words through which the human race announced its coming of age with no less clatter than that which had accompanied the revelation of its infancy on Mount Sinai.

The blond hero kept company with the dawn. His strong soul preferred marching men to the iniquitous pomp with which his monarch paraded, shining opalescently on the shoulders of his hungry vassals like a saint carried on a litter by barefoot porters. His king persecuted him, England persecuted him, but his wife helped him.

God pity the heroic heart whose noble enterprises found no welcome at home! He left his house and regal wealth, armed his ship, wrote from his ship: "The happiness of America is intimately bound up with the happiness of Humanity. She is going to become a cherished and safe asylum of virtue, of tolerance, of equality and of peaceful liberty." How great his soul, ready to give up all the privileges of fortune to follow a handful of poorly clad rebels on their march through the snow! He jumped off his ship, flew to the Continental Congress: "I wish to serve America as a volunteer and without pay." Sometimes things happen on earth that shed a heavenly splendor over it.

Manhood seemed to have matured within that youthful body. He proved to be a general's general. As he clutched his wound with the

---

[1] Marquis de Lafayette (1757–1834) was a French general who fought in the American revolution.

one hand, with the other he commanded his fleeing soldiers to turn about and win. With a flash of his sword he mustered a column that a traitor had dispersed.

If his soldiers were on foot, he was on foot. If the Republic had no money, he who was offering her his life, advanced his fortune. Behold a man who glittered as though he were all gold! When his fame restored to him his king's affection, he realized France's hatred toward England could be helpful in chasing the exhausted English out of America.

The Continental Congress girded on him a sword of honor and wrote to the King of France: "We recommend this noble man to Your Majesty's notice, as one whom we know to be wise in counsel, gallant in the field, and patient under the hardships of war." He borrowed the wings of the sea. France, the vanguard of nations, bedecked herself with roses to receive her hero.

"It is a wonder Lafayette is not taking with him to his America the furniture of Versailles," exclaimed the French Minister, as Lafayette crossed the ocean with France's help to the newborn Republic, with Rochambeau's army and de Grasse's navy.[2]

Even Washington was at the time despairing of victory. But French noblemen and American farmers closed against Cornwallis[3] and routed him at Yorktown.

Thus did the United States assure with France's help the independence they had learned to wish for in terms of French thinking. The prestige of a heroic deed is such that this svelte marquis has sufficed to keep united during a century two nations that differ in spiritual warmth, in the idea of life, and in the very concept of liberty— egotistical and selfish in the United States, and generous and expansive in France. Blessed be the country that radiates its light!

Let us follow the throngs that fill the streets, coming from every direction. It is the day of the unveiling of the monument consecrating the friendship between Washington and Lafayette.

---

[2] Count Jean Baptiste de Rochambeau was commander-in-chief of the French troops and François Joseph Paul de Grasse commanded the French fleet sent to assist the American colonists in the War of Independence.

[3] Marquis Charles Cornwallis commanded British forces during the War of Independence.

People of all tongues are present at the ceremony.

The rejoicing is to be found among the common people. Banners flourish in men's hearts; a few on men's houses. The emblazoned grandstand where the procession is to pass awaits the President of the Republic, the delegates from France, the diplomatic corps, the state governors, the army generals.

Sidewalks, portals, balconies, roofs begin to seethe with a joyous mass of people. Many fill the wharves to await the naval procession. The war ships, the fleet of steamers, the prattling tugboats that will carry the invited guests to Bedloe's Island, where the statue stands waiting on her Cyclopean pedestal, her face covered by the French flag. But most gather along the route of the grand parade.

Here comes a band. Here comes a fire brigade with its ancient fire engine raised on stilts. The firemen wear black trousers and red shirts. The crowds make room for a group of deliriously happy Frenchmen. Then comes another group in beautiful uniforms garnished with gold braid, full, striped trousers, plumed cap, fierce mustachios, slender figures, bubbling palaver and very black eyes: they are a company of Italian volunteers. From around a corner juts the elevated railroad. Up above, a crowded train; down below policemen branching out to their beats, their blue frock coats well buttoned up with gilt buttons. The rain fails to wipe out everyone's smiles.

Now the crowds step back onto the sidewalk, as the mounted police advance pushing against them with their horses' haunches. A woman crosses the street, her oilcloth coat filled with commemorative medals bearing on one side the monument, on the other the sculptor Bartholdi's[4] pleasing likeness. There goes an anxious-looking man making notes as he walks.

But what about France? Here there is not much talk of France, nor of Lafayette. Little do they know of him. No one is aware of the fact that a magnificent gift of the modern French people to the American people is being celebrated.

There is another statue of Lafayette in Union Square, also the work of Bartholdi, a gift of France. Only the men of letters and the old men with the cravats remember the admirable marquis. There is

---

[4] The statue had been sculpted by Frédéric Auguste Bartholdi (1834–1904).

a new life boiling in the enormous cauldron. This country where each man lives and toils for himself has really not much love for that other country which has fertilized every human seed with its blood.

"France," says one ingrate "only helped us because her king was an enemy of England." "France," ruminates another in his corner, "gives us the Statue of Liberty so that we will let her finish the Panama Canal in peace."

"It is Laboulaye,"[5] says another, "who gave us the statue. He would apply English brakes to French liberty. Even as Jefferson learned from the Encyclopedists the principles of the Declaration of Independence, so did Laboulaye and Henri Martin try to take to France the methods of government the United States had inherited from the Magna Carta."

Yes, indeed, it was Laboulaye who inspired Bartholdi. It was his idea: Go, he said, and propose to the United States the construction, jointly with us, of a superb monument in commemoration of their independence. Yes, the statue was to signify the prudent Frenchman's admiration of the peaceful practices of American liberty.

Thus was born the idea which grew like the streamlet that swells along its course from the mountaintop until at last it reaches the sea. On the grandstand sit the delegates from France, the sculptor, the orator, the journalist, the general, the admiral, and this man who joins the seas and cleaves the land. French tunes flitter over the city; French flags flap against balconies and wave on the tops of buildings. But what livens all eyes and gladdens all souls is not the gift of a generous land, received perhaps with insufficient enthusiasm, but the brimming over of human pleasure on seeing the instinct of our own majesty, which resides in the marrow of our bones and constitutes the root and glory of our life, rise with stupendous firmness, a symbol of captivating beauty.

Behold, they all reveal the exhilaration of being reborn! Is not this nation, in spite of its rawness, the hospitable home of the oppressed? The voices that impel and counsel come from within, from deeper than the will. Flags are reflected on faces, heartstrings are plucked by a sweet love, a superior sense of sovereignty brings to countenances a look of peace, nay, of beauty. And all these luckless

---

[5] The statue was originally proposed by French jurist and politician Edouard René de Laboulaye (1811–83).

Irishmen, Poles, Italians, Bohemians, Germans, redeemed from oppression or misery, hail the monument to Liberty because they feel that through it they themselves are uplifted and restored.

Behold how they run toward the wharves from which the statue can be seen, elated as shipwrecked people who descry a hopeful sail! These are the humblest, those who fear the main streets and the clean people: pale tobacco workers, humpbacked stevedores, Italian women with their colored shawls. They do not run brutally, disorderly as on ordinary holidays, but in friendly equable groups. They come from the east side, the west side, the congested alleys of the poor neighborhoods. Sweethearts act like married couples, husbands offer their arms to their wives, mothers drag their young along. They question each other, encourage each other; cram into the positions from where they think they will see better.

In the meantime, among the crowd's hurrahs, the lavishly decorated gun carriages roll along the broad streets; buildings seem to speak and hail each other with their flags; the elevated trains, like an aerial, disciplined, steaming cavalry seem to stop, paw, unload their riders on the beach; the steamers restlessly test the ties that hold them to their moorings, and out there, in the distance, wrapped in smoke, the enormous statue rises, greeted by all the incense burners on earth, crowned with clouds, like a mountain.

The greatest celebration is at Madison Square where, facing the impious monument of Farragut[6] which commemorates the North Americans' inglorious victory over Mexico, rises from the grandstand bedecked with United States and French flags from where the President is to watch the parade. He has not yet arrived, but everyone is anxious. The brown helmets of policemen protrude above the dark mass. Tricolored festoons hang from house fronts.

The stand is like a bunch of roses on a black background. Now and then a murmur spreads over the nearby groups as though their collective soul had suddenly been enriched, for Lesseps[7] has walked up, and then come: Spuller, Gambetta's friend, with his steely eyes and powerful head; bold Jaurès who gloriously led 12,000 soldiers,

---

[6] David Glasgow Farrugut (1801–70): a naval commander during the American war against Mexico and the Civil War.

[7] Viscount Ferdinand de Lesseps (1805–04): French diplomat and financier who built the Suez Canal but failed to build a canal across Panama.

closely pursued by the Germans, out of the battle of Mamers; Pellisier who although wounded at Nogent-sur-Marne applied his pale hand to the wheels of his cannon; Lieutenant Ney who, when his Frenchmen fled in panic from a trench on fire, opened his arms, steadied his feet firmly on the ground, his face embellished by the bronze-hued glare, pushed the cowards through the hellish mouth and then followed; Laussédat, the gray-haired colonel who with youthful hands built barriers against the Prussian arms; Bureaux de Pussy who kept his great-grandfather Lafayette's sword from falling to the enemy; Deschamps, the Mayor of Paris, who three times fell prisoner to the Germans and three times got away; Villegente, the young naval officer like a figure out of a Neuville painting; Caubert, lawyer and soldier, who wanted to organize a legion of lawyers and judges to hold Prussia back; Bigot, Meunier, Desmons, Hielard, and Giroud, who have served the Fatherland bravely with purse or pen; and Bartholdi the creator of the statue, who planted on the buttress of Fort Belfort his sublime lion and cast in silver for Gambetta that pathetic, cursing Alsace, whose eyes, melancholy as great men's eyes are, reveal all the sadness of the standard bearer dying on his Alsace's bosom, and all the faith of the child by her side in whom the Motherland is reborn.

Familiarity with what is enormous cannot but engender light. The habit of conquering matter imparts to sculptors' faces an air of triumph and rebellion. The very capacity to admire what is great makes one great, much more so to model it, caress it, give wings to it, to extract from our mind the idea which, by means of our arms, our deep glances, our loving strokes, gradually curves and illumines the marble or the bronze.

This creator of mountains was born a free soul in the Alsatian city of Colmar, stolen from him later by the German foe, and in his eyes, inured to the sight of Egyptian colossi, liberty's beauty and grandeur took on the gigantic proportions and eminent majesty to which the Fatherland rises in the minds of those who live bereft of her. Bartholdi wrought his sovereign statue out of all his Fatherland's hopes.

Never did man create anything of real beauty without deep suffering. That is why the statue advances as though to step onto the promised land; that is why she bows her head and there is a widow's expression on her face; that is why she stretches her arm, as though to command and to guide, fiercely toward the sky.

Alsace! Alsace! cries every inch of her. The sorrowing virgin has come more to ask for a French Alsace than to light the way for world liberty.

Smiles and thoughts are but an abominable disguise, a tombstone when one lives without a Fatherland or when a part of it falls prey to the enemy's clutch. An atmosphere of drunkenness perturbs judgment, shackles words, quenches verses, and then whatever a nation's minds produce is deformed and empty, unless it expresses the soul's craving. Who feels more deeply the absence of a good than he who has possessed it and lost it? From the vehemence of sorrows stems the greatness of their representation.

There is Bartholdi, greeted lovingly by his comrades as he takes his place on the grandstand. A vague sadness veils his face; in his eyes shines a chaste grief; he walks as in a daze; looks where there is nothing to see; his unruly locks falling across his forehead bring to mind cypresses and shattered banners.

And there are the deputies: all have been chosen from those who fought most bravely in the war in which Alsace was lost to France.

Over there sits Spuller, Gambetta's friend. At the reception given by the French Circle of Harmony in honor of their compatriots there had been vague talk full of compliments, talk of historic brotherhood, of generous abstractions. Then Spuller appeared, a veritable lion. At first his speech was like a prayer, he spoke slowly, sadly as one burdened with some pain. Over the august, tearful silence he gradually draped his flaming words; when he drew them to a close the whole audience sprang to its feet; Spuller was sheathed in an invisible flag; the air seemed to vibrate like a smitten sword: Alsace! Alsace!

Now Spuller moves with bowed head, as those who are preparing to charge always do.

The French delegates gathered on that grandstand together with President Cleveland and the country's personages surrounding him watched the gala parade with which New York celebrated the dedication of the statue: rivers of bayonets, miles of red shirts, gray, blue and green militiamen, a spot of white naval caps, a miniature model of the *Monitor* on a truck led by a boy in navy uniform.

The artillery in its blue uniforms passes by; the police, marching heavily; the cavalry, with their yellow lapels; on either hand the sidewalks black with people. The "hurrah!" raised at the foot of Central Park passed on from mouth to mouth and died amid the rumble of the Battery. Then pass Columbia University students wearing their square caps; then carriages bearing invalids, veterans and judges; and then Negro groups. Bands are heard; an anthem follows them all the way.

The gallant Seventh Regiment militia gets applause from the grandstand; the 22nd Regiment militiamen are handsome in their campaign capes; two German girls who came with one company hand the President two baskets of flowers; almost speechless, a child dressed in blue presents Lesseps with a silk banner for Bartholdi; the golden clarion notes of the *Marseillaise* fly over the procession; the President salutes bareheaded the tattered flags; as they pass the grandstand each company dips its colors and each French militia officer kisses the hilt of his sword. There are frantic cheers from the stand, sidewalks and balconies when armless sleeves, bullet-riddled flags, wooden legs pass by.

An old man in a dove-colored cloak drags himself along. Everyone wants to shake his hand. There was a time in his youth when he was a volunteer and pulled a fire engine as bravely as now he drags his old bones. He had broken his arms catching in them a child in flames, and his legs trying to protect an old man from a falling wall. He is followed by firemen dressed as in days of old and pulling their engines by means of ropes. Just as the oldest engine of all, lovingly cared for, brightly polished and laden with flowers, comes shaking on its fragile wheels behind the young redcoats, one of the formidable new engines dashes through the crowd to put out a fire nearby. It leaves the air stricken and warm in its wake. The smoke is black, the horses black. It knocks down carts, runs over people. Puffs of sparks redden its smoky mane.

Then the hook-and-ladder wagon flies by, followed by the enormous pumper as noisy as the artillery.

A bell sounding like an order is heard and the masses respectfully step aside to allow the passage of an ambulance with a wounded person. The regiments can still be heard far away. The golden clarion notes of the *Marseillaise* still hover over the city.

Then, when the hour came to draw away the flag that veiled the statue's face, everyone's heart swelled and it seemed as though the sky had become covered with a canopy of eagle wings. People rushed to the boats as impatiently as would bridegrooms.

Even the steamers, dressed to look like great wreaths, seemed to smile, chatter and bustle about as merrily as girls at a wedding feast.

Everyone's thoughts were uplifted by a deep feeling of respect as though the festival of liberty evoked all those who have died in its quest. Over our heads a ghostly battle was being waged! Oh, the lances, the shields, the statuesque dead, the superb agonies! One fighter's shadow alone was as great as a public square. They stood up straight, stretched out their arms, glanced down on men as if they were creating them, and then vanished.

The brightness which suddenly cleaved the dark atmosphere was not from the rays of the sun, but caused by clefts between the shields through which the splendor of the battle pierced the mist. They fought, they fell, they died singing. Such is the triumphal hymn which, better than the sounds of bells and cannon, becomes this statue made, rather than of bronze, of all the sunshine and poetry in the human soul.

From the time the parade was over, until dusk brought an end to the celebrations on the island where the monument stands, New York City and its bay were like one great cannon volley, a ringing of bells, a column of smoke.

The docks, bereft of their steamboats, looked like toothless gums. The continuous cannon volleys increased the rain. Two hundred ships made their way through the brown fog to the island like a procession of elephants. Like pregnant pigeons, the curious steamships crowded around the figure, which could be seen indistinctly towering above them. There was billing and cooing. Bursts of music came from the steamships like detached wings. Even those who have not suffered for freedom can understand the frantic joy that crazed all souls when, at last, their eyes caught sight of that figure whom all address as a beloved mistress.

There she stands, at last, on her pedestal taller than the towers, splendid as a storm and kind as the sky! In her presence eyes once again knew what tears are. It was as though souls opened and flew to take refuge among the folds of her tunic, to whisper in her ear, to perch on her shoulders, to die like butterflies in her light. She seemed alive, wrapped in clouds of smoke, crowned by a vague brightness, truly like an altar with streamers kneeling at her feet! Not even Rhodes's Apollo, with the urn of fire on his head and the dart of light in his hand, was higher; nor Phidias's all gold-and-ivory Jupiter, son of the age when men were still women; nor the Hindus' statue of Sumnat, inlaid with precious stones like their fancy; nor the two thirsty statues at Thebes, captive at the desert soul on their chiseled pedestals; nor the foul colossi guarding by the mouth of a cavern the temple at Ipsambul. She is greater than the Saint Charles Borromeo in crude bronze on the hill at Arona by the lake; greater than the Virgin at Puy, a low-flighted conception on the mount overlooking the hamlet; greater than the Cheruscian Armenius who rises over the Teutoburg gate summoning with his sword the German tribesmen to rout Varus's legions; greater than the Niderwald "Germania," a sterile armored beauty who opens not her arms; greater than Schwanthaler's "Bavaria," who proudly crowns herself on the Munich plain, with a lion at her feet; over and above the churches of all creeds and all the buildings of men. She rises from out of a star-shaped pedestal, "Liberty Enlightening the World," without any lion or sword. She is made of all the art there is in the Universe, even as Liberty is made of all the sufferings of mankind.

She has Moses's Tablets of the Law, Minerva's uplifted arm, Apollo's flaming torch, the Sphinx's mysterious expression, Christianity's airy diadem.

Even as mountains rise out of the depths of the earth, so has this statue, "an immense idea in an immense form," sprung from the brave aspiration of the human soul.

Man's soul is peace, light and purity. Simply clad, Liberty seeks heaven as her natural abode. Girdles are painful to Liberty; she disdains crowns that hide her forehead; she loves nakedness as symbolic of Nature; Liberty stands pure in the light from which she was born.

Thus the tunic and the peplum befit Liberty as a protection against unlove and impure desire. Sadness also becomes her, that sadness which will only leave her eyes when all men love each other. It is right that she be barefoot, as one who only feels life in her heart. The diadem, made of the fire of her thoughts, emerges naturally from her temples, and even as a mountain ends in its peak so does the statue taper to the torch above in a condensation of light.

At the foot of the statue, the grandstand built for the occasion from fresh pine trees and adorned with virgin flags seemed as small as a poppy. The more favored guests occupied the platform in front of the stand. The whole island was like one human being.

How the people roared when their President, who had come up as they had from the worker's bench, stepped into the official launch to go and accept the image in which every man seems to see himself redeemed and uplifted! Only an earthquake is comparable to such an explosion.

The rumble of cannon smothered out the clamor of men. The steam compressed in the boilers of factories and ships escaped in unison with a mad, stirring, wild jubilation. At times it seemed as though the soul of the Indian charged across the sky yelling its war cry; or that churches knelt, their belfries bent over, their bells pealing; or that from the steamers' chimneys came, now weak, now strident, the cock's crow, the symbol of victory.

What was enormous became childlike: steam rushed in the boilers; lighters frolicked through the fog; the crowds on the steamers nagged the bands; stokers, garbed in gold by the glare of the fire, poked coal into the furnaces; through puffs of smoke one could see sailors standing on the yards of navy vessels.

At the grandstand the commander-in-chief of the American army called in vain for silence, waving his black three-cornered hat. Nor did the Reverend Storrs's prayer, lost in the confusion, quiet the bustle. But Lesseps did conquer it, Lesseps with his 80-year-old head bare in the rain. The magnificent spectacle was unforgettable. The great old man had not simply stood but jumped to his feet.

A small man: he would fit in the hollow of the Statue of Liberty's hand, started to speak. His voice was so firm and fresh that the illustrious gathering, fascinated, enraptured, hailed that human monument with an interminable cheer. Compared to this man, accustomed to severing continents in order to join seas, what was all that clatter, the clamor of machines, the cannonade from the ships, the monument which towered above him?

Why, he even provoked laughter there in front of the statue with his first words! "That steam, American citizens, which has done so much good to the world, at this moment I find very obnoxious and harmful."

Marvelous old man! Americans do not like him because he is doing, in spite of them, what they have not had the courage to do. But with his first words he won them over. Then he read his speech written in his own hand on big, white, loose sheets of paper. He spoke familiarly or gave familiar form to graver matters. From the way he phrases his sentences we can see how it has been easy for him to reshape the earth. Within his every idea, no bigger than a nutshell, is contained a mountain.

As he speaks he moves incessantly; he turns to every side so as to face everyone. When he utters some phrases he drives them home with a movement of his head. He speaks a martial French, resonant like bronze. His favorite gesture is to raise his arm rapidly. He knows the land should be trodden victoriously. His voice as he talks on grows stronger instead of weaker. His short phrases are wavy and pointed like pennants. He was invited by the American government as the foremost Frenchman of his time.

"I have hastened to come," he says as he lays his hand on the flag of France draped in front of the rostrum; "the idea of erecting the Statue of Liberty does honor to those who conceived it as it likewise does to those who with understanding have received it." To him France is the mother of nations and with exceptional skill he mentions without contradiction the opinion expressed by Hepworth Dixon: "An English historian, Hepworth Dixon, in his book *New America*, after having said of your constitution that it is not a product of the soil, and that it does not emanate from the English idea, adds it can, on the contrary, be regarded as an exotic plant born in the atmosphere of France."

He does not deal in symbols but in objects. Things exist, in his opinion, according to what they are good for. The Statue of Liberty leads him to his Panama Canal. "You like men who dare and persevere. I say, like you, 'Go ahead!' We understand each other when I use that term!"

Oh, benevolent old man! Before he sits down, rewarded by the applause even of his opponents, astounded and won over, let thanks reach him from us "down there," from the America which has not yet had her fiesta, because he remembered our peoples and pronounced our forgotten name on that historic day when America consecrated Liberty, for who have better known how to die for her than we? Or loved her more?

"Until we meet again in Panama, where the 38 stars of North America will soon float at the side of the banners of the independent States of South America, and will form in the New World, for the benefit of all mankind, the peaceful and prolific alliance of the Franco-Latin and the Anglo-Saxon races!"

Good old serpent charmer! Lucid soul who sees the greatness of our hearts under our bloodstained garments! The other America loves you because you spoke of Liberty as though she were your daughter!

Before Senator Evarts got up to offer the statue to the President of the United States on behalf of the American Commission, the audience, stirred by Lesseps's words, insisted on greeting Bartholdi, who, with becoming modesty, stood and gratefully acknowledged the tribute. Senator Evarts's speeches are characterized by noble language and lofty content, and his eloquence, deft and genuine, reaches the heart because it is born of the heart.

But his voice fades when he read from narrow sheets his speech depicting France's generosity in phrases like ribbons and pompons. After Lesseps he seemed a stooping reed: his head is all forehead; his inspiration finds difficulty in shining through his lean, parched face; he is dressed in a frock coat with turned-up collar and a black cap on his head.

Before he concluded his speech someone mistakenly thought the expected moment had arrived when the banner covering the face of the statue would be drawn, and the navy, the ships, the city broke out in a unanimous din that seemed to ascend to high heaven from a shield of resounding bronze. Astounding pomp! Sublime majesty! Never did a people incline with greater reverence before any altar! Men at the foot of the pedestal, stunned by their own smallness, looked at each other as if they had fallen from above. Far away the cannon boomed, masts disappeared in the smoke, the growing clamor spread through the air. In the distance the statue seemed like a huge mother among the clouds.

President Cleveland seemed entirely worthy of speaking in her presence. His style too has marrow, his accent is sincere, his voice warm, clear and powerful. He suggests more than he explains. He said such broad, lofty things as sound well before a monument. His left hand rested on the rostrum rail, his right he sank under the lapel of his frock coat. His glance had that challenge which becomes honest winners.

Shall we not forgive for being haughty one who knows he is surrounded by enemies because he is pure? His mind is compensation for his overflowing fleshiness. He looks what he is, kind and strong. Lesseps glanced upon him affectionately as if wanting to make friends.

He too, like Lesseps, bared his head to speak. His words brought forth applause not so much for the pompous phrase and commanding gesture, as for their vibrating tone and sound sense. If the statue could be melted into words, they would say the same: "This token of the love and esteem of the French people proves the kinship between republics and assures us that we have a firm ally across the Atlantic in our efforts to recommend to all men the excellence of a government built on the will of the people." "We are not here today to bow our heads before the image of a warlike and fearful god, full of wrath and vengeance, but to contemplate joyfully our own goddess guarding the gates of America, greater than all those the ancients worshiped, a goddess who instead of wielding the bolts of terror and death, raises to heaven the beacon that lights the way to man's emancipation." The long applause that rewarded this honest man came from loving hearts.

Then Chauncey Depew, "the silver orator," began the main oration. It must have been good when he was able to hold untiringly the public's attention at a late hour.

Who is Chauncey Depew? All that talent can be without generosity. Railroads are his business, millions his figures, emperors his public, the Vanderbilts his friends and Maecenas. Men are of little concern to him, railroads of much. He has a preying eye, a broad, haughty brow, a hooked nose, a thin, narrow upper lip, a long, pointed, close-shaven chin. He is idolized here because his speech is brilliant and harmonious, his will aggressive and sharp, his judgement keen and sure. On this occasion his fresh, versatile style did not sparkle as it often does in his much praised after-dinner talks, nor did he present a point with irrefutable logic as when he pleads a case as lawyer and railroad executive, nor had he adversaries to browbeat mercilessly as he is reputed doing at the malignant, fearful performances of political meetings. Instead, he told in fiery phrases the generous life of him who, not satisfied with having helped Washington found his nation, returned— blessed be the Marquis de Lafayette!— to ask the North American Congress to free "his Negro brothers."

In ardent paragraphs he described the friendly talks between Lafayette and Washington at the latter's modest Mount Vernon home and the speech with which the Marquis, "purified by battles and privations," took leave of the American Congress, in which he saw "an immense temple of liberty, a lesson to all the oppressors and a hope to all the oppressed of the world."

The year of 1793 did not appall him, nor the dungeon at Olmütz tame him, nor Napoleon's victory convince him. To one who really feels liberty in his heart, what are persecutions but challenges, or unjust empires but soap bubbles? It is such men of instinct that guide the world. They act first and reason after. Thought corrects their errors, but lacks the virtue of sudden action. The feel and push. Thus by the will of nature it is written that things should be in the history of man!

Chauncey Depew looked like a magistrate when, shaking his arm and a trembling forefinger over his head covered with a silk cap, he summarized admirably the benefits man enjoys in this land founded on liberty; and with all the fire of a charger that feels his loins sorely spurred, he transformed his hidden fear into bravery, rose up in the name of free institutions to attack the fanatics who, under their protection, would seek to defeat them, and having learned the lesson of the social problem spreading over the United States, this "silver-worded" gentleman humbled the pride for which he is noted and drew out inspired strains to utter as his own the very phrases which are the gospel of the workers' revolution.

Oh, Liberty, how convincing is thy shadow: those who hate thee or use thee bow before the commanding gesture!

Then a bishop appeared on the rostrum. He raised an age-bitten hand; all around the men of genius and of power stood up. There was a magnificent silence while he blessed in the name of God the redeeming statue. Guided by the bishop the audience intoned a slow, soft hymn, a mystic doxology. A sign from the top of the torch indicated the ceremony was over.

Streams of people, fearful of grim night, rushed to the narrow wharves, without concern for age or rank. Bands were heard vaguely as though lulled by the evening twilight.

The weight of joy rather than the weight of people seemed to load down the ships. Cannon smoke covered the official launch that carried the president back to the city. High above, the astonished birds circled fearfully around the statue as though it were the top of a new mountain. Men felt their hearts were firmer within their breasts.

When, among shadows, the last boats left the shores of the island, now transformed into an altar, a crystal-clear voice breathed out a popular melody which passed from ship to ship. Garlands of lights, reddening the sky's canopy, shone from the cornices of buildings. A song, at once soft and formidable, spread at the statue's feet and along the river. A united people, pressed together on the sterns of ships, gazing toward the island, with an unction fortified by night, sang: "Farewell, my only love!"

New York, October 29, 1886

The Munkácsy Christ

At the end of 1886, the Hungarian painter Michael Lieb, who was known as Munkácsy (1844–1900), visited the United States. The contents, form and intention of his work had a marked national character, linked to the desire for independence of the Hungarian people. As in other previous occasions, Martí avails of a feature article to enhance values very much in accordance with the ideas and criteria rooted in his own spirit. This article, published in La Nación, *Buenos Aires, January 28, 1887, essentially focuses on the Hungarian painter's masterpiece* Christ Before Pilate.

Today we will follow all of New York to see the painting of Christ by the Hungarian artist Munkácsy. Painters, poets, journalists, clergy, politicians are shouting "Elhem, elhem!" meaning "Hurrah!" wherever Munkácsy appears in his current visit to New York. They cheer his name as if to enhance the fame and fortune of his canvas. Yesterday the city's distinguished men gave him a banquet and upon the wall, above his head with its heavy shock of hair, "Istem-Hozot" or "God brought you to us" was spelled out in letters of flowers. The luxurious manner with which he was treated while traveling is reminiscent of the way Rubens lived— a man who wanted everything dripping with gold and silver, and who even enjoyed seeing the pomp and splendor of jewels upon feminine flesh itself. In Washington he was celebrated with great feasts, brocade tablecloths, all hung with red damask, the wealth of kings. But his sublime Christ, in the modest tabernacle where it is on view, is receiving even more honor than the artist. By some secret magic of the paintbrush, the white linen robe gives forth a great light which dominates and intensifies everything around it, restfully drawing together all varied movement of the whole, and investing with captivating majesty a solitary body from which the linen cloth hangs in graceful folds.

Ah, one has to fight to fully understand those who have fought! To fully understand Jesus it is necessary to have come into the world in a darkened manger with a pure and devout spirit, and to go through life touched by the scarcity of love, the flowering of cupidity, and the victory of hate. One must have sawed wood and kneaded bread amid the silence and transgressions of men. This Michael Munkácsy, now married to a rich widow who lends the charm of a palace to her house in Paris, was in his early years the "poor little Miska" from Munkács. He was born in a fortress in the days when the Russians were laying waste to Hungary, and when the entire lovely country of forests and vineyards looked like a cupful of colors shattered by a horse's hoof.

Those souls never saw the sun. People were starving to death. Munkácsy's mother died of hunger. His father died in prison. The robbers born in wartime killed all who remained in the house and left no one alive but him, close to the body of his aunt. The child never knew how to laugh. A poor uncle put him to work as a carpenter's apprentice. He worked a 12-hour day for a peso a week. Some school children, grieved to see that sad but eager face, taught him to read and write, and he caressed those letters with his eyes.

Not knowing why, he began painting the chests in the carpentry shop with heroic scenes of Hungarians and Serbians wearing their shaggy helmets, close-fitting boots and curved daggers. Finally, his uncle began to prosper and sent him away to regain his strength. The place seemed like heaven to Miska, for there he saw a portrait painter who managed his colors so well that they brought to life at will all those heroes that the boy had painted upon the carpentry shop chests. Miska pleaded with the portrait painter so fervently that he succeeded in staying with him to learn to paint. He was such an apt pupil that within a few months he gave drawing lessons, and painted the family of a tailor so much to "Sr. Cloth Cutter's" liking that the man paid him for his work with an overcoat.

In those days he was already an avid reader, and the heroic types and periods in history assumed the task of invading his soul with light—a soul that death, war, and the orphanage had clothed like a darkened funeral parlor. But the Hungarians worship Nature, with their stubborn black eyes, naked passions, open homes and a free and joyous countryside. Their music is epitomized by Liszt, their poetry by Petofi, their orators by Kossuth. They drink new wine from wineskins, and love with a consuming ardor. When playing their spirited music they have the storm-tossed mane of a charger, the voice of a flower and the call of a dove. This is the land of those colorful Gypsies and their gay and picturesque caravans, their love-making with the scent of early fruits, their curly headed vagabonds who fall in love with the queens.

Life flowers and overflows there, comes out of cannons and rules and preserves its regal aspect even in vice and effeminacy; all those vagabonds resemble princes whimsically disguised as beggars. Foreign ideas troubled Munkácsy as if they were bridles. His love of Nature was racial and inborn, and he preferred life to books. He found it absolutely necessary to create, and had that thirst for truth, unknown to the learned, that makes men great. Men are like the stars, for some of them give out the inner light and others shine with the light they reflect. How could Munkácsy paint his gloomy memories, but with the sorrows of his soul, the very colors that have given him no joy? One can see what he carried in his inner self; man places himself above Nature and alters her light and harmony at will. This is how poor Miska trained his impatient hand; and since he came from those who have their own intrinsic law and color, from which the artist in him overflowed, he always searched in his subject for the picturesque. But it was from his soul, which too seldom saw the sunlight, that he extracted the lugubrious tones so well fortified by his own superiority, from which only love and the kind of glory that attracts enlightenment were later to be separated. In that black bed of pitch, however shone the eyes of a Gypsy.

And did that courageous, direct, self-possessed man have to amuse himself by clothing mummies, by fondling masks, by grouping academies? Not at all. Life is full of enchantment and the picturesque. When he felt his strength mature and given praise in exhibition halls and competitions, that which occurred to him to paint, with much uproar from the usually placid Knaus, was a living sign, a famous canvas entitled *The Last Day of the Condemned Man*. The man under sentence is praying face down upon a table whose white tablecloth sets off a crucifix standing between a pair of candles. His poor moaning wife leans against the dreary wall; their little daughter stands between them; at the door to the cell a soldier holds back the crowds. The painter put into that work all his poor man's pity, the color of his solitary soul, his new man's courage.

He was awarded the Paris prize; his art and his very existence have grown with legendary beauty and swiftness. Every one of Munkácsy's canvases is an attack. He is a well-known artist in the outside world, but in his own home his wife's affection gives him the courage to earn that fame. She praises his creations, returns to his hands the palette laid aside by his sense of futility or despair; she alights upon his shoulder like a hummingbird, to whisper into his ear in such a way that he fails to realize that her voice is not his own, that arm too high, that eye not attentive enough, that slightly brutal foot a slur upon her Miska. She drives away the last vestiges of his sadness. She softens his daring groupings, brings green and blues to his studio. Not the umber; that she cannot make disappear completely, for when a soul is baptized by darkness some salt is left upon the brow, like a diamond rose, and there is a pleasure in darkness. White does not attract him either, for this takes the painter out of himself with epic boldness.

Every day, the force of ideas nourished the creativity of this spirit that evolved the pulsating beings of his canvas principally from inside himself, with little aid from books, and because of his admiration for intellectual power he began to feel a deep affection for the blind and wasted Milton as being representative of the finest model of the strength and beauty of ideas. And then, to further emphasize his indigence and depression, he rose higher to a love for Christ before whose triumphant light he grouped the most fearsome and active power on earth: egoism and envy. He has intentionally brought together apparently insurmountable difficulties, and has been eager to make the human mind triumph by means of its own splendor. He has succeeded in investing an ugly figure with supreme beauty, and in dominating with a figure in repose all the ferocity and brilliance of the passions animatedly contending for that figure.

That is his Christ. This is his strange concept of Christ. He does not see him as charity, as charming resignation, as immaculate and absolute forgiveness not at all applicable to human nature. The pleasure of controlling one's anger is applicable indeed, but man's nature would be less lovely and efficacious if it were able to stifle its indignation in the presence of infamy, which is the purest source of strength.

He sees Jesus as the most perfect incarnation of the invincible power of the idea. The idea consecrates, inflames, attenuates, exalts, purifies; it gives a stature that is invisible but can be felt; it cleanses the spirit of dross the way fire consumes the underbrush; it spreads a clear and secure beauty which reaches the soul and is felt in it. Munkácsy's Jesus is the power of the pure idea.

There he is in a loose-fitting robe, thin and bony. His wrists are bound, his neck stretched out, his tight lips partly open as if to make way for the final bitterness. One feels that evil hands have just been placed upon him; that the human pack of hounds surrounding him has begun to sniff at him as if he were a wild animal; that he has been harassed, beaten, spat upon, dragged by force, has had his robe torn to shreds, and has been reduced to the lowest and most despicable condition. And that instant of extreme humiliation is precisely the one which the artist chooses to make him emerge with a majesty that dominates the powers of the law before him, and the brutality pursuing him, without the aid of a single gesture or a visible muscle, thus making Christ emerge with the dignity of his garments, the height of his stature, the exclusive use of white pigments, and the mystical aureola of painters!

And there is no more assistance from the head, from the noble downcast eyes in their hollow eye sockets, from the sunken cheeks, the tight-lipped mouth revealing a human courage still, the calm and admirable forehead above the temples sparsely covered with hair like a canopy over the brows.

The secret of that figure's singular power are the eyes! Anguish and aspiration are clearly seen in them as are resurrection and life eternal! The winds can strip trees bare, men can topple thrones, fire from the earth can decapitate mountains; but even without the violent and sickly stimulus of fantasy, one can feel that his glance, by means of his natural power, will continue to shed its fire.

All things will bow before those eyes which focus all the love, affirmation, splendor and pride that the spirit can hold. Jesus is near the four wide steps leading to Pilate's council chamber, and Pilate appears to be prostrate before him. Pilate's tunic is also white, but Jesus's robe, through no visible trick of the brush, shines with a light quite unlike that of the cowardly judge.

Wrath runs rampant beside him, insolence is bold, the law is being debated, loud are the demands for Jesus's death. But those courageous and inquiring eyes, those frenetic and impudent faces, those talking and shouting mouths, those angry upraised arms, instead of deflecting the strength and light of his fulgurant figure, focus upon it and put it into sharp relief by contrasting his sublime energy with the base passion surrounding him.

The scene is set in the vast and austere praetorium. Through the entrance in the background, which has just admitted the multitude, one can see a patch of glorious sky shining like the wings of Muzo's blue butterflies.

At the left of the canvas the excited crowd pushed toward the figure of Jesus. The painter refused to place him in the center, to have that one extra difficulty to overcome. A magnificent soldier raises his lance to drive away a peasant, and the man shouts and waves his arms—an imposing figure! There is that bestial type among the people—beardless, with a large mouth, flattened nose, wide cheekbones, small gelatinous eyes, low forehead! He overflows with that insane hatred of despicable natures for the souls who dazzle and shame them with their splendor. And without any artful effort or violence in contrast, the painting most forcibly projects its two-fold moral and physical opposition: the virtuous man who loves and dies, and the bestial man who hates and kills.

At the right is the Roman Pilate, his white toga bordered with the red of the patricians; one can guess by the softness of the folds that it is made of wool. The modeling of Pilate's figure is astounding; in a recess of the council chamber he seems to be alive. His eyes bespeak his troublesome thoughts, his fear of the populace, his respect for the accused, his hesitation in lifting one hand from his knee as if wondering what is going to become of Jesus.

Caiaphas the fanatic can be compared with the finest creation in art. His head turned toward the praetor, he gestures imperiously to the crowd that demands Jesus's death; that white-bearded head rebukes and compels; from those lips come cruel and impassioned words.

Two doctors seated to the left in the council chamber look at Jesus as if they had never been able to fully understand him.

Beside Caiaphas an old man has his eyes fixed upon Pilate whose head is bowed. A wealthy Sadducee, white-turbaned and white-bearded, gives Jesus his total attention; richly clothed and self-satisfied, he is seated upon a bench, his right arm bent, his left resting upon his thigh; he is the detested rich man of every age! Wealth has made him swell with a brutal pride; humanity is his footstool, he is worshiped for his purse and its bulging contents. Between him and Caiaphas some priests argue about this legal case, one with a stern expression in his eyes, one with the assurance of a petty lawyer. Another, leaning against the wall as he stands upon a bench, calmly surveys the turbulent scene. Behind the Sadducee and close to Jesus, a marvelously realistic peasant leans over the railing in a violent posture to see the prisoner face to face. Above the peasant's head and beside the column of the arch that wisely divides the scene, a young mother with babe in arms fixes her devout eyes upon Jesus— eyes and figure so reminiscent of Italian Madonnas. There in the background, to break the row of heads, stands a bearded Bedouin holding out his brutal arm to Jesus.

It is impossible to see this gigantic canvas without having one's mind, already weary of so much inferior, patchwork and fallacious art, assaulted by the memory of that era of fixed ideals in which painters treated their churches and palaces in the grand manner.

That light from the captive Christ, which draws the eye to him as the inevitable end of one's perusal of the canvas; that sturdy and spacious arch which instead of robbing the Christ of effect heightens and completes it; that forceful, new and lively group of men; that knowledge of how to make the most exquisite colors stand out from the somber background without the use of artifice— colors as warm and rich and mellow as those of the old Venetian school; that sure and harmonious concept in which none of the less important figures lose power and relief when subjugated to the central and principal one; those eloquent facial expressions that tell of their owner's consuming passion; that masterful boldness of detail, contempt for artifice, contrasts and direct light; that truth, grace and movement, and the patch of sky which from a distance inflames and perfects them— all these things indicate that the poor Miska of Munkács village, who now lives in Paris like the king of painters, is one of those magnificent spirits, so rare in this age of pressure and crisis, who can intimately embrace a human idea, reduce it to its component parts, and reproduce it with the energy and intensity required of works that are worthy of the approbation of the ages.

Not in vain has this painting been shown triumphantly throughout Europe. Not in vain did Paris give the admirable Valtner the medal of honor for his brilliant etching of *Christ Before Pilate*. Not in vain, in this century whose chaotic and preparatory greatness could not be reduced to symbols, does this canvas of Munkácsy move and excite both the critics and the people at large, even if some of its figures are indeed violent, and if some of its composition may appear to have been added to the main idea as an afterthought, for decorative effect, and even if the artist's faith in the religion he commemorates has been lost.

True genius never rushes to the admiration of men who need to be great in spite of themselves. But can it be merely a faculty for composing in the grand manner, a strength and brilliance in the use of color, a harmonious grace in arranging the figures, an impact of the work as a whole— can it be all this, in these days of rebellious beliefs and new subject matter, that assures such wide popularity to the familiar matter of a religion gone down to defeat?

This painting contains something besides the pleasure produced by harmonious composition and the liking induced by an artist who impetuously addresses and splendidly completes a courageous work of art. It is the man in the painting who delights and arrests one's judgement. It is the triumph and resurrection of Christ, but as he lives his life and because of his human strength. It is the vision of our own strength in the pride and splendor of virtue. It is the victorious new idea aware that its light can free the soul without any extravagant and supernatural communion with creation; it is ardent love and disdain for self that took the Nazarene to his martyrdom. It is Jesus without a halo, the man subdued, the living Christ, the human, the rational and courageous Christ.

It is the courage with which the Hungarian Munkácsy— his artist's intuition foreseeing what his study corroborated, understood and accomplished (for his passion and motives were always one), and ridding himself of legends and weakly portrayed figures— it is the courage with which he studied in his own soul the mystery of our divine nature, and with the brush and a free spirit stated that the divine resides in the human! But one's fondness for the pleasing error is so forceful, and the soul so certain of a more beautiful figure beyond this life, that the new Christ does not appear to be completely beautiful.

New York, December 2, 1886

The Funeral of the Haymarket Martyrs: A Terrible Drama

On May 4, 1886, a bomb exploded during a peaceful labor demonstration against police brutality in Chicago's Haymarket Square. In a wave of hysteria, a number of anarchists, anarcho-syndicalists and alleged anarchists were rounded up, and eight men were tried. Four of these, Albert R. Parsons, August Spies, George Engel and Adolph Fischer, were subsequently executed for this crime. A fifth (Louis Lingg) apparently committed suicide. Three others were convicted and imprisoned.

Martí's article, excerpted here, was published in La Nación, *Buenos Aires, January 1, 1888.*

Neither fear of social justice, nor blind sympathy on the part of those who initiate it, must guide nations in their crises, or the reporter of those crises. Freedom is well served only by the one who, at the risk of being taken for its enemy, is calmly preserving it from those whose mistakes are endangering it. He who excuses their wrongs and crimes because of an effeminate fear of appearing lukewarm in its defense does not deserve the title of defender of freedom. Nor should we pardon anyone who is incapable of controlling the hatred and antipathy that the crime inspires, or who passes judgement on social ills without knowing and weighing the historic causes from which they come, or the generous impulses they produce.

In a solemn procession of mourning followers, the flower-covered coffins containing the bodies of the four anarchists Chicago had sentenced to the gallows, and the man who, because he preferred not to die that way, exploded a dynamite bomb concealed in the thick curls of his young head of chestnut hair, have just been taken to their graves.

Accused of instigating or being a party to the frightful death of one of the policemen who suggested dispersing the group, these men were gathered to protest the death of six workers at the hands of the police, in an attack on the only factory to break the strike. Accused of having made and helped to throw— even if it were not thrown— the orange-sized bomb that knocked down the rear ranks of the police and left one dead, later caused the death of six more, and seriously wounded 50 others, the judge, in accord with the verdict of the jury, condemned one of the criminals to 15 years in the penitentiary and seven others to death by hanging.

Never since the War of the South, since the tragic days when John Brown died like a criminal for attempting single handed at Harper's Ferry what the nation, inspired by his bravery, attempted later as a crown of glory— never was there such interest in or such a hue and cry about a hanging in the United States.

Furious as a wolf, the entire Republic engaged in the fight to prevent the efforts of a benevolent lawyer, a girl in love with one of the prisoners and a Spanish-Indian half-breed mother of another— alone against an enraged country— from robbing the gallows of the seven human bodies it believed essential to the gallows' perpetuation.

The nation is terrified by the increased organization among the lower classes, by the sudden agreement among the working masses, who restrain themselves only in the presence of the rivalries of their employers. It is frightened of the impending separation of the country's population into the same two classes of privileged and discontented that cause so much ferment in European society. Therefore the Republic decided, by tacit agreement resembling complicity, to use a crime born of its own transgressions as much as of the fanaticism of the criminals in order to strike terror by holding them up as an example— not to the doleful rabble that will never triumph in a country of reason but to the tremendous emerging strata. The free man's natural aversion to crime, together with the harsh ill-will of the despotic Irishman who regards this country as his own and the German and Slav as the intruder, assumed on the part of the privileged sector— in this trial which has been a battle, an unfair hypocritical battle— the sympathies and almost inhuman aid of those who suffer from the same wrongs, the same desertion, the same bestial working conditions, the same heartbreaking misery whose constant spectacle fired the Chicago anarchists with such eagerness to right those wrongs that it dulled their judgment.

When the carpenters were already at work setting up the timbers for the scaffold, some who felt ashamed and others who dreaded a barbarous retribution went to plead for mercy to the governor, a feeble old man subservient to the supplications and flattery of the monied classes who were asking him, even at the risk of his life, to save the threatened society.

Until that time only three voices, not counting the professional defenders and natural friends of the victims, had dared to intercede for those unfortunate men who, on the pretext of a specific accusation that was never proved, and on the pretext of their having tried to establish a reign of terror, were dying as the prey of social terror. These voices belonged to Howells, the Boston novelist whose generosity caused him to sacrifice reputation and friends; Adler, the strong but cautious thinker who discerns a new world in the travail of our century; and Train, a monomaniac who spends all his time in the public square feeding the birds and talking with children.

Finally, in a horrible dance of death, turning and twisting and crammed into their white tunics, the accused men died.

Finally, without having been able to put more fire into the stoves, more bread into the pantries, more social justice into the distribution of wealth; without having instituted more safeguards against hunger for the useful members of society; without having been able to secure more light and hope for the hovels of the poor, or more relief for all that seethes and suffers, the nearly disjointed body of the man who, believing he was giving men a sublime example of love, tossed away his life with the weapon he thought was revealed to redeem them, was placed in a wooden coffin. Because of its unconscionable cult of wealth, and lacking any of the shackles of tradition, this Republic has fallen into monarchical inequality, injustice and violence.

The revolutionary theories of the European worker in the United States were like drops of blood carried away by the sea, whereas life in a spacious land and under a republican form of government enabled the recent arrival to earn his bread and lay aside a portion of his earnings for his old age, and in his own house.

But then came the corrupting war and the habit of authority and domination which is its bitter aftereffect. Then came the credit that stimulated the creation of colossal fortunes and the disorderly foreign influx. Then came the leisure of the war's unemployed, always ready, because of the need to maintain their well-being and because of the fatal inclination of those who have smelled blood, to serve the impure interests resulting from it.

The Republic changed from a wonderfully desirable village to a monarchy in disguise.

European immigrants denounced with renewed anger the wrongs they thought they had left behind in their own repressive countries.

The ill-will of the nation's workers, recognizing themselves to be the victims of the greed and inequality of a feudal people, exploded with a greater faith in the freedom they hoped to see succeed in the social realm as it was succeeding in the political.

Since the country's inhabitants are accustomed to winning without bloodshed through the power of the vote, and since they neither understand nor excuse those who were born in nations where suffrage is a tool of repression, they see nothing in the apathetic work of those of foreign birth but a new aspect of the old abuse that scourges their thinkers, challenges their heroes and curses their poets. But although the essential differences in political practices, and the disagreements and rivalries of the races already arguing about supremacy in this part of the continent, might have stood in the way of the immediate formation of a formidable labor party with identical methods and purposes, the common denominator of pain has accelerated the concerted action of all who suffer. A horrendous act was needed, no matter how much it might be a natural consequence of inflamed passions, so that those who hasten indomitably from the identical misfortune can interrupt their efforts to eradicate and repair, while their bloody recourses are condemned for being ineffective by men who, because of an insane love of justice, seize those who have lost their faith in freedom.

In the recently emerging West, where the commanding influence of an old society like that of the East, reflected in its literature and customs, puts fewer restrictions on the new elements; where a somewhat more rudimentary kind of life facilitates close relationships among men, more harassed and scattered in the larger and more cultured cities; where the same astounding rapidity of growth, accumulating mansions and factories on the one hand, and wretched masses of people on the other, clearly reveals the evils of a system that punishes the most industrious with hunger, the most generous with persecution, the useful father with the misery of his children—there the unhappy working man has been making his voice heard. In the West, where the impoverished day laborer is joined by wife and children in reading books that teach the causes of, and the cures for, their unhappiness; where the industrialists, justified in their own eyes by the success of their grand and glorious factories, are carrying to extremes, prejudiced by prosperity, the unjust methods and harsh treatment that keep them prosperous—there both the workers and their friends have been able to speak their minds. In the West, where German leaven coming out of the imperial country is keeping in ferment the harassed and intelligent laboring masses, putting upon the iniquitous land the three terrible curses of Heine; in the West, and especially in its major city Chicago, the discontented among the working masses, the ardent counsel of their friends, and the rage piled up by the effrontery and inclemency of their bosses, have found living expression.

Since everything tends toward the great and the small at the same time, just as water rises from the sea as mist and then condenses and returns to the sea again, so the human problem—condensed in Chicago because of its free institutions at the same time as it infused the Republic and the world with fear or hope, due to events in the city and the passions of its men—changed into a bitter and angry local problem.

Hatred for injustice changed into hatred for its representatives. Secular fury, enfeebled by inheritance, eating away and consuming like lava, is inherited by men who, out of their deep compassion, see themselves as holy beings, and this fury is concentrated upon those who persist in the abuses provoking it. When the mind starts working, it never stops; when anguish reaches the boiling point, it explodes; when speech begins to become inflammatory, it bursts its bounds; when vanity starts boasting, it acts as a spur; when hope is put into action, it ends in either triumph or catastrophe. "For the revolutionary," said Saint-Just,[1] "the only rest is the grave!"

What man motivated by ideas fails to realize that the harmony of all harmonies, where love presides over passion, is scarcely revealed to those great thinkers who, seated on the crest of time and blocking out the sun with their hands, see the world at the boiling point? What man who deals with men is unaware that, since they are more flesh than enlightenment, they barely recognize what seems self-evident; scarcely discern the surface; are hardly aware of anything but their own desires or threats; can scarcely conceive of anything but a frontal attack from the wind, or the apparent and therefore not always real expedient that can stop people from shutting the door on their hatred, pride or appetites? What man suffering from human wrongs, no matter how much he restrains his reason, fails to feel inflamed and misled by one of those social evils which might well keep in a state of constant madness those who watch their wives and children rotting in those social evils, especially when he examines them closely, as if they were slapping him in the face, burying him in the mud and staining his hands with blood.

Once those wrongs are recognized, the generous soul goes out to seek a remedy. Once the peaceful means are exhausted, the liberal soul resorts to violence for that remedy. Another person's

---

[1] Louis Antoine Saint-Just (1767–94): French revolutionary follower of Robespierre.

pain works in the generous soul the way a worm works in an open wound.

Was it not Desmoulins[2] who said: "As long as one embraces freedom, what matter if it be upon heaps of corpses?"

Blinded by generosity, dazzled by vanity, drunk on popularity, demented by constant transgression, by their apparent impotence in the struggle for suffrage, by the hope of being able to establish in an emerging region their ideal nation, the diligent leaders of these angry masses—educated in lands where the vote has barely commenced—do not stray from the present, do not dare to appear weak in the eyes of their followers, do not see that in this free Nation the only obstacle to sincerely desired social change lies in the lack of agreement on the part of those who seek that change. These diligent leaders, weary of suffering and with a vision of a universal phalanstery in their minds, do not believe that world justice can ever be brought about by peaceful means.

They pass judgement like cornered animals. All that is in process of growth they consider as growing against them. "My daughter slaves 15 hours a day to earn 15 cents." "I haven't had any work this winter because I belong to a labor union."

The judge sentences them.

The police, proud of the authority and uniforms that put fear into the hearts of the uncultured, manhandle and murder them.

The impoverished are cold and hungry, live in stinking houses.

America, then, is the same as Europe!

These wretched people fail to understand that they are merely cogs in the gears of society; if they are to change, all the gears must change. The hunted wild boar is deaf to the joyous music of the wind, to the song of the universe and to the grandiose movement of the cosmos. The wild boar braces its rump against the trunk of an obscure tree, sinks its fangs into the belly of its pursuer, and turns its victim's entrails inside out.

Where will those tired masses, suffering more and more each day, find that divine state of greatness to which the thinker must

---

[2] Camille Desmoulins (1760–1794): French revolutionary and journalist who led the march on the Bastille in 1789.

ascend to control the rage their unnecessary misery causes? They have tried every conceivable recourse. It is that reign of terror depicted by Carlyle: "Man's dismal and desperate battle against his condition and all that surrounds him."

Just as the life of man is concentrated in his spinal cord, and the life of the earth in its molten mass, there emerges from among those hordes of people swelling with pride and vomiting fire beings in whom all of life's horror desperation, and sorrow seems to have been fused.

They come from hell; what language must they speak but the language of hell?

Their speeches, even when read, throw sparks, mouths full of smoke, food but half digested, reddish vapors.

This is a horrible world; create another, as on Sinai amid the roar of thunder; as in '93, from a sea of blood! "Better to blow up 10 men with dynamite than let 10 men starve slowly, as they are doing in the factories!"

Montezuma's[3] pronouncement sounds again: "The gods are thirsty!"

A handsome youth, who has himself painted against a background of clouds, with the sun on his face, sits at a writing desk surrounded by bombs, crosses his legs and lights a cigar. As one fits pieces of wood together to make a doll's house, he explains the world of justice that will flower over the land when the impact of Chicago's social revolution, symbol of worldwide oppression, bursts forth.

But everything was words, meetings in corners, gun drills in one or another cellar, three rival newspapers circulating among 2,000 desperate readers, and dissemination of the most recent methods of killing. The guiltiest are those who, through the vainglory of freedom, permitted men to exercise it by means of the violence of their generosity!

When the workers showed a stronger will to better their condition, their employers showed an even stronger

---

[3] Montezuma II was the last Aztec emperor who died in 1520 during the Spanish conquest of Mexico by Hernán Cortés.

determination to resist them.

The worker believes he has a right to a certain security for the future, a certain amount of comfort and cleanliness for his house, a right to feed without worry the children he begets, a fairer share in the products of the work of which he is an indispensable factor, some time in the sun for helping his wife plant a rosebush in his yard, some corner in which to live that is not a stinking hole one cannot enter without nausea, as in the city of New York. And every time the Chicago workers asked for this in some way, the capitalists banded together and punished them by denying them the work that means their meat, their heat and their light. The bosses set the police on them, the police who are always eager to let their nightsticks fall upon the heads of the shoddily clothed. At times a policeman would kill some daring soul who resisted with stones, or some child. The workers were finally starved into returning to their jobs, spirits grim, misery further irritated, decency offended, meditating vengeance.

Heard only by their few partisans, the anarchists have been meeting year after year, organized into groups each of which kept a section under arms. In their three quite distinct newspapers they publicly preached social revolution, declaring in the name of humanity a war on existing society. They decided that a radical conversion could not be brought about by peaceful means, and recommended the use of dynamite as the holy weapon of the disinherited as well as methods of preparing it.

It was not in the treacherous shadows but in a direct confrontation with those whom they considered their enemies that they proclaimed themselves free and rebellious in order to emancipate mankind. They recognized that they were in a state of war, gave their blessings to the discovery of a substance which through its unique power was to equalize forces and save bloodshed, and strongly encouraged the study and manufacture of the new weapon with the same cool horror and diabolical calm as if they were writing a regulation treatise on ballistics. Reading these instructions, one sees bone-white circles in a sea of smoke; into the darkened room comes a ghost, gnawing on a human rib and sharpening its nails. To measure the entire depths of man's desperation, one must see if the horror that generally makes preparations calmly is getting the upper hand over that against which it is rebelling with a centuries-old fury; one must live in exile from one's homeland or from humanity... .

New York, November 13, 1887

Three Heroes

This is one of the stories written by Martí for La Edad de Oro (The Golden Age), *a "monthly publication for recreation and instruction" devoted to the children of America which was published in New York from July to October 1889.*

Once upon a time, a traveler arrived in Caracas as night was falling and, not pausing to even shake off the dust of the road, asked— no, not where he could eat or sleep, but how to get to the statue of Bolívar. They say that, alone with the tall, fragrant trees of the square, the traveler stood in front of the statue and tears ran down his cheeks, and the statue seemed to move, like a father when his son draws close to him. The traveler was right to do this, because all of us in the Americas should love Bolívar like a father— Bolívar and all the others who fought like he did so the Americas would belong to their own people. We should love them all: from the famous hero down to the very last soldier, the unknown hero. Men who fight to make their homeland free grow handsome in our eyes.

Liberty is every man's right to be respected and to think and speak without hypocrisy. In the Americas, in the past, nobody was respected or could think or speak. A man who hides what he thinks or does not dare to say it has no honor. A man who obeys a bad government and does not try to change it is not honest. A man who obeys unjust laws and allows those who mistreat his country to remain there has no honor. As soon as a child is big enough to think, he should think about everything he sees and suffer for those who cannot live with honor. He should work to give everyone the chance to live with honor, and he should be honest. A child who thinks about what is going on around him and does not want to do anything, not caring whether he is living with honor or not, is like a man who lives off a scoundrel and is on the way to becoming one. Some men are worse than animals, because animals need to be free to be happy: an elephant that is not free does not want to bear young; the Peruvian llama lies down and dies if an Indian speaks harshly to it or puts too heavy a load on its back. Men should have at least as much self-respect as elephants and llamas. Before the Americas were free, men lived like overloaded llamas. We, too, had to shake off our load or die.

Some men are happy even when they are not respected. Others suffer agonies when they see men around them with no self-respect. There must be a certain amount of honor and respect in the world, just as there must be a certain amount of light. When there are many men without honor, there are always others who embody the honor of many. They are the ones who rebel with a terrible force against those who rob the people of their liberty, which is the same as robbing men of their honor. They represent thousands of men, entire nations, human dignity itself. Such men are sacred. Bolívar, of Venezuela; San Martín, of the Río de la Plata; and Hidalgo, of Mexico, are three of these men. They should be forgiven for their mistakes, because the good they did outweighs their mistakes. Nobody can be more perfect than the sun. The sun burns with the same light that warms. The sun has spots. The ungrateful speak only of the spots. The grateful speak of the light.

SIMÓN BOLÍVAR

Bolívar was a short man. His eyes flashed, and when he spoke, his words were like a torrent. He always seemed to be about to leap on his horse. His country, his oppressed country, weighed on his heart and never let him live in peace. All the Americas were awakening. A single man is never worth more than a nation, but there are some men who never tire when their nation gets tired and who decide that it is necessary to fight before their nation does, because they have to consult nobody but themselves, while nations are composed of many men and cannot come to a decision so quickly. This was Bolívar's merit, that he did not tire of fighting for Venezuela's freedom, when it looked like Venezuela was tiring. The Spaniards had defeated him and made him leave his country. He went to an island so he could look at his country and think about it.

A generous Negro helped him when nobody else would; and one day he started fighting again, with 300 heroes, 300 fighters for freedom. He freed Venezuela, Nueva Granada, Ecuador and Peru. He founded a new nation: Bolivia. He and his barefoot, half-naked soldiers won wonderful battles. Everything around him was shaken up and filled with light. Generals fought at his side with supernatural courage. His army was filled with young men. Never before in the world had anyone fought so much or better for freedom. Bolívar fought for the Americas' right to be free, even more than for men's right to govern themselves. The envious exaggerated his defects. Bolívar died of a broken heart rather than from an illness, in the house of a Spaniard in Santa Marta. He died poor, but he left a family of nations.

MIGUEL HIDALGO Y COSTILLA

Mexico did not have many brave men and women, but the few it had were worth a lot. Half a dozen men and women worked to make their country free: a few brave young people, the husband of a liberal woman and a 60-year-old priest who loved the Indians. Ever since he was a child, the priest Hidalgo had been good and wanted to learn. Those who do not want to learn are bad. Hidalgo knew French, which was a thing of merit in those days, because few people knew that language. He read the works of the 18th-century philosophers who stated that man had the right to be respected and to think and speak without hypocrisy. He saw Negro slaves, and the sight filled him with horror. He saw people mistreating the Indians, who are gentle and generous, and he sat down with the Indians like an older brother and taught them the fine arts, which they learned quickly: music, which brings consolation; the breeding of silkworms, that produce silk; and the raising of bees, that give honey. He burned with inspiration, and he liked to build: he made kilns for baking bricks. His green eyes shone with enthusiasm.

Everybody said that he spoke very well, that he knew many new things and that the priest of the village of Dolores was very charitable. They said that he went to the city of Querétaro once in a while to speak with some brave men and with the husband of a good woman. A traitor told a Spanish commander that the friends in Querétaro were trying to free Mexico. The priest got on his horse like the rest of his people, who loved him dearly; the cattle herders and servants on the haciendas joined him, and they were the cavalry; the Indians went on foot, with clubs and bows and arrows or with slings and lances. A regiment joined him and seized a gunpowder train that was supposed to be for the Spaniards. He entered Celaya in triumph, to music and cheers. The next day, the Town Council met and made him a general, and a new Nation was born. He made lances and hand grenades. He gave speeches that, as a cattle herder put it, gave off heat and sparks. He freed the Negroes, and he returned the Indian lands to them. He published a newspaper called *The American Awakening*. He won and lost battles. One day, 7,000 Indians with bows and arrows would join him, and the next day he would be all alone. The bad people wanted to go with him to rob in the towns and to take revenge on the Spaniards. He told the Spanish leaders that, if he defeated them in battle, he would welcome them in his home as friends. That's how big-hearted he was! He was magnanimous, and he was not afraid that the bad soldiers who wanted him to be cruel would desert him. When his comrade Allende became jealous of him, he gave Allende the command. They were together looking for help when the Spaniards fell on them. The Spaniards took off Hidalgo's cassock and other religious clothes one by one, to humiliate him. And they took him out behind a wall and shot him in the head. He was wounded and fell down, covered with blood. There, they killed him. They cut off his head and hung it in a cage in the public granary of Granaditas, where he had his government. They buried the headless bodies. But Mexico is free.

JOSÉ SAN MARTÍN

San Martín was the liberator of the South, the father of the Argentine Republic and of Chile. His parents were Spaniards, and they sent him to Spain to be a soldier of the King. When Napoleon and his army marched into Spain to take away the Spaniards' freedom, all the Spaniards fought against Napoleon; even the old people, the women and the children fought. One brave boy from Catalonia made a whole company of Frenchmen run away one night because he kept shooting at them from a hideout in the mountains. Later on, the boy was found dead—killed by hunger and cold—but his face was shining with happiness.

San Martín fought very well in the Battle of Bailén, and they made him a lieutenant-colonel. He never talked much; he was like steel; he had an eagle's gaze, and nobody disobeyed him. His horse came and went through the battlefield like a thunderbolt through the air. As soon as he heard that the Americas were fighting for their freedom, he came here. He gave up his career to do his duty. When he arrived in Buenos Aires, he made no speeches; instead, he raised a squadron of cavalry. His first battle was at San Lorenzo. Brandishing his saber, San Martín went after the Spaniards, who were very sure of themselves, beating their drums; but they would end up without any drums or cannon or flags. The Spaniards were winning in the other nations in the Americas: the cruel Morrillo of Venezuela had expelled Bolívar, Hidalgo was dead and O'Higgins had to flee from Chile; but San Martín kept free the place where he was. Some men just could not stand slavery. San Martín could not, and he set out to free Chile and Peru. In 18 days, he and his army crossed the high, cold Andes. Hungry and thirsty, the men climbed higher and higher, into the sky. They were so high up, the trees looked like grass and the torrents roared like lions. San Martín found the Spanish army and cut it to pieces in the Battle of Maipú. He defeated the Spaniards decisively in the Battle of Chacabuco. He freed Chile. Then he and his troops got on ships and went to free Peru. But Bolívar was in Peru, and San Martín let him have all the glory. He went back to Europe sadly and died in the arms of his daughter Mercedes. He wrote his last will on a sheet of paper like the report of a battle. He had been given the flag that Pizarro, the *conquistador*, had taken with him four centuries before, and in his will, San Martín gave the flag to Peru.

A sculptor is wonderful because he can make a figure come out of a stone, but men who create nations are more than men. Sometimes they wanted what they shouldn't want, but what would a son not forgive his father for?

Our hearts are filled with tenderness when we think about these great founding fathers. Those who fight to free the people, like those who die in poverty and disgrace for defending a great truth, are heroes. Those who fight because they are ambitious or to enslave other people, to rise in rank or to take away the land that belongs to others are criminals, not heroes.

Mother America

José Martí delivered this speech on December 19, 1889, at the Latin American Literary Society of New York, in the presence of the delegates attending the Pan-American Congress being held in Washington. Presenting his Latin Americanist ideas, Martí warned about the potential danger posed by imperialist trends in the United States.

Ladies and gentlemen:

Our tremulous and exuberant thoughts, in the short time that discretion demands, are hard pressed to put into words the joy that overflows from our souls on this memorable night. What can the imprisoned son say when he sees his mother again from behind the bars of his cell? Talking is a small thing and almost impossible, more because of its personal and haphazard content and the throng of memories, hopes and fears than because of the certainty of not being able to give one's utterances worthy expression. For the man who sees himself surrounded by the nations we love with a religious passion, in the person of their illustrious delegates, whatever he could say would be intemperate and chaotic. When he sees how, by secret mandate, men have increased their stature and women their beauty to receive them; when he sees the dark and leaden air enlivened as if with the shadows of eagles about to take flight, of heads passing by and shaking their admonitory crests, of lands imploring, pale and stabbed, without the strength to pull the dagger out of their hearts, his words would be empty phrases. When he sees the shadow of the magnanimous fighter of the North, on the porch at Mount Vernon, give his admiring hand to the volcanic hero of the South, he vainly tries to gather the horde of feelings beating against his breast, like some over-patriotic spirit, and all he finds are discordant strophes and untamed odes with which to celebrate the visit of the absent mother in the house of Our America, and tell her, in the name of men and women, that the heart can find no better use than to wholly surrender to the messengers of the American nations. How can we pay our illustrious guests for this hour of joy? Why must we hide with the duplicity of ceremony what we see in these faces? Trim your rhetoric with other vignettes and bells and gold fringe; tonight we have biblical eloquence flowing as restlessly and cheerfully as a brook, from the generosity of the heart. Which of us will deny, on this night when no lies are told, that no matter how many roots our faith or affections or habits or business affairs may have in this land of unrestrained hospitality, no matter how lukewarm the faithless magic of ice may have left our souls, we have felt— ever since learning that these noble guests were coming to see us— as if there were more light in our houses, as if we were walking with a livelier step, as if we were younger and more generous, as if our earnings were greater and more certain, and as if in a vase without water there were flowers budding? And if our wives want to tell us the truth, are they not telling us with their loyal eyes that certain fairy feet never went through the snow more happily; that something asleep in the heart, in the incomprehension of foreign soil, has suddenly awakened; that a joyful canary has been flying in and out of the windows these days, back and forth incessantly and unmindful of the cold, with ribbons and bows in its beak, because for this celebration of Our America no flower seemed delicate and exquisite enough? All this is true. Some of us have been brought there by misfortune; others by legend; others by commerce; others by the determination to write, in a land that is still not free, the final stanza of the poem of 1810.[1] Others are ordered to live here by a pair of blue eyes, as their acceptable command. But no matter how great is this land, or how anointed the America of Lincoln may be for the free men of America— for us, in our very heart of hearts where nobody dares to challenge or take issue with our secret feelings, the America of Juárez[2] is greater because it has been more unhappy, and because it is ours.

---

[1] The liberation of Latin America from Spanish rule began in Caracas, Venezuela in 1810. By 1889, only Cuba and Puerto Rico remained colonies.

[2] Benito Juárez (1806–72) was born of Indian parents and was President of Mexico, 1861–71.

In apostolic days North America was born from freedom at its fieriest. The new breed of light-crowned men were not willing to bow before any other. Impelled by the mind, the yoke of human reason that was vilified in empires created at sword's point, or with diplomacy, by the great power-crazed Republic, broke into pieces from everywhere in those nations born of an amalgamation of smaller nations. Modern rights sprang from the small and autochthonous regions that had formed their free character in continuous struggle, and they preferred independent caves to servile prosperity. A king who came told a man who addressed him familiarly and did not remove his hat in his presence to establish the Republic. The 41 souls from the *Mayflower* together with their women and children, defy the sea and on an oaken table of an anteroom establish their community. They carry loaded muskets to defend their planted fields; the wheat they eat, they plow. A land without tyrants for the soul without tyrants is what they seek. In long jacket and felt hat comes the intolerant and irreproachable Puritan who despises luxury because men lie for it. In waistcoat and knee breeches comes the Quaker, and with the trees he fells he builds schools. Then comes the Catholic, persecuted for his faith, and founds a State where nobody can be persecuted for his faith. The gentleman arrives in fine woolen cloth and plumed hat, and his very habit of commanding slaves gives him the insolence of a king wherewith to defend his freedom. One of them brings in his ship a group of Negroes to sell, or a fanatic who burns witches, or a governor who refuses to listen to anything about schools. The ships bring men of letters and university scholars, Swedish mystics, fervent Germans, French Huguenots, proud Scotsmen, thrifty Batavians. They bring plows, seeds, bolts of cloth, harps, psalms, books. The settlers live in houses built with their own hands, masters and servants of themselves. And as a recompense for the tiring task of contending with Nature, the brave colonist found satisfaction in seeing the old woman of the house, in hairnet and apron, come with blessing in her eyes and a tray of homemade sweets in her hand while one daughter opens a hymnal and another plays a prelude on the zither or the clavichord. School was taught by rote and with the lash, but going to it through the snow was the best kind of schooling. And when couples trudged along the road, faces to the wind—the men in leather jackets and carrying shotguns, the women in heavy flannels and carrying prayer books—they were usually bound for church to hear the new minister who refused to give the governor power in the personal aspects of religion, or they were on their way to elect their judges or call them to account. No unscrupulous breed of men came from outside. Authority belonged to all, and was given to whomever they desired. They elected their own magistrates and governors. If the governor was unwilling to convoke the council, the "free men" did so over his head. The taciturn adventurer there hunted both men and wolves in the woods, and could sleep well only if he found a recently fallen tree trunk or a dead Indian for a pillow. And in the manorial mansions of the South, all was minuet and candlelight, and choruses of Negroes to greet their master as his coach drew up to the door, and silver goblets for the fine Madeira wine. But nothing in life was not food for freedom in the republican colonies that received certificates of independence from the king rather than royal charters. And when the Englishman, for granting them that independence in the capacity of master, levied a tribute which they resented, the glove that the colonies threw in his face was the selfsame one that the Englishman himself had put upon their hands. They led a horse to their hero's door. The nation that was later to refuse to help, accepted help. Triumphant freedom is like it: manorial and sectarian, with lace cuffs and a velvet canopy, more a matter of location than of human weakness, a selfish and unjust freedom teetering upon the shoulders of an enslaved race of men who before a century had passed hurled the litter to the ground with a crash. And ax in hand, out of the tumult and dust raised by the falling chains of a million emancipated men, emerged the woodcutter with the merciful eyes! Over the crumbling foundations of the stupendous convulsion rode Victory, proud and covetous. The factors that set the nation upon its feet appeared again, accentuated by war, and beside the body of the gentleman, dead among his slaves, were the Pilgrim (who refused to tolerate a master above him or a servant below him, or any conquests other than those made by the grain of wheat in the earth and by love in the heart) and the shrewd and grasping adventurer (born to acquire and to move forward in the forests, governed only by his own desires and limited only by the reach of his arm, a solitary and dreaded companion of leopards and eagles)— both Pilgrim and adventurer fighting for supremacy in the Republic and in the world.

And how can one fail to remember, for the glory of those who have known how to conquer, in spite of them, the confused and blood-soaked origins of Our America, although the faithful memory (more necessary now than ever) may be stained with untimely senility by the one whom the light of our glory— the glory of our independence— had hindered in the work of compromising or demeaning that America of ours? North America was born of the plow, Spanish America of the bulldog. A fanatical war took from the poetry of his aerial palaces the Moor weakened by his riches; and the remaining soldiers, reared to heresy on hate and sour wine and equipped with suits of armor and arquebuses, rushed upon the Indian protected by his breastplate of cotton. Ships arrived loaded with cavaliers in their half-cuirasses, disinherited second sons, rebellious lieutenants, hungry clergymen and university students. They brought muskets, shields, lances, thigh guards, helmets, backplates, and dogs. They wielded their swords to the four winds, took possession of the land in the name of the King, and plundered the temples of their gold. Cortés lured Montezuma into the palace he owed to the latter's wisdom or generosity, then held him prisoner there. The simple Anacaona invited Ovando to one of her festivities to show him her country's gardens, its joyful dances, and its virgins, whereupon Ovando's soldiers pulled their swords from beneath their disguises and seized Anacaona's land. Among the divisions and jealousies of the Indian people, the *conquistador* pushed on in America. Among Aztecs and Tlaxcaltecas, Cortés reached Cuauhtemoc's canoe. Among Quichés and Tzutuhils, Alvarado was victorious in Guatemala. Among the inhabitants of Tunja and Bogotá, Quesada marched forward in Colombia. Among the warriors of Atahualpa and Huáscar, Pizarro rode across Peru. By the light of burning temples the red banner of the Inquisition was planted in the breast of the last Indian. The women were carried off. When the Indian was free his roads were paved with stones, but after the Spaniard came he had nothing but cow paths used by the cow as she went nosing her way to the pasture, or by the Indian deploring how wolves had been turned into men. The Indian worked for what the Spanish commissioner ate. So many Indians died, like flowers that lose their aroma, that the mines had to shut down. Sacristans grew rich on the trimmings of their chasubles, and gentlemen went on walks, or burned the King's colors in a brazier, or watched heads fall in fights between viceroys and judges, or in rivalries among the commanders. When the head of a family wanted to mount his horse, he kept two Indian pages for the stirrups and two boys for the spurs. Viceroy, regent and town council were appointed from Spain; when the town councils assembled, they were branded with branding irons. The mayor ordered the governor to stay out of the town because of the harm he did to the Republic, ordered the councilman to cross himself when entering the town council, and ordered 25 lashes for any Indian who galloped his horse. Children learned to read by means of bullfight posters and highwaymen's jingles; the schools of rank and prestige taught them "contemptible chimeras." And when groups of people gathered in the streets, it was to follow the old hags who carried proclamations, or to talk in hushed voices about the scandal of the judge and the heavily veiled woman, or to go to the burning of a Portuguese where a hundred pikes and muskets led the procession, and where the Dominicans with their white crosses and the grandees with their staffs and rapiers and gold-embroidered hoods ended it. There were trunks full of bones carried on the back and flanked by torches; the guilty with ropes around their necks, their sins written upon their head coverings; the stubborn with pictures of the enemy painted upon their *sanbenitos*. There were the distinguished gentlemen, the bishop, the higher clergy; and in the church, between two thrones brightly lit by candles, the black altar. Outside, the bonfire. At night, dancing. The glorious Creole falls bathed in blood every time he seeks a way out of his humiliation, with no guide or model but his honor, today in Caracas, tomorrow in Quito, thereafter with the common people of Socorro! Either he buys, hand to hand, the right to have Bolivian councilmen in Cochabamba,[3] or he dies like the admirable Antequera,[4] professing his faith on the scaffold in Paraguay, his countenance glowing with happiness; or growing weak at the foot of Chimborazo, he "exhorts

[3] Cochabamba, Upper Peru, was the site of an armed uprising against Spain in 1730.

[4] José de Antequera protested against the power of the Jesuits and led an independence movement in Paraguay in 1767.

the people to strengthen their dignity." The first Creole born to a Spaniard—the son of Malinche—was a rebel. Juan de Mena's daughter, in mourning of her father, dons her festive attire and all her jewels, for the day of Arteaga's death is a day of honor for all of humanity! What is happening so suddenly to make the whole world pause to listen and marvel and revere? From beneath the cowl of Torquemada[5] comes the redeemed continent, bloody and with sword in hand! All the nations of America declare themselves free at the same time. Bolívar appears with his cohort of luminaries. Even the volcanoes acclaim him and publish him to the world, their flanks shaking and thundering. To your horses, all of America! And over plains and mountains, with all the stars aflame, redemptive hoof beats resound in the night. The Mexican clergy are now talking to their Indians. With lances held in their teeth, the Venezuelan Indians outdistance the naked runner. The battered Chileans march together, arm in arm with the half-breeds from Peru. Wearing the Phrygian or liberty cap of the emancipated slave, the Negroes go singing behind their blue banner. Squads of *gauchos* in calfskin boots and swinging their *bolas* go galloping in triumph. The revived Pehuenches, hair flying and feathered lances held above their heads, put spurs to their horses. The war-painted Araucanians, carrying their cane lances tipped with colored feathers, come running at full gallop. And when the virgin light of dawn flows over the cliffs, San Martín appears there in the snow crossing the Andes in his battle cape—crest of the mountain and crown of the revolution. Where is America going, and who will unite her and be her guide? Alone and as one people she is rising. Alone she is fighting. Alone she will win.

And we have transformed all this venom into sap! Never was there such a precocious, persevering and generous people born out of so much opposition and unhappiness. We were a den of iniquity and we are beginning to be a crucible. We built upon hydras. Our railroads have demolished the pikes of Alvarado. In the public squares where they used to burn heretics, we built libraries. We have as many schools now as we had officers of the Inquisition before. What we have not yet done, we have not had time to do, having been busy cleansing our blood of the impurities bequeathed to us by

---

[5] Tomás de Torquemada (1420–98): first Spanish Inquisitor-General, renown for his cruelty.

our ancestors. The religious and immoral missions have nothing left but their crumbling walls where an occasional owl shows an eye, and where the lizard goes his melancholy way. The new American has cleared the path among the dispirited breeds of men, the ruins of convents, and the horses of barbarians, and he is inviting the youth of the world to pitch their tents in his fields. The handful of apostles has triumphed. What does it matter if, when emerging as free nations and with the book always in front of our eyes, we saw that the government of a hybrid and primitive land (molded from a residue of Spaniards and some grim and frightened aborigines, in addition to a smattering of Africans and Menceys) should understand, in order to be natural and productive, all the elements that rose in a marvelous throng—by means of the greater politics inscribed in Nature—to establish that land? What does it matter if there were struggles between the city of the university and the feudal countryside? What difference if the servile marquis felt a warlike disdain for the half-breed workman? How important was the grim and stubborn duel between Antonio de Nariño[6] and St. Ignatius Loyola?[7] Our capable and indefatigable America conquers everything, and each day she plants her banner higher. From sunrise to sunset she conquers everything through the harmonious and artistic spirit of the land that emerged out of the beauty and music of our nature, for she bestows upon our hearts her generosity and upon our minds the loftiness and serenity of her mountains. She conquers everything through the secular influence with which this encircling grandeur and order has compensated for the treacherous mixture and confusing of our beginnings; and through the expensive and humanitarian freedom, neither local nor racial nor sectarian, that came to our republics in their finest hour, and later, sifted and purified, went out from the world's capitals. It was a freedom that probably has no more spacious site in any nation than the one prepared in our boundless lands for the honest effort, the loyal solicitude, and the sincere friendship of men. Would that the future might brand my lips!

Out of that troubled and sorely tried America, born with thorns upon her brow and with words and the heart's blood flowing out

---

[6] Antonio de Nariño was a Colombian independence fighter.

[7] Ignatius de Loyola (1491–1556) was the founder of the Jesuit order.

through the badly torn gag like lava, our eager strivings have brought us to Our America of the present, at once hard-working and heroic, frank and vigilant, with Bolívar on one arm and Herbert Spencer on the other. It is an America without childish jealousies or naive trust, fearlessly inviting all races to the fortunes of her home, because she knows she is the America of Buenos Aires' defense and of Callao's endurance, the America of Cerro de la Campanas and of the new Troy. And would she prefer the hates and appetites of the world instead of her own future, which is that of bringing equity and justice in an atmosphere of unrestricted peace, without a wolf's greed or a sacristan's admonitions? Would she rather disintegrate at the hands of her own children than undertake the grandiose task of becoming more firmly united? Would she desire to lie, because of neighboring jealousies, instead of following what is written by the fauna and stars and history? Or would she prefer to act as a legend to anyone who might offer her his services as a footboy, or go out into the world as a beggar to have her cup filled with terrible riches? Only self-created wealth and freedom earned by one's hand can endure, and it is for good. Whoever dares maintain that she would compromise, does not know Our America. Rivadavia,[8] the man always seen in a white cravat, said that these countries would save themselves, and so they have. The sea has been plowed. Our America also builds palaces, and gathers the useful surplus from an oppressed world. She also contributes her forests and brings it the book, the newspaper, the town and the railroad. And Our America, with the sun on her brow, also rises over deserts crowned with cities. And when the elements that formed our nations reappear in this crisis of their elaboration, the independent Creole is the one who prevails and asserts himself— not the beaten Indian serving as spur boy who holds the stirrup— and puts his own foot into it so that he can be higher than his master.

That is why we live here with such pride in Our America, to serve and honor her. We certainly do not live here as future slaves or dazzled peasants, but as people able and determined to help a man win esteem for his good qualities and respect for his sacrifices. The very wars that are thrown in her teeth by those who misunderstand

---

[8] Bernadino Rivadavia (1780–1845): leader of the Argentine independence movement and first president of the Argentine Republic.

her out of pure ignorance, are the seal of honor for our nations that have never hesitated to hasten the course of progress with the enriching sustenance of their blood, and that can display their wars like a crown. Devoid of the friction and daily stimulus of our struggles and passions that come to us from the soil where our children have not been reared—and from a great distance!—in vain does this country invite us with her magnificence, her life and its temptations, her heart and its cowardice, to indifference and forgetfulness. We are taking Our America, as host and inspiration, to where there is no forgetting and no death! And neither corruptive interests nor certain new fashions in fanaticism will let us be uprooted from her! We must show our soul as it is to these illustrious messengers who have come here from our nations, so they may see that we consider it faithful and honorable. We must convince these delegates that a just admiration and a usefully sincere study of other nations—a study neither too distant nor myopic—does not weaken the ardent, redemptive, and sacred love for what is our own. Let us allow them to see that for our personal good—if there is any good in the conscience without peace—we will not be traitors to that which Nature and humanity demand of us.

And thus, when each of them, content with our integrity, returns to the shores that we may never see again, he will be able to say to her who is our mistress, hope and guide: "Mother America, we found brothers there! Mother America, you have sons there!"

Our America

Nuestra América, one of Martí's most important writings, first appeared in La Revista Ilustrada de Nueva York *on January 1, 1891, and on January 30 of that same year, in* El Partido Liberal *of Mexico. Written during the period of the formation of the Cuban Revolutionary Party, this article presents the ethical and political principles of the future Cuban Republic.*

The conceited villager believes the entire world to be his village. Provided that he can be mayor, or humiliate the rival who stole his sweetheart, or add to the savings in his strongbox, he considers the universal order good, unaware of those giants with seven-league boots who can crush him underfoot, or of the strife in the heavens between comets that go through the air asleep, gulping down worlds. What remains of the village in America must rouse itself. These are not the times for sleeping in a nightcap, but with weapons for a pillow, like the warriors of Juan de Castellanos: weapons of the mind, which conquer all others. Barricades of ideas are worth more than barricades of stones.

There is no prow that can cut through a cloudbank of ideas. A powerful idea, waved before the world at the proper time, can stop a squadron of iron-clad ships, like the mystical flag of the Last Judgement. Nations that do not know one another should quickly become acquainted, as men who are to fight a common enemy. Those who shake their fists, like jealous brothers coveting the same tract of land, or like the modest cottager who envies the esquire his mansion, should clasp hands and become one. Those who use the authority of a criminal tradition to lop off the hands of their defeated brother with a sword stained with his own blood ought to return the lands to the brother already punished sufficiently, if they do not want the people to call them thieves. The honest man does not absolve himself of debts of honor with money, at so much a slap. We can no longer be a people of leaves, living in the air, our foliage heavy with blooms and crackling or humming at the whim of the sun's caress, buffeted and tossed by the storms. The trees must form ranks to keep the giant with seven-league boots from passing! It is the time of mobilization, of marching together, and we must go forward in closed ranks, like silver in the veins of the Andes.

Only those born prematurely are lacking in courage. Those without faith in their country are seven-month weaklings. Because they have no courage, they deny it to others. Their puny arms—arms with bracelets and hands with painted nails, arms of Paris or Madrid—can hardly reach the bottom limb, so they claim the tall tree to be unclimbable. The ships should be loaded with those harmful insects that gnaw at the bone of the country that nourishes them. If they are Parisians or from Madrid, let them go to the Prado, to swan around, or to Tortoni's, in high hats. Those carpenter's sons who are ashamed that their fathers are carpenters! Those born in America who are ashamed of the mother who reared them, because she wears an Indian apron; and those scoundrels who disown their sick mother, abandoning her on her sickbed! Then who is a real man? He who stays with his mother and nurses her in her illness, or he who puts her to work out of sight, and lives at her expense on decadent lands, sporting fancy neckties, cursing the womb that carried him, displaying the sign of the traitor on the back of his paper frock coat? These sons of Our America, which will be saved by its Indians and is growing better; these deserters who take up arms in the armies of a North America that drowns its Indians in blood and is growing worse! These delicate creatures who are men but are unwilling to do men's work! The Washington who made this land for them, did he not go to live with the English, at a time when he saw them fighting against his own country. These unbelievers in honor who drag that honor over foreign soil like their counterparts in the French Revolution with their dancing, their affectations, their drawling speech!

For in what lands can men take more pride than in our long-suffering American republics, raised up among the silent Indian masses by the bleeding arms of a hundred apostles, to the sounds of battle between the book and the processional candle? Never in history have such advanced and united nations been forged in so short a time from such disorganized elements. The presumptuous man feels that the earth was made to serve as his pedestal because he happens to have a facile pen or colorful speech, and he accuses his native land of being worthless and beyond redemption because its virgin jungles fail to provide him with a constant means of traveling the world, driving Persian ponies and lavishing champagne like a tycoon. The incapacity does not lie with the emerging country in quest of suitable forms and a utilitarian greatness; it lies rather with those who attempt to rule nations of a unique and violent character by means of laws inherited from four centuries of freedom in the United States and 19 centuries of monarchy in France. A decree by Hamilton does not halt the charge of the plainsman's horse. A phrase by Sieyès does nothing to quicken the stagnant blood of the Indian race. To govern well, one must see things as they are. And the able governor in America is not the one who knows how to govern the Germans or the French; he must know the elements that make up his own country, and how to bring them together, using methods and institutions originating within the country, to reach that desirable state where each man can attain self-realization and all may enjoy the abundance that Nature has bestowed in everyone in the nation to enrich with their toil and defend with their lives. Government must originate in the country. The spirit of government must be that of the country. Its structure must conform to rules appropriate to the country. Good government is nothing more than the balance of the country's natural elements.

That is why in America the imported book has been conquered by the natural man. Natural men have conquered learned and artificial men. The native half-breed has conquered the exotic Creole. The struggle is not between civilization and barbarity, but between false erudition and Nature. The natural man is good, and he respects and rewards superior intelligence as long as his humility is not turned against him, or he is not offended by being disregarded—something the natural man never forgives, prepared as he is to forcibly regain the respect of whoever has wounded his pride or threatened his interests. It is by conforming with these disdained native elements that the tyrants of America have climbed to power, and have fallen as soon as they betrayed them. Republics have paid with oppression for their inability to recognize the true elements of their countries, to derive from them the right kind of government, and to govern accordingly. In a new nation a government means a creator.

In nations composed of both cultured and uncultured elements, the uncultured will govern because it is their habit to attack and resolve doubts with their fists in cases where the cultured have failed in the art of governing. The uncultured masses are lazy and timid in the realm of intelligence, and they want to be governed well. But if the government hurts them, they shake it off and govern themselves. How can the universities produce governors if not a single university in America teaches the rudiments of the art of government, the analysis of elements peculiar to the peoples of America? The young go out into the world wearing Yankee or French spectacles, hoping to govern a people they do not know. In the political race entrance should be denied to those who are ignorant of the rudiments of politics. The prize in literary contests should not go for the best ode, but for the best study of the political factors of one's country. Newspapers, universities and schools should encourage the study of the country's pertinent components. To know them is sufficient, without mincing words; for whoever brushes aside even a part of the truth, whether through intention or oversight, is doomed to fall. The truth he lacks thrives on negligence, and brings down whatever is built without it. It is easier to resolve our problem knowing its components than to resolve it without knowing them. Along comes the natural man, strong and indignant, and he topples all the justice accumulated from books because he has not been governed in accordance with the obvious needs of the country. Knowing is what counts. To know one's country and govern it with that knowledge is the only way to free it from tyranny. The European university must bow to the American university. The history of America, from the Incas to the present, must be taught in clear detail and to the letter, even if the archons of Greece are overlooked. Our Greece must take priority over the Greece which is not ours. We need it more. Nationalist statesmen must replace foreign statesmen. Let the world be grafted onto our republics, but the trunk must be our own. And let the vanquished pedant hold his tongue, for there are no lands in which a man may take greater pride than in our long-suffering American republics.

With the rosary as our guide, our heads white and our bodies mottled, both Indians and Creoles, we fearlessly entered the world of nations. We set out to conquer freedom under the banner of the virgin. A priest, a few lieutenants and a woman[1] raised the Republic of Mexico onto the shoulders of the Indians. A few heroic students, instructed in French liberty by a Spanish cleric, made Central America rise in revolt against Spain under a Spanish general. In monarchic garb emblazoned with the sun, the Venezuelans to the north and the Argentines to the south began building nations. When the two heroes[2] clashed and the continent was about to rock, one of them, and not the lesser, handed the reins to the other. And since heroism in times of peace is rare because it is not as glorious as in times of war, it is easier for a man to die with honor than to think with logic. It is easier to govern when feelings are exalted and united than after a battle, when divisive, arrogant, exotic or ambitious thinking emerges. The forces routed in the epic struggle—with the feline cunning of the species, and using the weight of realities—were undermining the new structure which comprised both the rough-and-ready, unique regions of our half-breed America and the silk-stockinged and frock-coated people of Paris beneath the flag of freedom and reason borrowed from nations skilled in the arts of government. The hierarchical constitution of the colonies resisted the democratic organization of the republics. The cravated capitals left their country boots in the vestibule. The bookworm redeemers failed to realize that the revolution succeeded because it came from the soul of the nation; they had to govern with that soul and not without or against it. America began to suffer, and still suffers, from the tiresome task of reconciling the hostile and discordant elements it inherited from a despotic and perverse colonizer, and the imported methods and ideas which have been retarding logical government because they are lacking in local realities. Thrown out of gear for three centuries by a power which denied men the right to use their reason, the continent disregarded or closed its ears to the unlettered

---

[1] A reference to Father Miguel Hidalgo, guerrilla leader José María Morelos and Doña Josefa Ortiz de Domínguez (wife of the chief magistrate of Querétaro).

[2] San Martín and Simón Bolívar.

throngs that helped bring it to redemption, and embarked on a government based on reason—a reason belonging to all for the common good, not the university brand of reason over the peasant brand. The problem of independence did not lie in a change of forms but in change of spirit.

It was imperative to make common cause with the oppressed, in order to secure a new system opposed to the ambitions and governing habits of the oppressors. The tiger, frightened by gunfire, returns at night to his prey. He dies with his eyes shooting flames and his claws unsheathed. He cannot be heard coming because he approaches with velvet tread. When the prey awakens, the tiger is already upon it. The colony lives on the Republic, and Our America is saving itself from its enormous mistakes—the pride of its capital cities, the blind triumph of a scorned peasantry, the excessive influx of foreign ideas and formulas, the wicked and unpolitical disdain for the aboriginal race—because of the higher virtue, enriched with necessary blood, or a Republic struggling against a colony. The tiger lurks against every tree, lying in wait at every turn. He will die with his claws unsheathed and his eyes shooting flames.

But "these countries will be saved," as was announced by the Argentine Rivadavia, whose only sin was being a gentleman in these rough-and-ready times. A man does not sheathe a machete in a silken scabbard, nor can he lay aside the short lance merely because he is angered and stands at the door of Iturbide's[3] Congress, "demanding that the fair-haired one be named emperor." These countries will be saved because a genius for moderation, found in the serene harmony of Nature, seems to prevail in the continent of light, where there emerges a new real man schooled for these real times in the critical philosophy which in Europe has replaced the philosophy of guesswork and phalanstery that saturated the previous generation.

We were a phenomenon with a chest of an athlete, the hands of a dandy, and the brain of a child. We were a masquerader in English breeches, Parisian vest, North American jacket and Spanish cap. The Indian hovered near us in silence, and went off to hills to baptize his children. The Negro was seen pouring out the songs of his heart at night, alone and unrecognized among the rivers and wild animals.

---

[3] Augustín Iturbide (1783–1824): Mexican independence leader who was briefly declared emperor.

The peasant, the creator, turned in blind indignation against the disdainful city, against his own child. As for us, we were nothing but epaulets and professors' gowns in countries that came into the world wearing hemp sandals and headbands. It would have been the mark of genius to couple the headband and the professors' gown with the founding fathers' generosity and courage, to rescue the Indian, to make a place for the competent Negro, to fit liberty to the body of those who rebelled and conquered for it. We were left with the judge, the general, the scholar and the sinecured. The angelic young, as if caught in the tentacles of an octopus, lunged heavenward, only to fall back, crowned with clouds in sterile glory. The native, driven by instinct, swept away the golden staffs of office in blind triumph. Neither the European nor the Yankee could provide the key to the Spanish American riddle. Hate was attempted, and every year the countries amounted to less. Exhausted by the senseless struggle between the book and the lance, between reason and the processional candle, between the city and the country, weary of the impossible rule by rival urban cliques over the natural nation tempestuous or inert by turns, we begin almost unconsciously to try love. Nations stand up and greet one another. "What are we?" is the mutual question, and little by little they furnish answers. When a problem arises in Cojímar, they do not seek its solution in Danzig. The frock coats are still French, but thought begins to be American. The youth of America are rolling up their sleeves, digging their hands in the dough, and making it rise with the sweat of their brows. They realize that there is too much imitation, and that creation holds the key to salvation. "Create" is the password of this generation. The wine is made from plantain, but even if it turns sour, it is our own wine! That a country's form of government must be in keeping with its natural elements is self-evident. Absolute ideas must take relative forms if they are not to fail because of an error in form. Freedom, to be viable, has to be sincere and complete. If a Republic refuses to open its arms to all, and move ahead with all, it dies. The tiger within sneaks in through the crack; so does the tiger from without. The general holds back his cavalry to a pace that suits his infantry, for if its infantry is left behind, the cavalry will be surrounded by the enemy. Politics and strategy are one. Nations should live in an atmosphere of self-criticism because it is healthy, but always with one heart and one mind. Stoop to the unhappy, and lift them up in your arms! Thaw out frozen America with the fire of your hearts! Make the natural blood of the nations course vigorously through their veins! The new Americans are on their feet, saluting each other from nation to nation, the eyes of the laborers shining with joy. The natural statesman arises, schooled in the direct study of Nature. He reads to apply his knowledge, not to imitate. Economists study the problems at their point of origin. Speakers begin a policy of moderation. Playwrights bring native characters to the stage. Academies discuss practical subjects. Poetry shears off its Zorrilla-like locks and hangs its red vest on the glorious tree. Selective and sparkling prose is filled with ideas. In the Indian republics, the governors are learning Indian.

America is escaping all its dangers. Some of the republics are still beneath the sleeping octopus, but others, under the law of averages, are draining their lands with a sublime and furious haste, as if to make up for centuries lost. Still others, forgetting that Juárez went about in a carriage drawn by mules, hitch their carriages to the wind, their coachmen soap bubbles. Poisonous luxury, the enemy of freedom, corrupts the frivolous and opens the door to the foreigner. In others, where independence is threatened, an epic spirit heightens their manhood. Still others spawn an army capable of devouring them in voracious wars. But perhaps Our America is running another risk that does not come from itself but from the difference in origins, methods and interest between the two halves of the continent, and the time is near at hand when an enterprising and vigorous people, who scorn and ignore Our America, will even so approach it and demand a close relationship. And since strong nations, self-made by law and shotgun, love strong nations and them alone; since the time of madness and ambition— from which North America may be freed by the predominance of the purest elements in its blood, or on which it may be launched by its vindictive and sordid masses, its tradition of expansion, or the ambitions of some powerful leader— is not so near at hand, even to the most timorous eye, that there is no time for the test of discreet and unwavering pride that could confront and dissuade it; since its good name as a Republic in the eyes of the world's perceptive nations puts upon North America a restraint that cannot be taken away by childish provocations or pompous arrogance or parricidal discords among our American nations— the pressing need of Our America is to show itself as it is, one in spirit and intent, swift conquerors of a suffocating past, stained only by the enriching blood drawn from the scarves left upon us by our masters.

The scorn of our formidable neighbor, who does not know us, is Our America's greatest danger. And since the day of the visit is near, it is imperative that our neighbor knows us, and soon, so that it will not scorn us. Through ignorance it might even come to lay hands on us. Once it does know us, it will remove its hands out of respect. One must have faith in the best in men and distrust the worst. One must allow the best to be shown so that it reveals and prevails over the worst. Nations should have a pillory for whoever stirs up useless hatred, and another for whoever fails to tell them the truth in time.

There can be no racial animosity, because there are no races. The theorist and feeble thinkers string together and warm over the bookshelf races which the well-disposed observer and the fair-minded traveler vainly seek in the justice of Nature where man's universal identity springs forth from triumphant love and the turbulent hunger for life. The soul, equal and eternal, emanates from bodies of different shapes and colors. Whoever foments and spreads antagonism and hatred between the races, sins against humanity. But as nations take shape among other different nations, there is a condensation of vital and individual characteristics of thought and habit, expansion and conquest, vanity and greed which could— from the latent state of national concern, and in the period of internal disorder, or the rapidity with which the country's character has been accumulating— be turned into a serious threat for the weak and isolated neighboring countries, declared by the strong country to be inferior and perishable. The thought is father to the deed. And one must not attribute, through a provincial antipathy, a fatal and inborn wickedness to the continent's fair-skinned nation simply because it does not speak our language, nor see the world as we see it, nor resemble us in its political defects, so different from ours, nor favorably regard the excitable, dark-skinned people, or look charitably, from its still uncertain eminence, upon those less favored by history, who climb the road of republicanism by heroic stages. The self-evident facts of the problem should not be obscured, because the problem can be resolved, for the peace of centuries to come, by appropriate study, and by tacit and immediate union in the continental spirit. With a single voice the hymn is already being sung; the present generation is carrying industrious America along the road enriched by their sublime fathers; from Río Grande to the Straits of Magellan, the Great Semí, astride its condor, spreading the seed of the new America over the romantic nations of the continent and the sorrowful islands of the sea!

San Martín

Published in 1891 in the album of El Porvenir, *New York, this article highlights the figure of José de San Martín, one of the forefathers of American independence who, for 12 years, was the standard-bearer of the struggle for liberation waged by the peoples of America against Spanish colonialism.*

One day, when the stones in Spain were bounding to the footsteps of the French, Napoleon's eyes fell upon a lean and sunburned officer wearing a blue and white uniform. Approaching him, he read on the button of his dress coat the name of his corps: "Murcia!" He was a poor son of the Jesuit village of Yapeyú, raised in the open among Indians and half-breeds, who after 22 years of Spanish wars took firm hold of the crumbling uprising in Buenos Aires, bound the rebellious Creoles by oath, drove away the royal fleet at San Lorenzo, assembled the army of liberation in Cuyo, and crossed the Andes to greet the dawn in Chacabuco. From Chile, freed by his sword, he went by way of Maipú to liberate Peru, and in Lima promoted himself to the rank of Protector, with gold palms on his uniform. Suffering self-defeat, he yielded his command to Bolívar, withdrew, abdicated, passed through Buenos Aires alone, and died in France in a cottage filled with light and flowers, holding his daughter's hand. He proposed kings for America, artfully used the national resources for his own glory, retained the dictatorship—visible or concealed— until by his mistakes he was consumed in it, and certainly never reached the sublime merit of publicly and voluntarily laying aside his national empire. But smoldering in his Creole head was the epic idea that hastened and gave balance to American independence.

His veins flowed with the blood of a soldier from León and a granddaughter of *conquistadors*; his father was governor of Yapeyú on the banks of one of America's great rivers. He learned to read on the mountain slopes and grew up in the town as a gentleman's son in the shade of the palms and the *urundays*. He was taken to Spain to learn dancing and Latin in a school for the sons of noblemen. At the age of 12 the child "who seldom laughed" became a cadet. When as a Spanish lieutenant-colonel of 34 he returned to fight against Spain, he was no longer the man forged by the wind and rain of the pampas deep in his America, but the soldier who, in the glow of his native memories, had nurtured in the shadows of the Masonic Lodge of Lautaro, among young patricians and noblemen from Madrid, the will to work systematically and according to plan for American independence. Under the command of Daoiz and in the war with Napoleon, he had learned from Spain how to defeat Spain. He fought the astute and imaginative Moor, the pompous Portuguese and the brilliant Frenchman. He fought beside the Englishman who dies saluting, with all his buttons buttoned so that he does not disrupt the line of battle. When he left his ship at Buenos Aires with his Moorish cutlass that had flashed in Arjonilla and Bailén and Albuera, all he brought with him was his reputation for boldness, and all he demanded was "unity and direction," "a system that will save us from anarchy," and "a man who can lead an army." The war progressed as expected when a set political plan was not the driving force, for it is then a foray rather than a war, and a breeding ground for tyrants. "No army can exist without officers." "A soldier must be a soldier through and through." San Martín came from Spain with Alvear, an ambitious patriot from an influential family. Within a week he was given the task of organizing the corps of mounted grenadiers, with Alvear as his sergeant-major. The skills of the professional soldier dazzle the hesitant heroes of revolutions, those immature heroes who cannot put their ideas on horseback. They confuse what is merely the soldier's regular task with genius, and the well-intentioned but ignorant man confuses procedure with greatness. Among recruits, a captain is a general. San Martín was in the saddle, and he would never dismount until he reached the palace of the Peruvian viceroys. He selected his officers from among his friends, and these from persons of quality. The regulars never left the rank of lieutenant, the cadets came from distinguished families, the soldiers were strong and well built, and every one of them, at all hours of the day, he commanded: "Head up! A soldier must hold his head up!" He called each of them not by his name but by the name of a war. With Alvear and the Peruvian Monteagudo he founded the secret Lodge of Lautaro "to work systematically and with a plan for America's independence, and for her happiness, proceeding with justice and honor," so that "when a brother fills the role of supreme governorship, he will not of his own accord be able to appoint diplomats or generals, governors or judges, high officials, in the clergy or the military"; "to strive to understand public opinion"; "to help one another and carry out their sworn purposes, on pain of death." He assembled his squadrons man by man. He himself taught them to manage the saber: "The first high and mighty Spaniard you see, split his head open like a watermelon." He brought his officers together in a secret corps, accustomed them to accuse each other and bow to the will of the majority; with them he laid out the pentagon and the defenses on the drill field. He threw out of the squadron anyone showing fear under fire, or laying hands upon a woman; brought out the salient quality of every soldier; imbued military life with the ritual and mystery of the Church; honed his men to a cutting edge, setting each man like a stone in a piece of jewelry. He appeared with them in the square when their Lautaro Lodge rebelled against the triumvirate government. A cavalier on a magnificent bay horse, he led them in attacking the Spaniards disembarking at San Lorenzo; closing his two flanks over them, "with lance and cutlass" he sent them flying out of their saddles. Although pinned under his horse, he still gave orders and brandished his sword; a grenadier died clutching the Spanish flag; the grenadier who freed him from the animal fell at his feet; Spain fled, leaving her artillery and her dead behind.

But Alvear was jealous, and his party in the Lautaro Lodge "that governed the government" was stronger than San Martín's. San Martín engaged in an active correspondence with politicians. "To exist comes first, and we will see how later." "We must have an army, an army with officers of a mathematical turn of mind." "The last royalist must be thrown out of here." "I will resign my military commission the moment there are no more enemies left in America." "Let us strive together and we will be fee." "This seems to be a revolution of sheep, not men." "I am republican by conviction and principle, but I will sacrifice even this for the good of my native land." Alvear fought against the Spaniards in Montevideo as a general, and San Martín was sent as a general to upper Peru where not even the patriotism of Salta[1] was strong enough to raise the spirits. He was then sent to Cuyo[2] as an administrator. That was the logical place for him, for those were his people; he would make his fortress in that exile; from those heights he would pour himself over all the Americans! There in that remote place, through his own efforts and with the Andes as counselors and witnesses, he created the army with which he was to cross them. Alone, he planned a family of nations under the protection of his sword; he alone saw the risk run by freedom in every American nation as long as all were not free. While there is a single enslaved nation in America, the freedom of all the rest is in jeopardy! He laid his hand upon the devoted region, to be counted on as a leavening force by anyone who is determined to influence public affairs unaided. He was thinking of himself and of America, because his nobility and the pure gold of his character never permitted him to consider the various nations as different entities, but in the heart of his enthusiasm he could not see the continent as anything but one united American nation. Like all men of instinct he knew about local political facts and the hidden purposes in actions; but like all of them he failed— misled by success and flattery and self-confidence— because of confusing his native wisdom with that knowledge and art of manipulating the intangible and determining elements in a nation, skills attained, through a combination of talent and cultivation, only by the highest genius. That same redeeming concept of America, which would lead the sister nations to an effective unity of spirit, hid from his eyes the differences, necessary for freedom, between the American states, which make unity impossible. He failed to see, as would the profound statesman, the fully matured nations that had evolved from backwardness; he saw only the nations of the future that were bubbling and writhing with birth pangs inside his head. And in his mind he dealt with them as a patriarch deals with his sons. There is something formidable indeed in the clash between a man of decisive

---

[1] In 1813 San Martín won a major victory over loyalist forces in the Argentine province of Salta.

[2] San Martín was appointed governor of Cuyo in September 1814.

will and the accumulated work of centuries!

But for the time being the administrator of Cuyo saw only that he had to bring about America's independence. He believed and he commanded. And assigned by whatever fate to a region as sober as himself, he inspired love in its people, who recognized in him the very qualities they saw in themselves. He became their natural uncrowned king. Perfect governments originate from a people's identity with the man who rules affectionately and with a noble purpose, since identity itself is not enough if the noble purpose is lacking, for nobility is innate in every people. The day arrived when San Martín, confused in the rarefied air, sought to rule in Peru with purposes troubled by the fear of losing his glory; in the interest of his tottering command, he carried to extremes his honest belief in the need to have America governed by kings. At times his pride caused him to put his own interests ahead of America's, when the first thing a public figure must do in times of construction or reform is to renounce the personal, not favoring himself except in what he is worth to the country. On his own account he tried to test a government of rhetoric in a more highly cultivated country that lacked the vigor of its uncurbed originality. But in Cuyo, still close to the justice and freshness of Nature, nothing stood in the way of success for that man who ruled realistically, prepared breakfast with his own hands, sat beside the working man, saw to it that the mule was shod in a humane manner, granted audiences in the kitchen between the stewpot and the cigar, and slept in the open on a steer hide. There the neatly planted earth looked like a garden; the spotless houses standing among the vineyards and olive trees looked newly whitewashed. There the men pounded to pliancy the skins sewn by the women, and even the mountaintops seemed polished by hand. He stood out among those industrious people, a harder worker than they; among those early risers, the one who knocked on their doors in the morning. He meted out justice with common sense, reserving his reproaches and derision for the lazy and hypocritical. That man could be silent as a black cloud, yet spoke with the force of a thunderbolt. To the priest: "Here, the only bishop is myself; preach me a sermon on the sanctity of America's independence." To the Spaniard: "Would you like me to take you for a good man? Well, then, let six Creoles vouch for you." To the town gossip: "Ten pairs of shoes for the army for having berated the patriots." To the sentinel he threw out of the powder mill for having entered with spurs on: "One gold doubloon!" To the soldier who claimed his hands were tied by an oath taken before the Spaniards: "The firing squad will untie them for you!" He left some ransomed prisoners penniless "to ransom others!" He ordered a meeting of executors to pay a tribute: "The deceased would have given more to the revolution!" The American revolution was crumbling all around him in the thrust of the reconquest. Morillo came; Cuzco fell; Chile fled; from Mexico to Santiago the cathedral bells rang out the *Te Deum* of victory; the disorganized regiments took to the mountains in tattered bands. And in the continent-wide catastrophe San Martín decided to raise his army with a handful of men from Cuyo, invited his officers to a banquet, and with a voice as vibrant as a bugle offered this toast: "To the first shot fired upon Chile's oppressors across the Andes!"

Cuyo belonged to San Martín, and he rose up against the dictator Alvear, the rival who blundered when he rashly accepted the resignation sent him by San Martín at the height of his activities. Cuyo kept its governor who seemed to be declining in favor of his replacement, who explained to the provincial council his detailed reasons for breaking his word and who allowed his militiamen to go into the square out of uniform to demand Alvear's resignation. Enraged, Cuyo dismissed the one who dared to succeed, with a paper appointment, the man appointed by Nature; and San Martín had Cuyo, the place that could not give him up because he carried within him the redemption of the continent— that friend of the harness-makers to whom he returned intact the saddles required for the country, of the mule drivers whose mules he returned after their service in the army, of the farmers who proudly brought him seed corn for the troops to plant in their little patches of ground, of the region's notables who trusted the honest administrator and placed in him their hopes of ridding their heads and their properties of the Spaniard. San Martín charged the inhabitants of Cuyo for breathing; even the sprouting root paid a tax. But first he had fired them with such a passion for the freedom of their country, and with such pride in Cuyo, that whatever tax he imposed they considered tolerable, especially since San Martín, with his understanding of men, did not encroach upon local customs but exacted the new taxes by means of the old methods: town council approval. Cuyo would save America. "Give me Cuyo and with its help I will ride into Lima!" Cuyo had faith in anyone who had faith in it, and praised to the skies the man who thought highly of it. In Cuyo, at the gateway to Chile, he created, complete from boots to ships, the army with which he was to liberate it. His men, the defeated; his money, from Cuyo's people; their meat, the jerked beef wrapped in dough that lasts for a week; shoes, the *gaucho's* sheepskins boot drawn together over the instep; clothes, tanned hides; water flasks, horn; sabers honed to a razor's edge; bugles for music; cannon cast from bells. Dawn found him in the arsenal, counting pistols; in the munitions depot he could tell one cannonball from another. He hefted them bodily, dusted off the powder, and carefully replaced them on the pile. He put an inventive priest in charge of the arsenal, and the army went out of there equipped with gun carriages and horseshoes, canteens and cartridges, bayonets and mechanical devices; that lieutenant-priest, at 25 pesos a month, was hoarse for the rest of his life. San Martín built a saltpeter plant and a powder mill. He drew up the military code, organized the medical corps and commissary. He established an academy for officers, because "an army cannot exist without officers who are also mathematicians." Early in the morning when the sun hit the mountain peaks, there were field maneuvers, with San Martín's saber flashing everywhere among the green recruits, the mounted grenadiers, and his beloved Negroes. He would take a swallow from his canteen and say: "Here, let me fix your rifle!" "Your hand, brother; that was a fine shot." "Come, *gaucho*, some swordplay with the governor!" At a blast from the bugles the expert horseman was off, galloping from group to group, hatless and radiantly happy: "Faster, faster, while the daylight lasts; battles are won on the drill field!" He sent his officers to fight bulls: "I need these madmen to defeat the Spaniards!" With the stragglers from Chile, the liberated slaves, the conscripts, the vagrants, he gathered together and transformed 6,000 men. One sunny day he led them into the flower-decked city of Mendoza, put his general's staff into the hand of Our Lady of Carmen, dipped the blue flag three times in the silence following the roll of drums, and said, "My soldiers, this is the first flag of independence to be blessed in America; swear to defend it with your life, as I am swearing!"

The 4,000 mounted fighting men started crossing the Andes in four columns, with a groom for every 20 horses. There were 1,200 riflemen, 250 artillery men with their 2,000 cannon balls, and nine hundred thousand rounds of ammunition. The two center columns were flanked by a column on either side. Fray Beltrán marched ahead with his 120 wielders of the pickax and crowbar shouldering their implements, his drays and poles to protect the 21 cannon, his rope bridges for crossing rivers, his grapples and cables to rescue those who might lose their footing. At times the men walked along the edge of a precipice, at times made their way upward by hugging the slopes. When a body of men intended to fall upon the Chacabuco valley like lightning, those men had to live near the lightning. Out of the mass of snow rose the shimmering hulk of Aconcagua. Below them the condors wheeled among the clouds. There the rattled Spanish troops were waiting, wondering from which direction the blow would fall, their forces scattered by San Martín's subtle espionage and policy of attrition, so that they could avoid a confrontation with his concentrated strength. San Martín dismounted from his mule, wrapped himself in his cape, and slept with a stone for a pillow and the Andes all around him.

It was 24 days later at dawn when to the sound of drums, O'Higgins's[3] flank, jealous of Soler's, gained the summit by which the surrounded Spaniards might escape. Back in Cuyo, San Martín had been surrounding them in his mind's eye, hill by hill. Battles are won behind the eyebrows. The fighting man must have the terrain in his pocket. At noon the terrified Spaniard recoiled before the picket guards in the valley, to fall at the onslaught of the horses from the mountains. The liberating cavalry ran through the enemy infantry like a whirlwind and left the gunners lying over their own cannon. San Martín threw his full force against the ineffectual ranch walls used by the enemy as fortifications. The last of the royalists took to their heels through the fields and marshes. Among the 500 dead lay the two halves of a gun shining in the grass. And after winning the struggle that liberated Chile and assured America of her freedom, San Martín wrote a letter to "admirable Cuyo" and had the cloth of his cape turned.

---

[3] Bernardo O'Higgins (1780–1846): independence fighter in Argentina and Chile.

Chile wanted to name him governor with absolute powers, but he declined the offer. In Buenos Aires he resigned his commission of brigadier-general "because I have given my word not to accept any military rank or political office." The city fathers enshrined his portrait, decorating it with battle trophies, and his fellow countryman Belgrano ordered a pyramid built in his honor. But what San Martín wanted from Buenos Aires were troops, weapons, money, ships for cutting off Lima by sea as he planned to do by land.

With his Irish aide-de-camp he returned by way of the field of Chacabuco and wept over the fate of his "poor Negroes" who fell there in the cause of American freedom. In Buenos Aires he set in motion the secret power of the Lautaro Lodge, and backed his friend O'Higgins, who was his director in Chile, against the rival ambitions of his enemy Carrera. From his elegant home in Santiago, where he would have no silver plate or salaried retainers, he set about undermining the influence of the Peruvian viceroy. He sighed from the depths of "the sorrow gnawing away at my sad existence" for "two months of peace in the good city of Mendoza." Astride his horse at the Archbishop's doorway he harangued the Chileans defeated in Cancharrayada, and then emerged in triumph from the bloody field of Maipú, with Lima before him.

He leaped from his battle steed to an Andean mule; threatening to resign, he forced Buenos Aires, prodded by the Lodge, to send him funds for the expedition in Peru. He carried on a correspondence with his faithful friend, the Argentine director Pueyrredón, about the plan that ended in sending a Lodge member to the courts of Europe in quest of a king—just as the Chilean fleet, victorious in the Pacific, came under the command of the Englishman Cochrane who had left his country rather than "see it unmercifully oppressed" by a monarchy, and just as Bolívar was planting the republican flag in nation after nation. And when Chile and Argentina—faced by San Martín's threat of withdrawing his army across the Andes, leaving O'Higgins without support and the road to Chile and Argentina open to the Spaniards—were forced to submit to his demands for further help; when Cochrane had opened the sea route to Peru with his daring raids; when he was finally about to descend upon the Lima palaces with his reinforced army, assuring America of independence and himself of glory, Buenos Aires recalled him to throw back a Spanish expedition that was thought to be already upon the high seas, to protect the government against the rebellious federalists, and to support the monarchy that San Martín himself had recommended. He refused. He rose up with the army he could never have assembled without the aid of his country, was acclaimed supreme commander of his troops at Rancagua, and as an independent captain carrying the Chilean colors, turned toward Peru to rout the Spaniards, leaving his strife-torn country behind him. "The war will never end until Lima is in our hands!" On this campaign "hang the hopes of this vast continent." "I must follow the call of destiny...."

Who was that man in gold-embroidered uniform, driving through the mild air of Lima in his elegant state coach drawn by six horses? He was the Protector of Peru,[4] who by his own decree proclaimed himself all-powerful ruler, wrote a constitution fixing all power in his hands and establishing the political system, who freed the unborn children of slaves, abolished torture and the lash, and accomplished both good and evil through his fiery minister Monteagudo. He was the man who, on the very day the constitution was put into effect, created the order of nobility—the Order of the Sun; the man who had the breast band of the ladies of Lima inscribed "To the patriotism of the gentler sex"; the "emperor" ridiculed by the popular songs of the day; the "King José" laughed at by his Lodge brothers in the flag room. He was San Martín, abandoned by Cochrane, denied by his troops, detested in Buenos Aires and Chile, thrown into confusion at a meeting of the "Patriotic Society" when he applauded the speech of a priest who favored a king and begged to have some empty-headed fellow sent to Europe to look over an Austrian or Italian or Portuguese prince for Peru. Who was that grim and lonely man leaving the ball after that titanic meeting in Guayaquil, the ball where Bolívar, aglow with victory, unchallenged leader of the armies coming from Boyacá and sweeping the Spaniards before them, waltzed among the modest ladies and riotous soldiers? He was San Martín, who convoked Peru's first constitutional congress and stripped himself before it of his red and white sash; who stepped out of his state coach in a Peru turned against the

---

[4] San Martín was named Protector after Peru's independence was proclaimed July 28, 1821.

Protector because "the presence of a successful military figure is frightening to emerging countries, and I am growing weary of hearing it said that I want to become king." He left Peru to Bolívar "who won it by his hand," because "there is not enough room in Peru for Bolívar and me without a conflict that would be a worldwide scandal, and San Martín will not be the one to give the royalists a Roman holiday." In the dark of night he quietly bade farewell to a faithful officer, arrived in Chile with 120 gold doubloons in his purse, only to find that he was hated. In Buenos Aires they whistled at him in the streets, unaware that because of his sincere patience when luck was against him he had reached a truer greatness than his ambition had sought in vain.

Cured of the blindness and temptations of power, this man who had accomplished one of Nature's designs, and had secured the triumph of the continent so well that even his own defection could not endanger the American effort, emerged in all his beauty. He, whose vision had brought three free nations into being, lived, as it were, a life of dedicated exile, never involving himself in the affairs of men. He learned from his own experience that a leader's greatness does not lie in his own person, although so it may seem, but in the degree to which he serves the greatness of his people; they rise higher while following him, and fall when they put his leadership behind them. He would weep when he saw an old friend, and died facing the sea with his heart in Buenos Aires, seated in his armchair, white-haired and serene, no less majestic than the snows of Aconcagua in the silence of the Andes.

With All, for the Good of All

Speech delivered by Martí on the evening of November 26, 1891, at the Cuban Lyceum in Tampa, Florida, during the gathering organized by Cuban emigrés in that city. By that time, Martí had abandoned all his journalistic, diplomatic and literary activities to devote himself entirely to revolutionary tasks. This speech provoked a famous controversy that fortunately ended with the rapprochement of former combatants of the so-called Ten Year War (1868–1878) and the new generation (the so-called New Pines) represented by Martí.

Cubans:

For suffering Cuba, the first word. Cuba must be considered an altar for the offering of our lives, not a pedestal for lifting us above it. And now, after calling forth its most cherished name, I shall lavish the tenderness of my soul upon these generous hands that come to give me strength— surely not inopportunely— for the agonizing task of building. Now, with our eyes placed higher than our heads, and my own heart torn out of my body, I shall not egoistically thank those who think they see in me the virtues they desire both from me and from every Cuban. Nor will I merely thank the genial Carbonell or the fearless Rivero for the magnificent hospitality of their words and the fervor of their generous affections. But I shall give all the gratitude in my soul to them, and through them in all those loving people who have stood up in the face of the ambitious landowner who spies upon us and divides us; to these virtuous people in whom the free strength of our industrious country is being tried; to these cultured people whose writing desks stand beside their work benches, and for whom the thunderings of Mirabeau stand beside the arts of Roland— answer enough for the contemptuous of this world; to this temple bedecked with heroes and built upon men's hearts. I embrace all those who know how to love. And I have within my heart the star and the dove.

Periodic respect for an idea that one cannot abjure without disgrace is not bringing us together here, reluctantly and through sheer effort. Nor is it the ever ready and at times too ready response of patriotic hearts to fame or a position of power, or to some hero who fails to crown his untimely longing for death with the higher heroism of repressing that longing, or to a beggar who under the cloak of the mother country goes about with his hand held out. The one who comes here will never be disfigured by flattery, nor is this noble people receiving him a servile and easily led people. My breast swells with pride, and at this moment I love my country even more than before, and I now have an even greater faith in its serene and well-ordered future—a future rescued from the serious danger of following blindly, in the name of freedom, those who make use of their yearning for it to bend it to their own purposes. Still more firmly do I believe in a Republic of open eyes, neither foolish nor timid, neither haughty nor professorial, neither over-cultured nor uncultured, for I can see—by the sacred affirmations of the heart when we are together on this night of brain and brawn, together for now and for later, together for as long as patriotism prevails—I can see those Cubans who put their free and frank opinions above all things, and one Cuban who respects them.

For if in my country's affairs I were permitted to offer one benefit to everyone—one fundamental benefit to be a basic principle of all my countrymen, and without which the other benefits would be faulty and insecure—this is the one I would choose: I want the first law of our Republic to be the Cuban cult of full dignity for man. Every true man must feel upon his own cheek the slap upon any other man's cheek. Nations are vilified from the cradle by the habit of resorting to personal cliques, fomented by notorious or fraudulent interests, in defense of freedoms. Set your souls afire and let them shine and crackle like lightning for the sake of truth, and follow it in freedom, you honest men. Put this tender consideration above all things, this manly tribute of each Cuban to the other. Neither mysteries, nor calumnies, nor willful injuring of reputations, nor long and crafty preparations for the baneful day of ambitions. Either the Republic is founded upon the integral character of every one of its sons—the habit of working with his hands and thinking for himself, the putting of his whole self into what he does, and respect, like family honor, for everyone's wholehearted effort; enthusiasm, in short, for a man's honor—or the Republic is not worth one of our mothers' tears or a single drop of our heroes' blood. We are striving for truth and not for dreams. We are striving to liberate Cubans and not to intimidate them. We are striving to peacefully and equitably adjust the rights and interests of Cuba's loyal inhabitants and not to establish, at the gateway of the continent, of the Republic, the frightful administration of Veintimilla, or the bloody possessions of Rosas, or the lamentable Paraguay of France! Better to fall under the excesses of our fellow countrymen's imperfect characters than to profit from the credit acquired with the guns of war or the words that defame character! This is my sole claim to these affections that have come in time to strengthen these hands of mine that never tire in the service of true freedom. Cut them off, those of you whom I passionately desired to lift higher, and—I do not lie!—I will cherish that violence because it comes to me out of the fury of my own land, and because for its sake I will see a Cuban heart show courage and rebellion! Above all, let us band together in this faith. Let us join hands, in avowal of this decision, where all may see them, and where there is no forgetting without punishment. Let us bar the way to a republic which fails to come through methods worthy of a man's integrity, for the benefit and prosperity of all Cubans!

Of all Cubans! I wonder what tender mystery there is in this sweetest of words, or what purest of pleasures in this very word of man. It is so beautiful already that if pronounced as it should be, the air would seem to be a golden halo and Nature a throne or a mountaintop! One says "Cuban" and a sweetness like a gentle brotherhood suffuses the heart, and the strongbox of our savings opens by itself, and we hasten to set another place at table, and the enamored heart stretches its wings to give shelter to anyone born in the same land as ourselves, even if misdeeds confuse him, or ignorance misleads him, or anger infuriates him, or he is bloodied by crime! It is as if some divine arms we cannot see were gathering all of us onto a breast in which the blood still flows and the heart still sobs! You must create, there in our country, in order to give us dedicated work later on.

You must create, there where the corrupt proprietor rots whatever he looks upon, a new Cuban soul, hostile and bristling—a proud soul, different from that magnanimous and home-loving soul of our ancestors and illegitimate daughter of the misery that sees vice go unpunished, and of the useless culture that finds employment only in the dull contemplation of itself! Here where we keep watch for the absent ones, where we rebuild the house that topples upon our heads down there, where we create what must replace the things destroyed for us there—here, no word so closely resembles the light of dawn, no consolation enters our hearts with greater joy, than this ardent and ineffable word: Cuban!

For that is what this city is; it is the entire Cuban emigration; that is what we are accomplishing in these years of work without savings, families without pleasure, life without zest and a furtive death! To our fatherland crumbling to pieces down there, and blinded by corruption, we must take the devout and farseeing country being built here! To what is left of the country down there—everywhere being eaten away by gangrene beginning to gnaw at the heart—we must unite the friendly country to which we have come, here in our loneliness, accommodating our souls to all the realities with the firm hand that affection demands from within and without—realities so well concealed down there (in some because of despair and in others because of Babylonian pleasure) that although there are great certainties and great hopes and great risks, they are little less than unknown, even by experts! So what do they know down there about this glorious night of resurrection, about the methodical and resolute faith of our spirits? What do they know down there about the continuous and growing rapport of us Cubans away from the island whom the 10 years of mistakes and Cuba's natural fickleness and other malevolent causes have not succeeded in at last dividing? Indeed they have succeeded in becoming so intimate and affectionate a unifying force that all one can see is an eagle taking flight, a sun rising and an army advancing. What do they know down there about these subtle treaties, that nobody draws up or can terminate, between the despairing country and the waiting emigrés? What do they know about this character of ours, strengthened cautiously and by daily effort and cruel testing? What do they know about the brave and industrious and free people we are going to take to them? What does the man dying in the night know about the one awaiting him at dawn? Any stevedore can load a ship, and any artillery man can light a cannon fuse; but it has not been that lesser task, of mere opportunity and result, which is our duty; it has been the task of avoiding the harmful consequences, and hastening the happy ones, of the next and inevitable war, and of cleansing it of the naturally human neglect and indifference and envy that might needlessly and inexcusably put this war where they put the last one. It has been a task of disciplining our free souls in the knowledge and order of our country's genuine elements, and in this work which is the sun and air of freedom, so that, with the creative forces of a new situation, they may comprise without danger those inevitable remains of the difficult crises needed to produce those forces. And in this sublime task our hands will ache more than once. But the dead are commanding and counseling and keeping watch, and the living are listening to them and obeying; and in the wind there are sounds of adjutants passing by carrying orders, and the sound of flags unfurling! Let us band together, Cubans, in this other faith: with all, and for all: the inevitable war, so our country may respect and desire and support it, and the enemy not kill it for us at its height, because of location or staff or lack of men: the revolution of justice and reality for the recognition and unrestricted practice of the true freedoms.

Not even the brave men of war who are listening to me now agree with these scrupulous analyses of public affairs, because the enthusiast considers criminal even the delay of good sense in putting his enthusiasm to work. Nor do our wives, so attentively listening to us here, dream of anything but returning to tread their own land where their comrades will not be living bitterly and sullenly as they are living here. And the child, brother or son of heroes and martyrs, nourished by their legends, thinks of nothing but the beauty of dying in the saddle, fighting for his country, beside a palm tree!

This is my dream, the dream of us all. Palm trees are waiting brides, and we must establish justice as tall as the palms! This is what we wanted to say. The war of impulse, which collapsed in disorder, must at the insistence of national wrongs be followed by the war of necessity, feeble at first and with little chance of success without the encouragement of that strong and intelligent love of right whereby the souls most eager for it pick up from the grave the flag dropped upon it by those least in need of justice and weary of the first effort. Cubans in their independence are seeking their rights as men, and independence must be sought with man's entire soul. Let disconsolate Cuba turn her eyes to us! For with the logs in the road the children are testing the strength of their newfound arms! Wars break out, when there are reasons, because of the impatience of a brave man or a kernel of corn! For the Cuban spirit is forming ranks, and the confused masses are like the dawn! For the enemy, less surprised today and less concerned, does not have the wealth which he had to defend the last time. And we must not entertain ourselves with bickering about locality, or with vying for posts of command, or with national envies or insane hopes as much as we did then! Because outside of Cuba we have love in our hearts, our eyes upon the coast, our hands upon America, and a gun in our holsters! Then who can fail to read all this in the air in letters of light? And in letters of light it must be read that in this new sacrifice we are not seeking mere forms, or the perpetuation of the colonial spirit in our lives, with the latest in Yankee regimentals. What we are seeking is the essence and reality of a republican country of our own, without some people's sickly fear of a wholesome expression of all ideas and the honest use of all energies, and on the part of others the fear of that robbery of man which consists in the attempt to prevail in the name of freedom by means of ruthless actions in which the rights of others to freedom's methods and guarantees are set aside. Of course, the coxcomb politicians will be thrown out, for they forget how necessary it is to come to grips with what cannot be suppressed, and face-powder patriotism will start grumbling on the pretext that people, in the sweat of creating, do not always smell like garden pinks. And what are we to do about it? Without the worms that enrich the soil, no sumptuous palaces would be built! We have to enter truth with our shirt sleeves rolled up, the way a butcher enters a carcass of beef. All truth is sacred, even without the scent of garden pinks. Everything has ugly, bloody entrails. When the artist makes his wonderful jewelry, at first the gold in his crucible is muddy. It is from life's foulness that fruits derive their nectar and flowers their color. Man is born out of the pain and darkness of the maternal womb, out of the scream and the sublime rending, and from a distance and to human eyes, those magnificent forces and streams of fire leaping and fusing in the furnace of the sun only look like sunspots! Progress to those who do not fear the light; charity to those who tremble at its rays!

I would not regard that flag so fondly (resolved, as I am, to know that what is most sacred is taken as an instrument of interest by the world's bold victors) if I did not believe that out of its folds must come total freedom when the cordial recognition of every Cuban's integrity, and of a just means of resolving the conflicts in his affairs, robs of all reason those counselors of confused methods who deem terrible only that stubborn passion which refuses to recognize all there is in his just and equable demands. Drive a nail through the tongue of the popular flatterer, and hang it in the breeze like an ignominious flag where it may be a warning to those who further their own ambitions by vainly aggravating the pain of the sufferers, or hiding from them the essential truths of their problems, or kindling their anger. And beside the tongue of the flatterer, nail the tongue of the one who withholds justice!

Let the flatterer's tongue be nailed there for all to see, as well as that of those who use as a pretext the exaggerations to which ignorance is entitled and whoever does not use every means to put a stop to ignorance, refusing to respect whatever of man's pain and sacred agony exists in the exaggerations: it is more comfortable to curse in judicial robes than to study, sympathetically, wholly immersed in human sorrow! Life's judges must be put into life's prisons if they wish to learn justice. Let the one who judges everything know everything. Let the one at the top judge neither hastily nor with bias. Let the one at the bottom judge neither with bias nor hastily. The jealous man must not censure the well-being which he secretly envies. The powerful must not disregard the moving poem and the bloody sacrifice of the man who has to dig the bread he eats, or the sacrifice of his long-suffering companion wearing her crown which the unjust cannot see, or the sacrifice of their children who do not have what belongs to other men's children around the world! Better never to have unfurled that flag from its staff if it were not to shelter all heads equally!

Little does he know of our country, little does he know of it—the man who is unaware of what it holds as spirit of the present and guarantee of the future, a powerful aggregate of that original freedom which man by himself creates out of the land's substance and the pain he sees and his own ideas and proud nature. Flesh-and-blood politicians must rely more upon this genuine and vigorous freedom, which can sin only through lack of the culture it is easy to place in it, than can paper politicians rely upon that freedom of dilettantes schooled in the catechisms of France or England. We are men, and we are not going to want paper-doll governments but intellectual effort cast in the mold of our country. A man knows little about our nation if he fails to observe that, together with this natural impulse that rouses it for war and will not allow it to sleep during peace, it has been reared by study and experience and a certain explicit knowledge that our lovely land affords. He knows little about it if he does not see the accumulation of human and cultivated forces of order— a phalanx of broad intelligence enriched by love for man without which intelligence is no more than scourge and crime. He is not well acquainted with our country if he overlooks the intimate harmony (a result of common sorrow) among Cubans of natural law, without history or books, and among Cubans who have put into their studies the passion they were unable to put into building their new country— so fervent a brotherhood among the abject slaves of life and those of an annihilating tyranny— that because of this unanimous and burning love of justice in those of one occupation and those of another; that due to this equally sincere human ardor of men who hold their necks erect because their heads are held high by nature, and men whose necks are bent because fashion demands the display of a handsome back; because of this vehement country where those whom various states of culture might drive apart are drawn together by the same dreams and honesty— due to all this our Cuba, free in the harmony of equality, will tie down the colonial hand which in its own time will not fail to fall upon us, disguised in the glove of the Republic. And beware, Cubans, for some gloves are so like the human hand that they cannot be distinguished from it! Of all who come demanding power, Cubans, you must ask them in broad daylight, where the hand can be clearly seen, "Hand or glove?" But there is really no reason to be afraid or to quarrel. The very thing we must combat, we need. What holds peoples in subjection is as necessary to them as what urges them ahead; in the family household the father, always active, is as necessary as the mother, always timid. There is a male policy and a female policy. A locomotive with a boiler to make it run and without brakes to stop it in time? In the affairs of nations it is necessary to man the brakes with one hand and stoke the boiler with the other. And from too much steam, and from too much braking, nations hereabouts are suffering.

Then what is there for us to fear? A lessening of our enthusiasm, the illusory quality of our faith, the small number of us with untiring spirits, our disorganized hopes? Well, I look around this hall and can feel the firmness and stability of the earth under my feet, and I say: "You lie." I look into my heart, which is only a Cuban heart, and I say: "You lie."

Are we to fear the habits of authority practiced in war and, in a certain sense, salved by a daily disdain for death? Well, then, I do not know the valiant Cuban soul, or the wisdom and experience in Cuban judgement, or to what extent the old authorities would have to rely upon the untried authorities, or the admirable agreement between republican thinking and the heroic action which honors, almost without exception, those Cubans who bear arms. But since I do recognize all this, to anyone who says we must expect from our veterans this criminal self-love, this disregard of homeland for their own interests, this iniquitous treason against their country, I tell him: "You lie!"

Or will we have to discard our fear of the trials and tribulations of war stirred up by corrupt people in the pay of the Spanish government, or our fear of walking barefoot, a common thing in Cuba because, amidst thieves and their accomplices, nobody in Cuba has shoes any more except those very thieves and their accomplices? Well, since I know that the very one who writes a book to stir up the fear of war has said in verse— very good verse, to be sure— that the *jutías*[1] supply every need of the Cuban countryside— and I know that Cuba is full of *jutías* again, I return to those who want to frighten us with the very sacrifice we desire so much, and I tell them: "You lie!"

Must we be afraid of the Cuban who has suffered most from

[1] Common Cuban rodent.

being deprived of his freedom in the country where the blood he shed for it has made him love it too much to be a threat to it? Will we fear the Negro—the noble black man, our black brother—who for the sake of the Cubans who died for him has granted eternal pardon to the Cubans who are still mistreating him? Well, I know of black hands that are plunged further into virtue than those of any white man I have ever met. From the Negro's love for a reasonable freedom, I know that only in a greater natural and useful intensity does his differ from the white Cuban's love of freedom. I know that the black man has drawn his noble body to its full height and is becoming a solid column for his native liberties. Others may fear him; I love him. Anyone who speaks ill of him I disown, and I say to him openly: "You lie!"

Must we fear the Spaniard in Cuba? The armed Spaniard who could not defeat us by his bravery, only by our envy—for no other reason but our envy? Are we to be afraid of the Spaniard whose fortune is in El Sardinero or La Rambla and who will slip away with his fortune because it is the only country he has? Or shall we fear the Spaniard whose property is in Cuba because he is fond of the land and his children have roots there, and due to them and the fear and punishment will offer little resistance? Are we to fear the simple Spaniard who is as fond of freedom as are we ourselves, and who, together with us, is seeking a just country which is better than fondness for an incapable and unjust one? Or the Spaniard who with his Cuban wife suffers from irremediable desertion and the wretched future of the children born to them with the stigma of hunger and persecution, with the decree of exile within their own country, with the death sentence in life which is the Cuban's heritage? Should we be afraid of the good liberal Spaniard—my Valencian father, my bondsman from the North, the man from Cadiz who watched over my feverish sleep, the Catalonian who swore and cursed because he did not want the Creole to escape with his clothes, the man from Málaga who carried the feeble Cuban out of the hospital upon his back, the Galician who dies in alien snows returning from delivering the monthly bread ration to the home of the general acting as commander-in-chief of the Cuban war? In Cuba a man fights for his freedom, and there are many Spaniards who love freedom! Those Spaniards will be attacked by others, and I will help the former as long as I live! To the one who does not realize that those Spaniards are merely so many other Cubans, we say: "You lie!"

And must we fear the alien snows? Those who do not know how to fight with their fists in this life, or who measure other people's hearts by their own timid ones, or who believe that nations are merely chessboards, or who are so steeped in slavery that they need someone to hold their stirrup for them to extricate their foot— those people will seek in a nation of hostile and alien components the Republic which assures them of well-being only when it is administered for them in accord with their own character, and when it is bright and shining. To those who believe that Cubans lack the spirit and capacity to live for themselves in a land created by their own valor, I say: "You lie!"

And to the elegant young dandies who today sneer at this holy revolution whose foremost leaders and martyrs were men born to the marble and silk of fortune, this holy revolution which, in the shortest time and by the redemptive virtue of just wars, made brothers of the heroic first-born and the landless peasant, the master of men and his slaves. To those paperweight Olympians who step down from their slanderous tripods to ask, terrified and willing to submit, if this or that fighter has set foot upon the ground for the purpose of mollifying the soul with whom he can divide the power tomorrow; to the presumptuous who knowingly foment the deception of those who believe that this magnificent movement of souls, this burning idea of justified redemption, this sad but firm desire for the inevitable war, is only the stubbornness of an unruly tramp, or the escapade of an unemployed general, or the noisy chatter of persons who enjoy the wealth that can be kept only by collaborating with dishonor, or the threat of a mob of laborers with hate for a heart and waste paper for brains— a mob that can be led, as with a bridle, wherever the first ambitious man who flatters it, or the first despot who waves a flag before its eyes, cares to take it; to all the elegant dandies or Olympians, and to the presumptuous, I say: "You lie!" This is the mob of laborers, the coffer of our alliance, the baldric embroidered by a woman's hand where the sword of Cuba has been kept, the redemptive desert where one builds, forgives, foretells, and loves!

Enough, enough of mere words! We are not here for flattery, but to feel our hearts and see that they are sound and able; we are here to teach the despairing, the disbanded, the melancholic, the force of our idea and action, to teach them the proven virtue which assures them of happiness to come, to teach them our true stature, a stature having nothing of the presumptuous or the theorizer or the singsong chanter or the music fanatic or the chaser of clouds or the beggar. We are one, and we are able to march on to the end because we recognize the wrongs and will make certain that there is no backsliding. We have gathered together the scattered with absolute love and patience, and we have enthusiastically restored order to what was, after the catastrophe, distrustful confusion. We have brought about good faith, and we think we have succeeded in suppressing or repressing the wrongs that caused our defeat, and in gathering sincerely and for a lasting purpose the known or proposed elements whose unity will aid in carrying the imminent war to a successful conclusion. Now to form ranks! Nations are not founded upon mere hopes in the depths of a man's soul! Again I see those flags before me, giving orders. And the sea seems to be coming to us from Cuba, surging with hopes and sorrows and tearing down the barrier of this alien land where we are living, its turbulent waves crashing against these gates. Down there is our Cuba, smothered in the arms that crush and corrupt it! There it is, wounded in heart and mind, tied to the torture chair, presiding over the banquet where gold-trimmed cuffs lift poisoned wine to the lips of sons who have forgotten their fathers! And the father died fighting the second lieutenant, and the son, arm in arm with the second lieutenant, goes to the orgy to rot! Enough of mere words! Out of torn entrails let us build an unquenchable love of country without which no man, good or bad, can live happily. There she is, calling to us. We can hear her moan; she is being raped and mocked and turned gangrenous before our eyes. Our dearest mother is being corrupted and torn into pieces! So let us rise up at once with a final burst of heartfelt energy. Let us rise up so that freedom will not be endangered in triumph, by confusion or clumsiness, or impatience in preparing it. Let us rise up for the true Republic, those of us who, with our passion for right and our habit of hard work, will know how to preserve it. Let us rise up to give graves to the heroes whose spirit roams the world, alone and ashamed. Let us rise up so that some day our children will have graves! And let us place around the star of our new flag this formula of love triumphant: "With all, and for the good of all."

Our Ideas

On March 14, 1892, Martí published the first edition of Patria, *a journal intended to serve as the mouthpiece of Cuban exiles and to intensify the revolutionary propaganda campaign for the independence of Cuba and Puerto Rico. Five hundred and twenty-two issues appeared before it ceased publication on December 31, 1898, when the War of Independence (1895–98) ended.*

This journal comes into being because of the desire and with the resources of the independent Cubans and Puerto Ricans of New York to contribute, without pause or urgency, to the organizing of the free men of Cuba and Puerto Rico, in accord with the present-day needs and conditions of those islands and their future republican constitution. Its purpose is to maintain the intimate friendship which unites, and must unite, the various independent groups with one another, and also those good and useful men from many origins who persist in making sacrifices for our emancipation, or are sincerely beginning to work for it. The journal intends to explain and determine the country's real and vital forces and their sources of composition and decomposition, so that the recognition of our deficiencies and mistakes, and our dangers, will assure the task that could not be accomplished merely by the romantic and disorganized faith of our patriotism. Its function is to promote and proclaim virtue wherever it is found, and to unite and love and live in the passion for truth. It leaves at the door, because they deform the purest purpose, both the personal concern by which clouded judgement brings down to its own desires the sacred issues of justice and humanity, and the fanaticism which advises men to make a sacrifice whose feasibility and usefulness are unreasonable.

It is criminal for a man to promote a war that can be avoided, and to fail to promote an inevitable one. It is criminal for a man to see the arrival in his country of a conflict, fomented by provocation and favored by despair, and not prepare the country, or help prepare it, for that conflict. And the crime is greater when one recognizes, through previous experience, that a disorganized preparation can make the most glorious patriotism go down in defeat, or sow in the victorious country the seeds of its definitive dissolution. He who withholds his aid in preparing the war today is helping the country disintegrate. The simple belief in the likelihood of war is indeed an obligation on the part of whoever considers it honorable and wise to contribute to the purification of the likely war, or to prevent its turning sour. The strong foresee; the second-class citizen waits for the storm with folded arms.

For a country which was embroiled in war for 10 years and looks upon its heroes as loyal and active, war is the unavoidable consequence of a continuous denial, open or concealed, of the conditions necessary for the happiness of people who refuse to be corrupted and disorganized in their misery. And it is beside the point to wonder whether or not war is desirable, since no devout soul can desire war. All a man can do is to organize it in such a way that it will bring a republican peace, and when it is over, to see that the disturbances that brought it about—and that had to be encountered in the forward march of those American nations when political skill and the utilization of national strength for the task were not in the hands of all, as they are now—never again become necessary or justified. War is frightening only to mediocre souls incapable of preferring a dangerous dignity to a useless life.

The unfortunate war, upon whose sorrows a foresighted statesman must not tarry, is frightening in the present and relative sense; gold is a precious metal, and a gold coin is not given regretfully if one receives in exchange something of greater value. When a country lives in a state of silent warfare that embitters the most natural relationships and disrupts existence as if it had no roots, the precipitation of that indecisive state of war into a decisive war is a preservation of national strength that can be recommended. When two hostile entities in a country live with either admitted or unspoken aspirations for predominance, their living together can result only in the irremediable overthrow of one of them. When a nation, composed by the unfortunate hand of its rulers out of elements of hate and dissociation, emerges from the first test of war (over and above the dissentions that ended it) more united than when it entered it, the war becomes, instead of a hindrance to that nation's civilization, a new period of amalgam indispensable for uniting its diverse factors into a secure and useful republic. When in a country of Spaniards and Creoles there is to be a war— waged not against the Spaniards living there, but against dependence on a nation unable to govern a people who can be happy only without that nation— then that war can count as natural allies all those Spaniards who want to be happy.

War is a political process, and this process is appropriate in Cuba because it will definitively resolve a situation the fear of which keeps it in a state of confusion, and will continue to do so; because in the conflict between the country's rulers, now poor and in disrepute among themselves, and the naturally freedom-loving native, the war will bring the freedom needed to attain and enjoy a legitimate well-being; because the war will put the finishing touches on the unity and friendship of the regions and social entities without whose cordial and neighborly fellowship independence itself would be a hotbed of serious discord; because the war will give the industrious Spaniards, with their aid and neutrality, an opportunity to make people forget the blindness and cruelty with which in the previous struggle they stifled their children's virtue; and because the war will bring about a state of happiness greater than the efforts to be made on its behalf.

At the bottom of one's heart, and at a time when life weighs less than the infamy in which it crawls, war is the most beautiful and respectable form of human sacrifice. Some men think more of themselves than of their neighbors, and abhor the procedures of justice that can bring them risks or discomforts. Other men love their neighbors more than themselves, their children more than their own lives, the certain benefits of freedom more than the ever dubious benefits of an incorrigible tyranny, and expose themselves to death to enable their country to live. So when the contending elements in the islands show the impossibility of settling their differences fairly and honorably, and when the always partial agreement that they might attempt would never be sanctioned by the nation on which both depend— and would in any case be no more than a laudable and inadequate moratorium—then those who are incapable of sacrifice reject it.

But if war were to be the start of an era of revolt and jealousy which after an undeserved and improbable victory might turn the country, seasoned with our noble blood, into an arena of local disputes or into a stage for ambitious forays; if war were to be the hasty and disloyal consortium of cultured men whose needs were greater than their enterprise, and if it were to be the impatient and scornful authority which, for natural and in a sense noble reason, the military is in the habit of creating; if war meant that any one segment of our population would gain the upper hand, with a corresponding restlessness and decrease in power on the part of the others; and if it were not the way of adjusting in mutual respect the concerns of susceptibility and arrogance—then those who counsel and instigate such war should be accused of parricide. And in the struggle itself, which might not occur by design because of having been recommended but inevitably, honor would go only to those who had uprooted, or tried to uproot, its dreaded origins; and contempt would go to those who, either through fear or intrigue, helped prevent all the main parties to the struggle from joining forces, without unjust and unwise exclusions, in such a relationship that from the excisions the struggle would put glory beyond the danger of hallucination, and freedom out of reach of tyranny. But this journal comes to uphold the war that is eagerly desired both by the heroes of tomorrow, who fervently advocate it out of wisdom, and the heroes of yesterday, who derive their unscathed faith in its success from a lesson 10 years long—the only kind of war that the naturally free and thoughtful Cuban demands and supports. It is a war in which, according to the country's needs and desires, and with the lessons learned in previous efforts, all the factors of the imminent struggle, desirable or irremediable, are united in natural proportions. And with a grandiose and well-organized effort may it lead them to a victory that will not be discredited the next day by the endeavors of the victors, or the hopes of the discontented factions, and may there be no verbose and effeminate policies to hamper the use of national strength in the urgent labors of the task.

The sensible Cuban, who knows the reasons and excuses for mistakes, admires and loves those brave men who surrendered their guns to the sad occasion, not to the enemy, and whose spirits still shine with the unselfishness which the new heroes, in the impatience of youth, envy with filial jealousy. Through too many of the very conditions that give wars a special capability, or through the legitimate power that keeps in the heart what would be near it at the hour of death, wars breed habits of authority and companionship whose mistakes— serious at times— must not grow cold in those who can distinguish in them the essential ingredient of virtue: the son's gratitude. But the patriotic purity of the men who left their lives of luxury for the battlefield, the continuous contact between virtues and human nature occasioned by the long-drawn-out war, and the natural decency of whoever carries a sublimely tried heart in his breast, give Cuba a militia that does not, like other militias, place military glory above country. Plowing in the fields, counting in the banks, teaching in the schools, trading in the stores, working with a hero's hands in the factories, are today occupations of those who yesterday were fighting, drunk with glory, for their country's independence. And they are impatiently awaiting the generation that will emulate them.

The heart beats faster when, from the safety of foreign soil, it hails the men who, under the power of an implacable master, are silently preparing to topple him. It should be known, there where we have no desire to feed the threatening scaffold with the useless arts of conspiracy, that Cubans who seek from a foreign freedom only the methods of assuring their own, are too fond of their land to disrupt it without its consent. They would rather perish in exile than foment a war in which some Cuban, or some neutral inhabitant of Cuba, had to suffer as the conquered are suffering. The struggle undertaken to end one dissension must not give rise to another. Through the gates which we exiles may open— for being freer we are far less deserving— will come Cubans with the radical soul of the new country, Cubans who because of their prolonged enslavement will feel more intensely the need of replacing a government of prejudice and arrogance with a government through which the total energies of the country may flow freely and generously. A mere change of form would not warrant the sacrifice to which we are lending ourselves, nor would a single war be adequate to complete a revolution whose chief success resulted only in the change of location of an unjust government. One would have to defend, in the redeemed country, the popular policy in which through mutual recognition there would be a coming to terms in those segments of the population where selfishness or the technicality— the punctilio— would cause clashes. In the restless land bequeathed to us by an incapable government, new methods must build a realistic nation where emancipated lives, threatening no rights, can rejoice in the peace of all. This victorious innovation will have to be wisely and lovingly defended from those who see nothing in the revolution but the power of continuing to rule the country with the spirit they censured in their enemies. But this same excessive drift toward the past in republics has just as much right to respect and representation as has an excessive drift toward the future. And the determination to keep the country free so that a man may aspire to happiness by means of the full exercise of that freedom, will never change into a struggle of exclusion and scorn for those with whom we have wordlessly arranged a glorious and heartfelt engagement— as long as no Cubans of a stripe unknown until now are born, or as long as the idea of war is not in other hands. The war is being directed from outside of Cuba in such a way that, by the very magnitude that might alarm the easily frightened, it assures them of a peace that an incomplete war would disrupt. The war is being arranged in another country for the redemption and benefit of all Cubans. Grass grows thick in fallow fields; false ideas spread among impatient industrialists; the panic of need enters occupations devoid of intellects devoted until now mainly to the unproductive, bookshelf study of foreign civilizations, and to the discussions of rights that are almost always immoral. The revolution will mow down the grass; will reduce false industrial ideas to normal levels; will open to the mendicant intellect the genuine occupations that will assure, through man's independence, the independence of the country. Cuba is bursting with a mature glory, and it is time to strike.

The revolution will be for the benefit of all because all will have contributed to it. Due to a law which is beyond the hand of man to avoid, those who exclude themselves from the revolution, out of social objections or an arrogant sense of superiority, will be, in a way that does not clash with human rights, excluded from its honor and influence. Honor forbids a man to ask for his share in the triumph to which he refuses to contribute, and many a noble heart is perverted by a belief, in a certain sense justified, in the futility of patriotism. Patriotism should be censured when it is invoked to prevent friendship among all men of good will in the entire world, all who can see the growth of unnecessary wrongs and are honestly trying to alleviate them. Patriotism is a sacred duty when one fights to make one's country a happy place in which to live. It is painful to see a man insist upon his own rights when he refuses to fight for the rights of another. It is painful to see our cherished brothers, for the sake of defending their desire for wealth, refuse to defend the more important desire for dignity. It is painful to see men reduced, by a device exclusive to the working man, to an austerity more harmful than benign; because this isolation of the men of one occupation or a certain social circle—aside from the wise and proper agreements among persons of similar interests—encourages cliques and resistance on the part of members of other occupations and circles. Violent changes in leadership, and the continuous unrest which these shifts would bring about in the same republic, would be less beneficial to its children than a state of complete unity where, once the tools of daily work were laid aside, one man might be distinguished from another only by the warmth of his heart or the fire of his intellect.

For all Cubans, whether they come from the land of sun-burned skin or from countries where the light is gentler, the revolution in which all Cubans are involved, regardless of their color, will be equally just. If in the democratic system of equality one were to understand by "social equality" the inequality, unjust in any case, of forcing one part of the population—because it is a different color from the other—to set aside, at times harshly, in its dealings with the population of another color, the rights of friendliness and congeniality practiced by this same population among its own members—then "social equality" would be unjust for anyone who submitted to it, and wrong for those who wanted to impose it upon others. He who believes that a cultured and upright man, simply because he is black, would intrude upon the friendship of those who, because they reject social equality, would show themselves inferior to him, is grossly mistaken about the stalwart soul of the Cuban man of color. But if social equality means fair and respectful treatment without limitations of regard not justified by corresponding limitations of ability or virtue in men of any color who can, and do, honor mankind, then social equality is nothing more than recognizing the obvious impartiality of Nature.

Since it is a mark of loyalty for children to forgive the mistakes of their parents, and for friends of freedom to open their doors to all who love and respect it, the Cuban revolution will benefit not only Cubans and Puerto Ricans, but it will benefit all who esteem its purposes and abhor its blood. Having been born on Spanish soil is not what the oppressed inhabitants of the Antilles detest in the Spaniard; it is the aggressive and insolent occupation of the country where he embitters and atrophies the lives of his own children. The war is fought against the bad father, not the faithful one; against the arrogant and ungrateful sojourner, not the grateful and generous worker. The war is not fought against the Spaniard, but against the greed and incompetence of Spain. The Cuban son has received from his Spanish father the basic counsels of pride and independence; the father has removed his own military insignia so that his sons will not one day have to face him in battle; an illustrious Spaniard died on the gallows for Cuba; in wartime Spaniards have died beside Cubans. The Spaniard who detests the country of his children will be uprooted by the very war that he has made necessary. The Spaniard who loves children, and who prefers the victims of freedom to its executioners, will safely live in the republic he is helping to create. The war will not be fought for the extermination of good men, but for the necessary defeat of those who are opposed to their happiness.

The son of the Antilles, because of his obviously admirable nature, is a man whose temperate judgement equals his passion for liberty. And now that the country, as disorganized as it was 24 years ago, is abandoning a policy of useless peace that has been popular only when the country was on the brink of war and that has not taken all the available elements any further than where they were 24 years ago, the vigilant sons of Cuba are rising up to remedy the disorder with apostolic zeal and the wisdom of statesmen. And at the same time, they have been using the respite in bringing to light and eliminating the reasons for the tragic defeat. They have been uniting the emerging forces with their still useful elements so that the hand of the enemy, so skilled in persecution, will not fall upon those who, without this leavening of reality, might return to the inexperience and confusion responsible for making the robust glory of the last war result in blood and death. The fires are lighted and the word is spreading again. Weary of misery, the threat is crackling on the same timid hearth. The young go silently to worship at the heroes' graves. The bugle is sounding in the assemblies of Cubans abroad and on the island. This journal is beginning its life in the hour of danger, to watch over freedom, to be an invincible force for unity, and to prevent the enemy from again defeating us because of our disorganization.

Patria, New York, March 14, 1892

The Cuban Revolutionary Party

This article was written by Martí, but published unsigned on April 3, 1892, in Patria, *New York. The Cuban Revolutionary Party was being organized to unite all the different Cuban emigré groups in order to wage the "necessary war" that would free Cuba from the Spanish yoke.*

And the first thing to be said is that the Cuban independents, and the Puerto Ricans who love them as brothers, would abominate the word "party" if it merely meant a group or a sect or a redoubt where certain Creoles defended themselves from others. But the Cubans who have understood that in order to defeat a divided adversary the only thing needed is to unite— those Cubans use the word "party" as meaning that they are joining forces in a well-organized effort, and with a frank set of rules and a common purpose.

By "adversary" the free Cubans do not mean the Cuban who lives in agony under a regime he cannot shake, or the established foreigner who loves and desires freedom, or the timid Creole who will vindicate himself for today's laxity with tomorrow's patriotism. They mean the foreign government that stifles and corrupts the country's forces, and the colonial constitution that would prevent the peaceful practice of independence in the free fatherland. The adversary is the foreign government which, in the name of Spain, denies the rights of men to the sons of Spaniards, and stirs up hatred between fathers and sons; which impoverishes a portion of its dominions— the Antilles— to pay the debts of the entire nation, and to pay for the war that soaked with blood the country it provokes by its injustice. The adversary is the foreign government which, due to the continuous incursion of vicious and rapacious officeholders, is rotting a nation of people now forced to seek in immorality the sustenance they can no longer find in work; the government that permits in the important cities, and with the delinquent permission of Creoles eager to preserve their own security, the practice of freedoms which, in the true countryside and in the lesser cities, it punishes with the lash, stealthy exile or a dagger in the night. And the back that does not feel this—do not call it a Cuban back! No brother of the chastised can honorably sit down at the table of the castigator; should he do so, he would be dishonored! The adversary is the colonial constitution which might revive the germs of discord in independence itself, by regions and colors, for this discord is an integral part of the Republic and might perpetuate a pettifogging primacy in a country that must immediately enter into the work and balance of its true capacities. The Cuban Revolutionary Party must fight that alien government and the colonial constitution not with a the lost magic of names, but with positive and magnanimous spirit and with sure and rapid methods.

Parties usually spring up at propitious moments, sometimes from an executive board of halfhearted wills manipulated by a shrewd adventurer, sometimes from a conclave of interests more dragged along and grumbling than spontaneous and unanimous, sometimes from an ardent soul who inflames a phlegmatic mob with volatile passion, sometimes from the stubborn ambition of a man born for the flattery and complicity by which the word asserts itself. It could be merely a paper party written by faith and erased by the invisible hands of indifference. It could be the fervent and hasty work of a busybody who, in the confused ignorance of danger to his homeland, assembles some followers, their timid hearts sworn to sterile weariness. But the Cuban Revolutionary Party, born with great responsibilities at the moment of the country's decomposition, did not spring up out of a passing zeal, or from vociferous and incompetent desire, or from dreadful ambition; it was the result of the enterprise of an instructed nation proclaiming, even before the Republic and through that very Party, its redemption from the wrongs that have deformed republican life from the outset. It was born as one, from everywhere at the same time. And whoever believes that it was perishable or extinguishable, either from within or without, is mistaken. That which a group covets, dies. That which an entire people desires, endures. The Cuban Revolutionary Party is the Cuban people.

The Party's formation could not have been hastened without risking its success for lack of maturity, nor could its organization have been delayed without fatal danger to its honor at the very moment when public opinion was receptive to it and division on the island was making it necessary. It could not have been formed sooner, I say, because of lack of maturity. A watchful genius, when in accord with the people's spirit, can assemble the forces which, without vigorous impetus, might vanish in sluggish discontent or ephemeral sparks. But this same genius, who is useful and right only when he directs and accelerates the human soul, will probe in vain for the attainment of the political ideal, which must be the just composition of the true national factors, until these factors are no longer in process of adjustment. The unwary genius would harm rather than help the national effort if his attack disturbed those elements which had not yet achieved harmony. The genius of one period in history lies in attacking; the genius of another lies in waiting, which is far better.

The war in Cuba died as a result of internal and external causes. And from the beginning of the truce it was as laudable and necessary to strive for the correction of those incidental causes that tarnished and laid waste the unquenchable spirit of independence, as it was senseless to have claimed that the jealousies and suspicions that were able to do more after years of work than in a decade of glorious union, could have disappeared in a day. Neither time nor the law of man admits reduction, and a wave takes a while to wash a sluggish object from the beach. In Canadian military diversions, which after 14 years are finally making a timid attempt at a realistic policy, the Cuban heroes (together merely through expediency with those who served them as a revolutionary passport) when they met a divinely beautiful death, or wore upon their hats the black band of the matador, or celebrated the glories of the infantry in the mother country— those Cuban heroes were taking some cognizance of Cuba. In polite journeys to the midnight country, they spent all the time they could in harassing their hosts, in case the journeys were unprofitable; and years passed in demanding English laws from a policy of cant, and in pricking the punctilio of verbose professors. But during this interval which should not have been troubled, for with complete freedom its inefficiency might have been better tested, some lively elements shone both within the country and abroad—elements that should lift those amiable guests of the Plaza de Armas right out of their seats, astonished and respectful. The war left a residue of factors, to increase or decrease, that for personal rather than national reasons—and because of the discouragement of waiting for some energetic assistance from the poorly directed community abroad—surrendered the flag to the enemy. And when the enemy went out to look for it, it confessed its fear of seeing it fly atop El Morro before a year had passed.

The heroic countryside, tired of external ineptitude and upset by external intrigue, should not have been given the chance to entertain agrarian idleness in the civilian or military disputes raised by a prolonged and dispersed exercise of authority. A stationary army crumbles. The enthusiast abroad made futile sacrifices in blood and jewels to those who showed less impatience than the ones who came to them for guidance. It was a struggle between colonial hearts, introduced to liberty by surprise, and free hearts; the worm devoured the eagle. Left from the war were combatants scornful of the incompetent communities abroad; leaders out of words or with little to say until the weight of the defeat once again united them in a desire to rise out of it; and the harebrained Cubans living away from the island, suspicious among themselves and so discontented with their learned leaders, returned to the red and yellow flag much too soon, that they saw salvation only in those who wanted to go back to Cuba as riflemen. And a genuine science of government, which was not to be found, consisted in stopping the lively and virile militia from scorning those learned leaders—contemptible when they curb the spirit of the brave with their dreadful arrogance, and saintly when they rescue courage from the grave danger of offending freedom. A genuine science of government consisted in uniting, by means of a pure and continuous nobility, the Cubans abroad whom, with the abuse or obsolescence of authority or a silent desire for that science of government, the war left like malleable wax in the hand of the provocative spy, or of the renegade who would prevent the others from returning to the faith, or of the jealous man who stands in the way of whatever greatness he cannot lead, or of the ambitious one who profits from discord and isolation. A genuine science of government consisted in restoring to the Cubans living abroad their lost faith in the counsels of the mind; in protecting the heroes from their own impatience, and the homeland from the partial invasions fomented by its enemies; in preventing among the emigrants the class war which the apathetic politicians, for lack of foresight and justice, have permitted to flare up on the island; in renewing the soul of Yara[1] for the time when the disorganized land will again hold out its arms to its children; in saving the inevitable Republic from the wrongs that appeared in the first war; in uniting the suspicious militia, the Cubans abroad who must give it an opportunity, and the spirit of the country.

The strength of this labor was to be seen when the island's disorderly anguish and the emigrants' ability to organize for the island's salvation became a single effort. If when the policy of repression crumbled—like the cowardly obstacle it is—the leaking water could find no channel to carry the flow of this new power, the subtle labor would have been futile, either because of the hopeless scarcity of the work materials, or the laziness and incompetence of the workers. If when the danger appeared the emigrants had stood up to defy it, had stood up in strength and confidence, the labor would not have been futile.

And in just one day they did rise to the task, following no other voice or command but that of their unified spirit! Some today, others immediately thereafter, and then still others—all of them arguing the prime importance of enthusiasm—are proclaiming, with the fire that burns only when one is going to win, their determination to follow the personification of freedom and go to the war without hatred, thereby achieving an industrious and just Republic. In the presence of the flag that shelters within its folds the idea's master craftsman and the battle hero, these people are proclaiming their power of fusing heart and will in the determination to put into their lives all that has been vainly striving for peace, work and decency. They are not declaring war by wearing the frown of the *conquistador*, but with their arms held out to their brothers. Thus, from 12 years of silent and ceaseless effort, and purified by trials, the Cuban Revolutionary Party came into being.

---

[1] The first Cuban War of Independence began with the "Cry of Yara" on October 10, 1868, when plantation owner Carlos Manuel de Céspedes proclaimed the island's independence and freed and armed his slaves.

It is a great national effort originating spontaneously. It is, with no personal hand other than the hand that pours the molten metal into the mold, the revelation of all that is wise and generous in the Cuban soul. It is, without the impropriety of solicitude or the distribution of intrigue, the visible and moving union of all who have learned to purify their passions in a dedicated love of freedom. It is the magnificent proof that when the country that perishes in useless sacrifice is impelled to useful sacrifice, the farseeing Cuban neither permits nor disregards those dangers in which a passion for names or persons disturbs or bleeds the emerging republics. It is the gentle impetus of heroic love where inspired hearts, under the guidance of a strong and just mind, return to the days of the dawn of our redemption, the lessons learned. It is the visible result of the wisdom and justice of 12 laborious years. And if its methods conform to its origins and purposes, and if it applies itself wholeheartedly and to the full extent of its power, it will bring salvation. It will fail to bring salvation and perish only if it distorts and diminishes its sublime spirit.

My Race

This article published on April 16, 1893, in Patria, *New York, is one of several Martí wrote explaining the concept of racial equality as the basis of Latin American continental unity and, particularly, the unity of Cubans in their struggle for independence.*

"Racist" is a confusing word, and it should be clarified. Men have no special rights simply because they belong to one race or another. When you say "men," you have already imbued them with all their rights. Negroes, because they are black, are not inferior or superior to any other men. Whites who say "my race" commit the sin of redundancy; so do Negroes who say the same. Everything that divides men, everything that specifies, separates or pens them, is a sin against humanity. To what sensible white person would it occur to be vain about being white, and what do Negroes think about whites who are vain about being white and think they have special rights as a result? What must whites think about Negroes who are vain about their color? To insist on racial divisions, on racial differences, in an already divided people, is to place obstacles in the way of public and individual happiness, which can only be obtained by bringing people together as a nation. Nothing inherent in Negroes prevents them from developing their souls as men, and nothing that happens to them can limit their innate ability. This fact should be stated and demonstrated, for there is much injustice in this world and ignorant prejudice which passes for wisdom: there are still those who, in good faith, believe that Negroes are not capable of the same intelligence and courage as whites. It does not matter if you call this defense of Nature racism, because it is no more than natural honesty and a heartfelt cry for peace and the country's well-being. It is alleged that slavery does not imply inferiority in the enslaved race, since Gauls with blue eyes and blond hair were sold as serfs with shackles around their necks in the markets of Rome. This example helps make ignorant whites less prejudiced. Negroes have the right to maintain and prove that their color does not deny them any of the skills and rights of the rest of the human species.

What right do white racists, who believe their race is superior, have for complaining about black racists, who see something special in their own race? What right do black racists, who see a special character in their race, have for complaining about white racists? White men who think their race makes them superior to black men admit the idea of racial difference and authorize and incite black racists. Black men who proclaim their race—when what they are really proclaiming is the spiritual identity that distinguishes one ethnic group from another—authorize and incite white racists. Peace demands of Nature the recognition of human rights; discrimination is contrary to Nature and the enemy of peace. Whites who isolate themselves also isolate Negroes. Negroes who isolate themselves incite and isolate whites.

In Cuba, there is no fear of a racial war. Men are more than whites, mulattos or Negroes. Cubans are more than whites, mulattos or Negroes. On the field of battle, dying for Cuba, the souls of whites and Negroes have risen together into the air. In the daily life of defense, loyalty, brotherhood and shrewdness, Negroes have always been there, alongside whites. Negroes, like whites, are divided by their character—timid or brave, self-sacrificing or selfish—into the diverse parties in which men group themselves. Political parties form around common concerns, aspirations, interests and characters. Essential similarities are sought and found beneath superficial differences; the common purpose is the fusion of that which is basic in the analogous characters, even though they may differ in incidentals. In sum, the similarity of characters, which is a superior uniting factor, outweighs the inner frictions between men of varying color and the difficulties that, at times, result. Affinity of character is more powerful than the affinity of color. Negroes, consigned to the unequal or hostile pursuits of the human spirit, will never be able to join, nor will they want to join, against whites in like position. Negroes are too weary of slavery to enter voluntarily into the slavery of color. Ostentatious men who are governed by self-interest will combine, whether white or black, and the generous and selfless will similarly unite. True men, black and white, will treat one another with loyalty and tenderness, out of a sense of merit and the pride of everyone who honors the land in which we were born, black and white alike. Negroes, who now use the word "racist" in good faith, will stop using it when they realize it is the only apparently valid argument that weak men, who honestly believe that Negroes are inferior, use to deny them the full exercise of their rights as men. White and black racists would be equally guilty of racism. Many whites have already forgotten their color, as have many Negroes. Whites and Negroes are working together to develop men's minds, to spread virtue and to promote the triumph of creative work and sublime charity.

In Cuba, there will never be a racial war. The Republic cannot go backwards. Ever since the day of redemption for Negroes in Cuba, ever since the declaration of independence in Guáimaro on April 10, there has been no talk of whites or Negroes in the Republic. The civil rights, granted by the Spanish Government for political expediency, were already practiced prior to Cuba's independence and cannot now be denied— either by the Spaniards who, as long as they breathe in Cuba, will continue dividing black from white Cubans, or by those fighting for independence, who could never deny in freedom the rights which the Spaniards recognized in servitude.

As for the rest, everyone will be free in the sanctity of his home. Merit, the manifest and continuous evidence of culture, and inexorable trade will eventually unite all men. In Cuba, there is much greatness, in both Negroes and whites.

Simón Bolívar

This speech was delivered on October 28, 1893, to the Latin American Literary Society of New York, at a gathering held as a tribute to that outstanding Latin American hero. It was published on November 4, 1893, in Patria, *New York.*

Ladies and gentlemen:

With the contrite brow of the Americans who have yet to enter America, serenely aware of the true place and worth of the great son of Caracas in the spontaneous and manifold work of American freedom; with the reverence and awe of one who still sees before him, demanding his due share, that man whose majesty and magnanimity were like the raintree of the savannahs, like the rivers plunging in turmoil from the mountaintops, and like the large burning rocks that come thundering from the bowels of the earth, I bring the meager homage of my words, less profound and eloquent than my silence, to him who tore Pizarro's flag from the skies of Cuzco. Above the carping criticism, above the outbursts of praise and abuse, above even the shortcomings of that prince of freedom—black flecks on the condor's breast—the real man emerges radiant. He sears and enthralls. To think about him, peer into his life, read one of his speeches, catch a glimpse of one of his ardent and breathless love letters, is like feeling one's thoughts turn to gold. He burned with our own desire for freedom, he spoke with the voice of our own natures, his zenith was our continent's finest hour, his fall strikes at the heart. Pronounce the name of Bolívar and one sees in the mind's eye the mountain crowned less by snow than by the caped horseman, or the flooded Apure valley through which the liberators swirl forward, three republics in their knapsacks, to complete the redemption of a continent. Oh no! that man who never lived in repose cannot be discussed in calm. One must speak of Bolívar from the tribune of a mountain, or in thunder and lightning, or with a fistful of free nations in one's grasp, and tyranny beheaded at one's feet! No one need shrink from just admiration because it is perennially fashionable among certain kinds of persons to belittle the extraordinary; nor should a low desire for applause ever allow the bombastic phrase to silence the voice of sober judgement. Words can never express the mystery and brilliance of that mind at the disaster of Casacoima when, wracked with fever and deserted by his scattered army, he clearly saw the roads across the Andes over which he would carry freedom into the valleys of Peru and Bolivia. But whatever we say tonight, even if exaggerated, will enhance the occasion, for all of us gathered here are children of his sword.

Nor need the fear of offending the ladies keep us from voicing tribute, for one can speak freely of freedom in the presence of American women. The courageous daughter of the Paraguayan Juan de Mena who, when she learned that her fellow countryman Antequera was being hanged for a patriot, took off her widow's weeds and put on her festive clothes because "the day a just man dies gloriously for his country is a day of celebration"; the Colombian girl in her calico and homespun, who anticipated the patriots when she tore down the insolent edict on taxation in El Socorro, and set 20,000 men fighting; the wife of Arismendi, pure as the finest pearl of La Margarita, who, when led out on the battlements in full view of her husband shelling the fort, told her captors: "You will never force a word past my lips to make him shirk his duty"; the noble Pola, who sent her sweetheart into battle and died beside him on the gallows; or Mercedes Abrego of the handsome braids, who was decapitated for embroidering the Liberator's uniform with her finest golden thread; and those loyal companions of Bolívar's soldiers, who rode with their men as they breasted the raging streams that plunge from the Andean peaks, milestones of Nature, on freedom's march to Boyacá[1]— all these were women.

That man was truly extraordinary. He lived as if among flames, and he was a flame. He loved, and spoke flowers of fire. He revered

---

[1] Bolívar won a decisive victory at the Battle of Boyacá on August 7, 1819.

friendship, and the death of a loyal companion silenced all activity around him. He was sickly, yet with the speed of the fastest post his untried army swept everything before it from Tenerife to Cúcuta. He was a fighter, and at the height of the struggle, with all eyes turned to him in supplication, he ordered his horse unsaddled. He wrote, and it was the brewing of a mountain storm that bursts suddenly over the mist-filled valley, and then the sun breaks through and clouds drift around the peaks, while the valley below sparkles with fresh colors. Like the mountains, he was broad at the base, his roots deep in the ground, yet rising to a lofty crest, as if to better pierce a stubborn sky. One can see him knocking on the gates of glory with the golden hilt of his saber. He believed in heaven, in the gods, in the immortals, in the god of Colombia, in the genius of America, in his destiny. He was surrounded by a glory that inflamed him and stirred him to action. Is it not a sign of divinity to have conquered? He conquered men, swollen rivers, volcanoes, centuries, Nature! Would he have undone the work of centuries if he had not been able to build anew? Did he not unshackle races, disenthrall a continent, bring nations into being? Has he not covered more peoples with the banners of freedom than has any other conqueror with the banners of tyranny? Did he not address eternity from Mount Chimborazo, with Potosí,[2] one of history's most barbarous and tenacious creations, at his feet beneath the condor-studded flag of Colombia? Did not cities open their gates to him, and the powers of this life pay him homage? Did not his rivals, and all the gifted sons and beauties of the New World, bow to him in fear or adoration? He was as the thawing and life-giving sun, burning and shedding light. If there is a senate in heaven, he is surely there. He saw that world, golden with sunlight, and the seat of the rock of creation, the floor of clouds, and the roof of stars reminded him, in their sparkling movements across the sky, of his lances at Apure as they reflected the noonday sun; from those heights happiness and order descend upon men as if by paternal dispensation. But such is not the case in this world where the sum of divinity rises from the bloody and painful sacrifice and ideal of all mankind! He died in Santa Marta from the horror and frustration of seeing that star of his, which he

---

[2] Bolívar captured the silver-rich region of Bolivia, Potosí, from the Spanish on April 4, 1825, which signaled the end of Spain's colonial rule in South America.

considered immortal, dashed to pieces. He made the mistake of confusing the glory of having served, which grows and is a crown that no hands can take from his brow, with the mere accident of power that was his to wield. For human power—which is nearly always the corrupt employment and pursuit of those who seek it for themselves, although they do not deserve it and are lacking in courage, or the sterile triumph of one faction over another, or the pawn of interests and passions—only falls to virtue or genius in moments of crisis or transient righteousness when nations, moved by danger, acclaim the idea or unselfish motive in which they seek their redemption. But there sits Bolívar on the rock of creation in the American heaven, stern and vigilant, with the Inca beside him and flags clustered at his feet. There his is, still wearing his campaign boots, for what he failed to achieve has not been achieved to this day. Bolívar still has work to do in America!

At the turn of the century America was seething, and he was its crucible. The America of those days still stirs and rears its head, a huge larval creature like worms under the bark of old roots. From France and North America, under priests' cassocks and in the minds of worthy travelers, the revolutionary message has been coming to revive the discontent of the educated and well-bred Creole, governed from across the seas by the law of tribute and the gallows. In the measure that the rebellion grew in high places, leavened by the rebellious, and in a certain sense democratic, unrest of the second-born disinherited Spaniard, the Argentine *gaucho*, the Chilean *roto*, the Peruvian *cholo*, and the Venezuelan *llanero*—all were touched where their common affections lay. In the muffled upheaval, their defenseless faces furrowed by tears, bands of Indians wandered through the forests, taking comfort in pillage, like tongues of flames licking at some colossal funeral pyre. American independence came bleeding from the past century; Our America springs neither from Rousseau nor Washington, but from itself! Thus, in the sultry and fragrant nights of his manorial garden at San Jacinto, or along the banks of the mirrored waters of the Arauco where he may have guided the tiny feet of his wife who died in her prime, Bolívar would see, with fist clenched against his bosom, the specters come and go through the air, and they can find no rest until their task is finished!

In the dusk at Mount Avila, he surely must have seen the bloody retinue.

The Paraguayan Antequera passes by, the first of many, raising his severed head; there goes the entire family of a poor Inca, quartered before the eyes of their shackled father, gathering up their sundered limbs. Tupac Amaru[3] crosses his vision; then comes the king of the Venezuelan half-breeds, vanishing in the air like a ghost; then Salinas asleep in his blood, Quiroga[4] dead over his dish of food, and Morales[5] like a living carnage, because in Quito's prison the love of country never faltered. León, having no house to call his own because his lands were sown with salt, lay dying in his cave. There on hooks go the limbs of José España, who died smiling on the gallows, and there the still smoking torso of Galán, burned at the stake. Berbeo passes, more dead than anyone, although the hangman spared his life for fear of the patriots, because for one who has known the joy of fighting for the honor of his country, there is no greater death than to be alive while the shame of one's native land endures. The hero wrapped himself in this Indian, half-breed and white soul merged into a single flame, and found it constant and inextinguishable. In the brotherhood of a common cause he fused the disparate components in the flame of glory; he removed or curbed his rivals; he crossed the desert and challenged mountains; he sowed the Andean watershed with republics. And when he halted the march of his armies, because the Argentine revolution opposed its collective and democratic endeavor to his thrust, 14 Spanish generals, huddled on the slopes of Ayacucho,[6] laid down their Spanish swords!

From the coastal palms, put there as if to intone a perennial song of praise to the hero, the land climbs in terraces of silver and gold to the fertile plains that this American revolution slashed until the blood ran. Heaven has seldom seen more beautiful scenes, for the determination to be free never before stirred so many hearts, heroism never knew a setting of such natural grandeur, and the soul of an continent never entered so fully into that of one man. Heaven

---

[3] Tupac Amaru led an unsuccessful Indian uprising in Peru in 1781.

[4] Juan Facundo Quiroga was a dictator of Argentina.

[5] Augustín Morales was assassinated while President of Bolivia.

[6] Venezuelan, Chilean, Colombian and Argentine revolutionary forces united against Spain to win the battle of Ayacucho (December 9, 1824).

itself seems to have played a role, for those were battles worthy of it. It was as if all the heroes of freedom, and all the martyrs on earth, gathered in that beautiful firmament and hovered like a giant shield over the straits in which our souls were struggling, or fled in terror through the unjust heavens when the battle went against us! Heaven must have paused, in fact, to have seen such beauty—breathtaking waterfalls break loose from the eternal snows like runaway horses; age-old trees cling to the dark ravines like down or curly fleece; the ruins of Indian temples keep watch over the wilderness of lakes; the rugged towers of Spanish cathedrals pierce the valley mists; the craters smoke, and erupting volcanoes reveal the bowels of the earth. All the while, in every corner of the land, Americans are fighting for their freedom! Some of them gallop over the plains and are snuffed out in the clash with the enemy like candles in a gust of wind; others, the reins held between their teeth, swim the swollen rivers trailing their army pennants on the water; others, like a forest on the march, come in close order, their lances above their heads; others scale a volcano, and plant the flag of freedom on the rim of its fiery crater. But none so handsome as that man of lofty forehead above eyes that have devoured the face, whose cape billows behind him on his flying horse, whose breast is impervious to storm or rain of fire, whose sword sheds the light of freedom upon five nations! He reins in his black stallion, hair limp from the storm of victory, and reviews the ranks of those who helped him crush oppression: the Phrygian cap of Ribas,[7] the gentle horse of Sucre,[8] Piar's[9] curly head, Páez's[10] red cloak, Córdoba's[11] slashing whip, and the flag-wrapped body of the colonel carried by his soldiers. He stands breathless in the stirrups as Nature watches Páez and his handful of lancers charge and scatter the enemy anthill in the dust and shadows of Las Queseras. Eyes wet with tears, he watches as his army in gala attire

---

[7] José Félix Ribas was Bolívar's uncle who fought in the liberation movement.

[8] José Antonio de Sucre was Bolívar's lieutenant who commanded the revolutionary troops at Ayacucho.

[9] Manuel Carlos Piar, a mulatto from Curaçao, fought with Bolívar but was later executed as a deserter.

[10] José Antonio Páez (1790–1873): Venezuelan leader, who was made General-in-Chief by Bolívar after the victory at Carabobo.

[11] José Córdoba was one of the commanders at the battle of Ayacucho (1824).

makes merry on the eve of the battle of Carabobo,[12] pennants and ensigns flying, masses of men a living wall around the tattered battle flags, martial music playing everywhere, the play of sun on steel, and all through the camp the mysterious joy of a house in which a child is to be born! But he was handsomer than ever at Junín,[13] developed in the darkest night, while the last of the Spanish lances splintered in pale silence against the triumphant might of America.

And then a little later, his thoughts disconnected, his hair clinging to his sunken temples, his withered hand gesturing as if rejecting a world, the hero said on his death bed: "José, José! Let us go, for we are not wanted here. Where shall we go?" Only his government had fallen, but he may have thought that the Republic was collapsing; local jealousies and fears had been largely overcome in the enthusiasm of independence, and he may have discounted those forces for reality that reappeared after the triumph. He may have been fearful that rival ambitions would wreck the newly formed nations, and by hateful subjection he sought that political balance which is stable only when based on freedom, and infallible in a regime of justice, with the fewer restraints the better. Perhaps, in his dream of glory for America and for himself, he failed to realize that the unity of spirit, indispensable to the salvation and happiness of our American nations, suffered rather than benefited from his union based on theoretical and artificial forms that had no roots in reality. Perhaps the prophetic genius who proclaimed that the salvation of Our America lies in the unified action of our republics with respect to the rest of the world and the course of our own future, was unaware, because it was foreign to his temperament, class and education, of the moderating force of the popular will, of the open struggle between people of varying shades of opinion requiring nothing but the law of true freedom to be the safeguard of republics. The anxious father may have erred at the crucial moment for all political architects, when the voice of prudence counseled him to yield the command to new leaders, so that the title of usurper would not discredit or endanger his creation; while another voice, perhaps from the mystery of the greater creative idea, urged him to endure for its sake even the dishonor of being considered a usurper.

---

[12] Bolívar's forces, under Páez, defeated the Spanish at Carabobo, June 24, 1821.

[13] Site of a battle between Bolívar and Spanish troops.

And they were his heart's desire, those whose blood was spilled without him in the long and bitter conflict; those who found their own lives in his magnanimity and perseverance, and who took from him, because he determined their struggles and their future, the power to govern themselves according to the needs of their peoples! And the union of Bolívar and America in order to achieve independence— firmer than the attraction among the stars— disappeared, and one could see the disagreement between Bolívar— resolved to unite the countries of the revolution under a distant, central government— and the multi-headed American revolution born of the desire for local self-government. "José, José! Let us go, for we are not wanted here. Where shall we go?"

Where will Bolívar go? To the respect of the world and the affection of America! To this loving home where every man is indebted to him for that ardent satisfaction of feeling himself embraced by his own people whenever he is among Americans, and where every woman adoringly remembers that man who always dismounted from his horse of glory to give thanks for a wreath of a flower offered him by the hands of beauty! To the justice of nations able to see, beyond the possible error of rash or personal measures, the impetus Bolívar gave, through these very measures, to the basic ideas of America, like a powerful hand shaping molten lava. Where will Bolívar go? Arm in arm with men to defend from new greed and old prejudices the land where human existence will be happier and more beautiful! To peaceful nations like a father's kiss! To men of narrow viewpoints and fleeting opinions, to well-fed burghers and prosperous Harpagons, so that by the light of the blaze that was his existence they may see the brotherhood so essential to the continent, and the greatness and dangers in America's future! Where will Bolívar go? The last of the Spanish viceroys lay bedridden with his five wounds, three centuries were dragging from the tail of the plainsman's horse, and the Liberator, wearing his finest clothes under the cassock of victory, rode with his army as if bound for a ball. Crowds looked down from the hills, and standing out along the ridges were clusters of flags like flowers in a vase. Finally Potosí appears, scarred and bloody. The five flags of the new nations blaze with real flames atop a resurrected America. Cannons announce the hero's approach, and above heads bared out of respect and awe the crackle of gunfire echoes from peak to peak as each mountain repeats the salute. And so, as long as America lives, the echo of his name will pass from father to son in all that is best and manliest in our natures!

The Truth about the United States

Published on March 23, 1894, in Patria, *New York, this article reflects Martí's views about the virtues and vices of the Latin and Saxon peoples of the Americas.*

In Our America it is vital to know the truth about the United States. We should not exaggerate its faults purposely, out of a desire to deny it all virtue, nor should these faults be concealed or proclaimed as virtues. There are no races; there are only the various modifications of man in details of form and habits, according to the conditions of climate and history in which he lives, which do not alter the identical and the essential. Superficial men— who have not explored human problems very thoroughly, or who cannot see from the heights of impartiality how all nations are boiling in the same stew pot, and how one finds in the structure and fabric of them all the same permanent duel between constructive unselfishness and iniquitous hate— are prone to amuse themselves by finding substantial variety between the egotistical Saxon and the egotistical Latin, the generous Saxon and the generous Latin, the Saxon bureaucrat and the Latin bureaucrat. Both Latins and Saxons are equally capable of having virtues and defects; what does vary is the peculiar outcome of the different historical groups. In a nation of English, Dutch and Germans of similar background, no matter what their disagreements, perhaps fatal, brought upon them by the original separations between nobility and the common man who founded that nation together, and by the inevitable— and in the human species innate— hostility of greed and vanity brought about by aristocracies confronted with the law and self-denial revealed to them, one cannot explain the confusion of political customs and the melting pot of nations in which the *conquistador's* needs permitted the native population to live. With parricidal blindness the privileged class spawned by the Europeans is still barring the way to those frightened and diverse peoples.

A nation of strapping young men from the North, bred over the centuries to the sea and the snow and the virility aided by the perpetual defense of local freedom, cannot be like a tropical isle, docile and smiling, where the famished outgrowth of a backward and war-minded European people, descendants of a coarse and uncultured tribe, divided by hatred for an accommodating submission to rebellious virtue, work under contract for a government that practices political piracy. And also working under contract are those simple but vigorous Africans, whether vilified or rancorous, who from a frightful slavery and a sublime war have entered into citizenship with those who bought and sold them, and who, thanks to the dead of that sublime war, today greet as equals the ones who used to make them dance to the lash. Concerning the differences between Latins and Saxons, and the only way that comparisons can be drawn, one must study the conditions they may have shared. It is a fact that in those Southern states of the American Union where there were Negro slaves, those Negroes were predominantly as arrogant, shiftless, helpless and merciless as the sons of Cuba would be under conditions of slavery. It is supinely ignorant and slightly infantile and blameworthy to refer to the United States and to the real or apparent conquests of one or more of its territories as one total nation, equally free and definitely conquered. Such a United States is a fraud and a delusion. Between the shanties of Dakota and the virile and barbaric nation in process of growth there, and the cities of the East—sprawling, privileged, well-bred, sensual and unjust—lies an entire world. From the stone houses and the majestic freedom north of Schenectady, to the dismal resort of stilts south of St. Petersburg, lies another entire world. The clean and concerned people of the North are worlds apart from the choleric, poverty-stricken, broken, bitter, lackluster, loafing Southern shopkeepers sitting on their cracker barrels. What the honest man should observe is precisely that it was not only impossible to fuse the elements of diverse tendency and origin out of which the United States was created, within a period of three centuries of life in common or of one century of political awareness, but that compulsory social intercourse exacerbates and accentuates their principal differences and turns the unnatural federation into a harsh state of violent conquest. It is a quality of lesser people and of incompetent and gnawing envy, this pricking holes in manifest greatness and plainly denying it for some defect or other, or this going to great lengths of prediction, like someone brushing a speck of dust off the sun. But it is a matter of certification rather than of prophecy for anyone who observes how, in the United States, the reasons for unity are weakening, not solidifying; how the various localities are dividing and irritating national politics, not uniting with it; how democracy is being corrupted and diminished, not strengthened and saved from the hatred and wretchedness of monarchies. Hatred and misery are posing a threat and being reborn, and the man who keeps this to himself instead of speaking out is not complying with his duty. He is not complying with his duty as a man, the obligation of knowing the truth and spreading it; nor with his duty as a good American who sees the continent's peace and glory secure only in the frank and free development of its various native entities. As a son of Our America he is not fulfilling his obligations to prevent the peoples of Spanish blood from falling under the counsel of the smirking toga and the skittish interest, whether through ignorance or disillusionment or impatience, in the immoral and enervating servitude of a damaged and alien civilization. In Our America it is imperative to know the truth about the United States.

Wrongs must be abhorred, whether or not they are ours. The good must not be hated merely because it is not ours. But it is worthless and irrational and cowardly for inefficient or inferior people to aspire to reach the stability of a foreign nation by roads other than those which brought security and order to the envied nation, through individual effort and the adaptation of human freedom to the forms required by the particular constitution of that nation. With some people, an excessive love for the North is the unwise, but easily explained, expression of such a lively and vehement desire for progress that they are blind to the fact that ideas, like trees, must come from deep roots and compatible soil in order to develop a firm footing and prosper, and that a newborn baby is not given the wisdom and maturity of age merely because one glues on its smooth face a mustache and a pair of sideburns. Monsters are created that way, not Nations. They have to live of themselves, and sweat through the heat. With other people, their Yankee mania is the innocent result of an occasional little leap of pleasure, much as a man judges the inner spirit of a home, and the souls who pray or die therein, by the smiles and luxury in the front parlor, or by the champagne and carnations on the banquet table. One must suffer, starve, work, love and study, even in vain, but with one's own individual courage and freedom. One must keep watch with the poor, weep with the destitute, abhor the brutality of wealth, live in both mansion and tenement, in the school's reception hall and in its vestibule, in the gilt and jasper theater box and in the cold, bare wings. In this way a man can form opinions, with glimmers of reason, about the authoritarian and envious Republic and the growing materialism of the United States. With other posthumous weaklings of Second Empire literary dandyism, or the false skeptics under whose mask of indifference there generally beats a heart of gold, the fashion is to scorn the indigenous, and more so. They cannot imagine greater elegance than to drink to the foreigner's breeches and ideas, and to strut over the globe, proud as the pompom tail of the fondled lap dog. With still others it is like a subtle aristocracy which, publicly showing a preference for the fair-skinned as a natural and proper thing to do, tries to conceal its own humble half-breed origins, unaware that when one man brands another as a bastard, it is always a sign of his own illegitimacy. There is no more certain announcement of a woman's sins that when she shows contempt for sinners. It matters not whether the reason is impatience for freedom or the fear of it, moral sloth or a laughable aristocracy, political idealism or a recently acquired ingenuity—it is surely appropriate, and even urgent, to put before Our America the entire American truth, about the Saxon as well as the Latin, so that too much faith in foreign virtue will not weaken us in our formative years with an unmotivated and baneful distrust of what is ours. In a single war, the War of Secession, more concerned with whether the North or the South would predominate in the Republic than with abolishing slavery, the United States lost more men per capita than were lost in the same amount of time by all the Spanish republics of America put together, and its sons had been living under republicanism for three centuries in a country whose elements were less hostile than in any other.

More men were lost in the United States Civil War than in Mexico to victorious Chile in the naturally slow process of putting upon the surface of the New World, with nothing but the enterprise of popular instinct and the rhetorical apostolate of a glorious minority, the remote peoples of widespread nuclei and contrary races, where the rule of Spain had left all the rage and hypocrisy of theocracy, and all the indolence and suspicions of a prolonged servitude. From the standpoint of justice and a legitimate social science it should be recognized that, in relation to the ready compliance of the one and the obstacles of the other, the North American character has gone downhill since the winning of independence, and is today less human and virile; whereas the Spanish-American character today is in all ways superior, in spite of its confusion and fatigue, to what it was when it began to emerge from the disorganized mass of grasping clergy, unskilled ideologists and ignorant or savage Indians. And to aid in the understanding of political reality in America, and to accompany or correct with the calm force of fact, the ill-advised praise (pernicious when carried to extremes) of the North American character and political life, *Patria* is inaugurating, with today's issue, a permanent section devoted to "Notes on the United States." In it, we will print articles faithfully translated from the country's earliest newspapers, without editorial comment or changes. We will print no accounts of events revealing the crimes or accidental faults, possible in all nations, where none but the wretched spirit finds sustenance and contentment, but rather those structural qualities which, for their constancy and authority, demonstrate two useful truths to Our America: the crude, uneven and decadent character of the United States, and the continuous existence there of all the violence, discord, immorality and disorder blamed upon the peoples of Spanish America.

Manifesto of Montecristi: The Cuban Revolutionary Party

This document, published on March 25, 1895, under the title "The Cuban Revolutionary Party in Cuba," was written and signed by José Martí and Máximo Gómez in Montecristi, Santo Domingo. It expresses the essential ideas of the revolutionary movement and the policies of the war for independence that had begun in Cuba on February 24, 1895. Some days later, Martí and General Antonio Maceo would land in Cuba to join the revolutionary troops.

The revolution for independence, begun at Yara after glorious and bloody preparations, has led Cuba into another period of war, by virtue of the command and agreements of the [Cuban] Revolutionary Party abroad and on the island, and of the exemplary brotherhood in the Party of all the elements dedicated to the country's emancipation and security, for the good of America and the world. The elected representatives of the revolution, which is today confirmed, recognize and respect their duty to repeat to the country its precise objectives, without usurping the declarations and tone characteristic of the dignity of the established Republic alone. The revolution must not cause unjustified bloodshed in Cuba, nor lack a just hope of triumph, for it is born of justice and is alien to vengeance; its objectives compose the unquenchable war which today carries to its struggles, in a wise and stirring democracy, all the elements of Cuban society. Thus it will arrive at its logical victory.

The war is not— in the considered opinion of the men who are still representing it today, and of the general and responsible revolution that elected them— the insane victory of one Cuban party over another; it is not even the humbling of one mistaken group of Cubans. On the contrary, it is the solemn demonstration of the will of a country too sorely tried in a former war to plunge lightly into a conflict terminable only by victory or the grave. The war must not be undertaken without reasons sufficiently profound to overcome human cowardice in all its various disguises, and without a determination so respectable, for being signed by death, that it must impose silence upon those less venturesome Cubans who do not feel possessed of equal faith in the abilities of their country, or of the courage to free it from slavery.

The war is not a capricious attempt at an independence more fearful than useful, which would only have a right to delay or condemn those who might demonstrate the virtue and purpose of leading it to another safer and more viable one, and which a nation unable to support it must truly desire. It must be the disciplined product of the resolve of men of integrity who, in the serenity of experience, have once again determined to face the dangers they know. It must be the product of a sincere brotherhood of Cubans of the most diverse origins, convinced that it is in the conquest of freedom rather than in abject despair that they are acquiring the virtues necessary to the maintenance of that war.

The war is not directed against the Spaniard, for he, in the security of his children and out of respect for the country they will acquire, will himself be able to enjoy, respected and even loved, the freedom that will crush only those who improvidently leave the path. Nor will the war be born of disorder, alien to the tried and tested moderation of the Cuban spirit. And it will not be born of oppression. Those who promoted it, and can still make their voices heard, declare in its name and before the country their freedom from all hatred, their brotherly indulgence toward timid or mistaken Cubans, their radical respect for man's integrity in combat and his energy in supporting the Republic. They declare their certainty that the war can be organized in such a way that it contains the redemption inspiring it, the relationship in which one nation must live with others, and the reality of which it is made. The instigators are determined to respect the neutral and honest Spaniard, and see that he is respected, both during the war and after it is over, as well as to be merciful toward repentance, and inflexible only toward vice, crime and inhumanity. In the resumption of Cuba's war, the revolution sees no reason for merriment that might impede an impulsive heroism; it does see the responsibilities that should concern the builders of nations.

Let Cuba enter the war with the full assurance, unacceptable only to sedentary and halfhearted Cubans, of its sons' ability to obtain victory through the energy of the thoughtful and magnanimous revolution. Let it trust the Cubans' capacity—cultivated in the first 10 years of sublime fusion, and in modern practices of government and work—to save the country as a whole from the inconveniences and ordeals so necessary at the beginning of the century, when there was no communication or preparation, in the feudal or theoretical Republics of Spanish America. It would be culpable ignorance or perfidy to disregard the often glorious, and now generally accepted, causes of American disturbances resulting from the error of adjusting to foreign patterns of uncertain doctrine, or mere relation to their place of origin, the ingenuous reality of countries that know nothing about freedoms except the eagerness that secured them and the sovereignty gained by fighting for them. The concentration in the capitals of a merely literary culture; the Republics' erroneous attachment to the feudal customs of the colony; the creation of rival leaders resulting from distrustful and imperfect communication among the separated regions; the rudimentary state of the sole industry, be it agriculture or cattle raising; and the abandonment of and disdain for the prolific native race in disputes of belief or locality which these causes of the upheavals in American nations pursue—these factors are by no means the problems of Cuban society. Cuba is returning to the war with a democratic and cultured people, jealously aware of their own rights and the rights of others; aware of a much higher culture in its lowliest elements than in the plainsmen of Indian masses with whom, at the call of the foremost heroes of liberty, America's silent colonies changed from cattle ranches into nations. And at the crossroads of the world some brilliant sons—magnates or servants—are coming to Cuba from creative and sustaining work in the more capable nations of the world to enlist in the war, and they are bringing their own efforts on behalf of the country's misery and persecution. These are men who, from the first age of adjustment (now overcome), among the heterogeneous components of the Cuban Nation, went out to prepare, or on the island itself continued to prepare, with their own perfectionism, the nationality to which they are today contributing with the stability of their industrious persons and the security of their republican education. The patriotism of its fighters; the culture and generosity of its craftsmen; the realistic and modern employment of a vast number of its intelligentsia and resources; the peculiar conservatism of the peasant mellowed by war and exile; the intimate daily intercourse among the various sections of the country, and their rapid and inevitable unification; the mutual admiration of common virtues among Cubans who have progressed from the differences of slavery to the brotherhood of sacrifice; and the growing benevolence and aptitude of the freed slave— greater than those rare examples of his ill-will or straying from the path— all these factors assure Cuba, and without unfounded hopes, of a future in which the stable conditions and immediate work of a productive people in a just Republic will overcome the dissociation and partiality arising out of the indolence or arrogance sometimes brought about by war. There are other likely causes for this ignorance or arrogance, namely the offensive animosity of a minority of landowners deprived of their rights; the blameworthy haste with which a still invisible minority of discontented freedmen might, with regrettable violation of human nature and free will, aspire to a social respect that must surely come to them from a proved equality in talents and virtues alone; and the sudden dispossession, largely among learned city dwellers, of the luxury and relative abundance now coming to them from the colony's convenient and immoral taxes, and from the occupations that will have to disappear with freedom. A free people with work available to all, enclaved at the approaches to the wealthy industrial world, will replace advantageously and without hindrance, after a war inspired by the purest self-sacrifice and maintained consistent with it, the abashed nation where well-being is attained only in exchange for overt or tacit collusion with the oppression of the indigent foreigners who bleed and corrupt it. There is no distrust of Cuba, or of its ability to obtain and govern its independence, by those who, in the heroism of death and of the quiet building of the country, can see the gifts of harmony and good judgement shine continuously, in the great and the small. Only those who stand outside the true soul of their country, and judge it according to the arrogant concept of their own selves, with no more power of rebellion and creation than that which timidly appears in the servitude of their colonial tasks, can disregard these gifts.

Today cowardice might have to make use of another fear, on the pretext of prudence: an unreasoning fear of the Negro race, never justified in Cuba. The revolution, with its abundance of martyrs and of generous and obedient fighters, indignantly contradicts—as the long testing period of the communities abroad and the truce on the island is contradicting—the charge that the Negro race is a threat, a charge wickedly made by the beneficiaries of the Spanish regime in order to stir up fear of the revolution. In Cuba there are now Cubans of both colors who have put out of their minds forever, with the emancipatory war and the work in which together they are becoming proficient, the hatred with which slavery was able to divide them. Bitterness and a changed state of social relations, resulting from the sudden transformation of the foreigner into a "native," are less important than the Cuban white man's sincere esteem for the kindred spirit, the laborious culture, the free man's fervor and the amiable character of his Negro compatriot. And if the Negro race were to produce some filthy demagogues or avid souls, whose own impatience were to stir up that of their color, or in whom compassion for their own people might lead to injustice toward others—then with its gratitude and practical wisdom, its love of country, its conviction that it is necessary to deprive of authority the still prevailing opinion that the race is incapable of these qualities, and with the possession of all that is real in human rights, and with the enjoyment of and strong respect for all that is just and generous in the Cuban white man, the Negro race itself would eradicate the Negro danger single-handedly, with no help from the white man needed. The Cuban Negro's integrity and intelligence have been patently proved. This the revolution knows and proclaims, and so do the Cubans living abroad. The Cuban Negro has no schools of anger there, just as in the war there was not a single case of undue pride or insubordination. The Republic against which the Negro has never rebelled rests safely upon his shoulders. Only those who hate the Negro can see any hate in him, and only those who trafficked in similar unjust fear in order to control, with an undesirable authority, the hands that might rise to the task of expelling the corrupting occupant from Cuban soil.

Instead of the dishonorable rage of the first war, the revolution (which neither fears nor flatters) hopes to find among Cuba's Spanish inhabitants such affectionate neutrality and such real assistance, that because of them the war will turn out to be shorter, its disasters fewer, and the peace in which parents and their children will live easier and friendlier. We Cubans are starting the war, and we Cubans and Spaniards will end it. Let them not mistreat us, and we will not mistreat them. Let them show respect, and they will be respected. Steel replies with steel, friendship with friendship. There is no hate in Antillean hearts; the Cuban salutes in death the Spaniard whom the cruelty of the necessary army took away from his house and plot of ground to begin killing in men's hearts the freedom he himself so eagerly desires. Rather than salute him in death, the revolution would like to protect him in life; and the Republic will be a peaceful home for all honest and industrious Spaniards, so they may enjoy the freedom and benefits they will not find for a long time in the sluggishness, indolence, and political evils of their own land. This is the heart of Cuba, and its war will be conducted accordingly. What Spanish enemies will the revolution actually have? Possibly the largely republican army that has learned to respect our courage as we respect its courage, and in addition sometimes feels more like joining us than fighting us? Possibly the conscripts, trained in humanitarian ideals and opposed to shedding the blood of their fellow men for the sake of a useless scepter or an envious country? These conscripts are mowed down at the height of their youth in order to defend, against a nation that would gladly welcome them as free citizens, a throne unjustly controlling the nation betrayed by its leaders with the help of their concessions and profits. Could the Spanish enemies be the now human and cultured masses of artisans and clerks whom the inducement of the wealthy Spaniards dragged into crime and ferocity on the pretext of national duty? These Spaniards, with most of their fortune safe in Spain, are today showing less zeal than that with which they bled the land of its riches when the war surprised them on it with their entire fortune. Or could the revolution's Spanish enemies be the founders of Cuban families and industries, now weary of Spain's dishonesty and mismanagement, and like the Cubans vexed and oppressed? Could its enemies be those imprudent ingrates who, with no consideration for their own household peace or for preserving a fortune threatened more by the Spanish regime than by the revolution, may turn against the land that has changed them from sad peasants into happy husbands and fathers whose offspring know how to die without hate for the sake of assuring a free soil to the bloodthirsty father so that he can maintain a permanent state of discord between the Creole and the peninsular Spaniard? It is a free soil where an honest fortune may be kept without bribery and increased without anxiety, and where the son does not see, between his father's hand and his kiss, the abhorrent shadow of the oppressor. What fate will the Spaniard choose: an endless war, acknowledged or dissembled, that threatens or disturbs the ever uneasy and violent relations of the country, or the definitive peace that can never be achieved in Cuba except with independence? Will the Spaniards entrenched in Cuba provoke and stain with blood a war in which they may be the losers? And by what right can the Spaniards hate us if we Cubans do not hate them? The revolution fearlessly employs this kind of language because the decree to free Cuba at once from the irreparable ineptitude and corruption of the Spanish government—and to give all men of the New World free access to the island—is as peremptory as the will to see how Cubans, without lukewarm feelings or bitter memories, and how Spaniards, who because of their passion for freedom are helping to obtain it in Cuba, and how those who respect the present war, are redeeming the blood that in yesterday's war they caused to flow from the breasts of their sons.

In the forms that the revolution will take, well aware of its unselfishness, a cautious cowardice will doubtless find no reason for reproach—a cowardice which in the formal errors of the emerging country, or in its apparently slight progress toward republican status, could find some reason to deny it its due quota of blood. True patriotism will have no reason to fear for the dignity and future of the country. The difficulty with wars of independence in America, and those of its first ethnic groups, has not lain in the discord among its heroes and in man's inherent distrust and jealousy, but in the opportune lack of form contained by the spirit of redemption which, supported by lesser impulses, furthers and promotes war and its necessary practices, and which war must expedite and uphold. In the initial phases of the war the country must find such methods of government as satisfy both the mature and distrustful intelligence of its cultured sons and the conditions required for the aid and respect of other nations— methods that permit rather than hinder the full development and rapid conclusion of the war that is unfortunately necessary to national well-being. From its beginnings, the country must be built with viable forms originating in its own needs and character, so that an unsanctioned and unrealistic government will not lead it to partiality or to tyranny. Without attempting, by means of a disordered concept of its duty, to use the integral constitutional faculties with which the experienced and inexperienced elements are organized and arranged in their peculiar responsibility before the contemporary, liberal and impatient world, it is only just for the Cuban Revolutionary Party to declare its faith that the revolution must find forms assuring it of the unity and strength indispensable to a cultured war— assuring it of the enthusiasm of Cubans, the trust of Spaniards and the friendship of the world. For these experienced and inexperienced elements are moved alike by active impulse and pure idealism, men who, with the same nobility and impregnable title of their blood, are throwing themselves behind the guiding spirit of former heroes to open an industrious Republic to humanity. The duties and intentions of the revolution are these: to recognize and establish reality; to compose in a natural pattern the reality of ideas which produce or destroy the facts, and the reality of facts originating in those ideas; to organize the revolution with integrity, sacrifice and culture so that not one man's decency is damaged, not one Cuban feels his sacrifice to be futile or the revolution to be inferior to the culture of the country itself (not to the foreign and unauthorized culture that alienates the respect of virile men because of its ineffective results and the pitiful contrast between the genuine stupidity and arrogance of its sterile possessors). The revolution must be directed toward the profound knowledge of man's labor in the redemption and support of his dignity. It will be directed so that the powerful and capable war may promptly give the new Republic a foundation of stability.

From its inception the sound and vigorous war resumed by Cuba today, with all the advantages of experience, with assured victory for its final resolves, and with the lofty efforts of its deathless heroes— never recalled without the warmest feelings— has not been merely a pious longing to give a full life to the people who, under the growing immorality and occupation of an inept master, are disintegrating or losing their superior strength in the oppressed country or in Cuba's scattered communities abroad. The war is not an inadequate desire to conquer Cuba with the tempting sacrifice, the political independence, that would wrongfully rob Cubans of their strength if it did not offer them the hope of building a country with freedom of thought, equality of customs and peace through work. The war for the independence of Cuba— a knot in the sheaf of islands that the continental trade routes will cross within a few years— is an event of great human significance, and a timely service which the judicious heroism of the Antilles lends to stability and fair treatment among the American nations, and to the still uncertain balance in the world. It is touching and an honor to think that when a soldier fighting for independence falls upon Cuban soil, perhaps abandoned by the unwary or indifferent nations for which he is sacrificing himself, he falls for the greater good of mankind, for the affirmation of the moral Republic in America, and for the creation of a free archipelago where respectable nations may lavish the wealth which, as it circulates, must fall upon the crossroads of the world. It is hardly credible that with such martyrs and such a future, there were Cubans who bound Cuba to the decaying and uncultured monarchy of Spain, and to its paralyzed and vice-ridden misery! The duty of the revolution tomorrow is to again explain to the country and to the other nations the local reasons— although universal in idea and application— why the freedom-loving people of Yara and Guáimaro are once again embarking on a war worthy of the respect of its enemies and the support of nations, a war for the advancement and benefit of humanity because of its rigid concept of man's rights, and its abhorrence of useless vengeance and fruitless devastation. Today— while reverently proclaiming from the threshold of the world the spirit and doctrines which caused and are inspiring the total and humanitarian war in which the Cuban people, unconquerable and indivisible, are being united still further— let us, as leaders and guideposts of our nation, lawfully invoke the magnanimous founders whose labors are invigorating the grateful country. And let us invoke the honor which must prevent Cubans from wounding, by word or deed, those who die for them. Upon thus declaring in the name of our country, and attesting before it and before its free power of constitution, the identical work of two generations—the Delegate of the Cuban Revolutionary Party, created to organize and aid the present war, and the Commander-in-Chief, elected to it by all the active members of the Army of Liberation, by virtue of the common responsibility of their representation, and as an indication of the unity and solidity of the Cuban revolution, together do endorse this declaration.

Montecristi
March 25, 1895
José Martí M. Gómez

Campaign Diary: From Cabo Haitiano to Dos Ríos

Martí's diary begins on April 9, 1895, when the Cuban revolutionaries set sail for Cuba from Haiti. The diary was only published in 1940 as part of Máximo Gómez's Campaign Diary (Diario de Campaña del Mayor General Máximo Gómez, 1868–1899). *Martí's diary stops two days before he was killed at Dos Ríos on May 19, 1895.*

[April] 11: Boat. We leave at 11. Go round (4) Maisí,[1] sight beacon. I on the bridge. Dark at 7:30. Activity on board. Captain shows emotion. They lower the boat. Heavy downpour as we push off. Set the wrong course. Confused and conflicting opinions in the boat. Another downpour. Rudder lost. Back on course. I take forward oar. Salas rows steadily. Paquito Borrero and the General help out in the stern. We strap on our revolvers. Head toward clearing. Moon comes up red from behind a cloud. We land on a stony beach. La Playita (at foot of Cajobabo). I the last to leave the boat, bailing it out. Jump ashore. Great joy. We overturn the boat and the jug of water. Drink Málaga. Climb uphill over rocks, in thorns and mud. Hear a noise, make preparations, near a picket fence. Go round it and come to a house. Sleep on the ground nearby....

[April] 15: We greet the dawn in formation. A commission will be sent to Las Veguitas to purchase supplies in the Spanish store. Another for the ammunition left in the road. Another to look for a guide. Commission returns with salt, sandals, a cornucopia of sweets, three bottles of liqueur, chocolate, rum and... José arrives with some pork. Dinner: stewed pork with plantain and *eddo* root. In the

[1] Maisí is the eastern point of the island of Cuba.

morning... leftover stew, plantain, cheese for dessert and hot anise and cinnamon water. Colombié, a hunter with weak eyes, poor aim, comes to... with his yellow dog. By afternoon the people line up, the General, with Paquito, Guerra, and Ruenes leave for the ravine. Will he let us three stay alone? I'm resigned, but disappointed. Any possible danger? Angel Guerra comes calling me and Captain Cardoso. Gómez, moved and handsome, at the foot of the hill, in the pathway shaded by plantain, the ravine below, tells me that aside from recognizing me as a delegate, the Liberation Army, through its commanding officer, elected by a council of commanding officers, appoints me Major-General. I embrace him. All of them embrace me. At night, pork with coconut oil. Tastes good... .

[April] 25: Day of fighting. Straight through the woods we are nearing Arroyo Hondo, hostile in the first war but now in the claws of Guantánamo. We lose our way. Thorns tear at us. Lianas choke and lash at us. We go through a woods of green *jigüeras*: gourds on vines clinging to bare tree trunks and climbing over bare stretches of ground. People busy scooping out the gourds and smoothing their openings. At 11, heavy gunfire. Steady shooting echoed by sharp but hidden counterfire. The fighting seems to be right at our feet; the thud of three bullets hitting nearby trees. "How beautiful is faraway shooting!" says the amiable boy from San Antonio, a mere child. "Even more beautiful close at hand," says the old man. Keeping to our path we reach the bank of a brook. The gunfire becomes heavier. Magdaleno, sitting against a tree trunk, carves designs on his new gourd. We lunch on raw eggs, a sip of honey and some La Imperial chocolate from Santiago. Soon the news from the village reaches us. They have already brought in one dead and 25 wounded. Maceo came to look for us, and waits nearby; off to Maceo in high spirits. I wrote to Carmita: "On the battle route itself the victorious Cubans were waiting for us, jumping off their horses—horses they took from the Civil Guard. They embrace and applaud us, help us mount their horses, give us spurs." Why was I not horrified by the blood I saw in the road, or by the partly dried blood from a head already buried and resting on the dispatch case that one of our riders put under it for a pillow? And in the afternoon sun we began our victory march back to the camp.

They had set out at midnight, across rivers, through cane fields and bramble patches, to rescue us; they had almost reached us when they were attacked by the Spaniards. They fought for two hours without food, and fooled their hunger from the victory with hardtack. They began their eight-league march, first in the clear bright afternoon, then through arbors of thorns in the dark of night. The long column marched single file. Now the adjutants go by, running and shouting. We move about, both horsemen and foot soldiers, on the giddy heights. Each soldier enters the cane field and comes out with a cane stalk. (We cross the wide-gauge railroad tracks and hear the evening whistle of the sugar mills; at the end of the plain we see the electric lights.) "Column halt, there's a wounded man back there." The man drags his wounded leg and Gómez pulls him up behind him on his horse. Another wounded man refuses help: "No, friend, I'm not dead yet," and struggles on with a bullet in his shoulder. Those poor tired feet! The men sit at the roadside, rifles ready, and flash glorious smiles at us. There is an occasional cry of pain, but more laughing and happy conversation. "Make way!" and up rides mighty Lieutenant-Colonel Cartagena, who won his military rank in the big war, a flaming pine torch stuck like a lance into his leather stirrup. And more torches from time to time... setting fire to the dry leaves, which crackle and snap and send their shafts of flame and plumes of smoke skyward. The river sings to us. We wait for the weary. Guano palms are all around us in the shade. So the last drink, and then to sleep. Hammocks, firelight, stew pots, the camp is sleeping. Soon I will be asleep at the foot of a large tree, my machete and revolver beside me, my rain cape for a pillow. Now I am rummaging through my knapsack and taking out some medicine for the wounded. How affectionate the stars at 3 in the morning. At 5, wide awake, Colt strapped to my side, machete in my belt, spurs on sandals; and up in the saddle!

Alcil Duvergié, the brave, died: each burst of fire means a man. The bullet entered his head; they emptied a volley into the other sharpshooter; still another fell while foolishly crossing the bridge. And where are the wounded? With difficulty I round them up and put them near the man most seriously wounded, thought to be in shock, brought in on a stretcher made of a hammock suspended from a pole. Pressed into a corner of his mouth with some tobacco juice were his knocked-out teeth. He painfully sips a swallow of maraschino. And water for the wounded, where is it? They finally bring in a muddy bucketful. Evaristo Zayas, the obliging man from Ti Arriba, brings some fresh. And the medical assistant, where is the medical assistant who has not yet come to his wounded? The three others are complaining, in their rubber capes. Finally he comes, huddled in a quilt, alleging fever. And with everyone's help, with Paquito Borrero's tender aid, we take care of the wounded man in the hammock—a wound as large as the hole for an animal's nose ring, from a bullet that entered and left through the shoulder: one hole the size of a thimble and the other the size of a hazelnut. We wash the wound, disinfect it with iodoform, dress it with cotton soaked in carbolic acid. The other man wounded in the top of his thigh; the bullet went right through. Another, turned over on his stomach, still had the bullet in his back: there it is, on the way out, lodged in the swollen patch of red; the man's nose and mouth are eaten away by syphilis. The last of the wounded has his shoulder shot through also. They were shooting in a crouched position; one knee on the ground, and the low-flying bullets pierced those muscular backs. Antonio Suárez from Colombia, cousin of Lucía Cortés, Merchán's wife, received the same kind of wound. He has lost his way on foot and found us later.

[May] 17: Gómez sets out with 40 horsemen to harass the convoy at Bayamo. I stay behind, writing, and Garriga and Feria copy the "General Instructions" to the officers and commanders. A dozen men with me, under Lieutenant Chacón, with three men guarding the three roads; beside me, Graciano Pérez. Rosalío on his pony, mud up to the knees, kindly brings me lunch in his straw bag: "I'd lay down my life for you." From Santiago, which they recently left, come the Chacón brothers, one of whom owns the string of horses captured the day before yesterday, and their fair-skinned brother who has a college degree and is vain about it. Then there is José Cabrera, the Jiguaní shoemaker, honest and stuttering, and Duane, a black youth and kind of... in shirt sleeves, pants, and a wide belt, and ... Avalos, timid; and Rafael Vásquez, and Desidero Soler, 16 years old, whom Chacón treats like a son. Another son is here: Ezequiel Morales, 18, whose father was killed in the wars. And these who come tell me about Rosa Moreno, the widow from the country, who sent her only son Melesio, a boy of 16, to Rabí: "Your father died there; I can't go any more; you go." Plantains are being roasted and dried beef pounded soft with a stone in a mortar, for the recent arrivals. The floodwaters of the Contramaestre are very turbulent and muddy, and Valentín brings me a pitcher of sweetened boiled water, with fig leaves...

This is the end of Martí's diary.

PART 2

Letters

To mother

To My Mother, Leonor Pérez

Hanábana, October 23, 1862

Esteemed Mama,

First of all, I hope you are well, and also the girls, Joaquina, Luisa and Mama Joaquina. Papa received your letter on the 21st, since the mail didn't come on Saturday the 18th and he got it on Tuesday. He says that the mail couldn't get across the Sabanilla River, which makes it difficult to get to Nueva Bermeja and here. Papa doesn't hurt any more from his fall, but he itches from the time he lies down until he gets up, so he can't sleep, and he's been this way for three nights.

Now, I'm concentrating on taking care of my horse and getting him fat as a pig. I'm teaching him to walk while I rein him in, so he'll step elegantly. I ride him every afternoon, and he looks more polished every day. I still have something else with which to entertain myself and pass the time, the purebred rooster which Mr. Lucas de Sotolongo gave me. It is very handsome, and Papa takes very good care of it. Right now, Papa is looking for somebody who can trim its comb and is getting it ready for me so I can fight it this year. He says this rooster is worth more than two ounces.

Both the rivers that go by Mr. Jaime's farm and the Sabanilla—which the mail must cross—were very high on Saturday (the one near here came close to Mr. Domingo's fence), but they have gone down quite a lot since then.

That's about all. Give my love to Mama Joaquina, Joaquina, Luisa and the girls, and give Pilar a kiss for me. Your obedient son, who loves you passionately, sends you his love.

To mother

[Prison] November 10 [1869]

Mother,

I wrote you two days ago, sending the letter with a Frenchman who comes to see the Domínguezes (not the one who went there), and he told me that he hasn't been able to take the letter. He promised he would. Tell me if he does.

I also wrote you the day before yesterday, but I haven't found anyone to send the letters with, and I don't want to sent them out in the food carrier. Since I'm writing you today, I'm tearing up the letter I wrote the day before yesterday.

The prosecutor was here yesterday, and he seemed quite interested in asking about my case and how it was coming. I told him what he knew; but it's quite strange that the person who will be trying me should be asking me why I'm in jail. I've been told that somebody spoke to him about me. The Domínguezes and Sellén will finally be released, and I'll still be locked up. Prison doesn't frighten me very much, but I can't stand being in prison for a long time. This is the only thing I ask: act quickly, because nothing should be done to one who hasn't done anything. At least, they can't make any accusations that I am unable to disprove.

I'm very sorry to be behind bars, but I'm getting a lot out of prison. It has taught me many lessons that will be useful in my life— which I predict will be short— and I won't fail to make use of them. I am 16, yet many old people have told me I seem old. And they're right, in a way, because while I have all the recklessness and excitement of youth, I also have a small— and wounded— heart. Really, you suffer a lot, but I suffer more. God grant that, someday when I am happy, I may tell you of the problems in my life!

I am in prison, and that is the unvarnished truth, but I don't need anything, except for some small change for coffee every so often, and this is the first time I've wanted any. When you don't see your family or anyone else you love for some time, it isn't hard to get through a day without drinking coffee. Papa gave me five or six coins on Monday. I gave two or three away and lent two.

Bring one of the girls with you on Sunday.

This is an ugly school, because, even though some decent women come here, so do some others who aren't—four of them every day. Thank God, the bodies of women don't move me. Their souls are the important thing, and, if their souls are ugly, they can offer their attractions elsewhere. Prison can do just about anything except change my views on this.

While here, I haven't written any poetry. In one sense, I'm glad, because you know what kind of verses I write.

Everybody here talks to me about Mr. Mendive, and that makes me happy. Send me some books of poetry and a big one called *El Museo Universal* (*The Universal Museum*).

Your blessing on your son.

Pepe

To Amelia

[New York, January 1882]

Amelia,[1]

My beautiful Amelia, before me, like a rare jewel of soft, pure light, I have your affectionate letter. It conveys your serene, unblemished soul, free of wild impatience. It expresses your tender spirit, which wells forth from you like the essence of the first May flowers. I want you to protect yourself from violent, traitorous winds and hide when you see them go by; like birds of prey in the air, the winds sweep the earth, seeking the essence of the flowers. All the happiness of life, Amelia, lies in not confusing the eagerness to love which you feel at your age with the sovereign, deep, overwhelming love that flowers in your soul only after long examination, the most thorough knowledge and true and prolonged company of the person to whom you entrust your love. In our land, there is a disastrous custom of confusing loving feelings with the decisive, unchangeable affection that leads to a marriage that cannot be dissolved, without breaking the hearts of the separated lovers. The man and woman who feel drawn together by their mutual feelings, sometimes born of the budding soul's eagerness to open itself to the wind and our desire to experience love, rather than of another's inspiring love in us— instead of such a bachelor's and maid's confessing their mutual attraction and differentiating it from love, which should be something else and comes later (if at all) and has no occasion to arise except after marriage, those two relative strangers are forced into an affection that cannot have stemmed from anything except intimate knowledge of each other. Relations of love in our land begin where they should culminate. An intelligent woman with a stern soul should distinguish between the intimate and keen pleasure which comes close to being love but yet falls short of it,

---

[1] Amelia is one of Martí's sisters.

which she feels on seeing a man who appears to be worthy of being esteemed, and that other, definitive, magnificent love, which, since it is the ineffable attachment of one spirit to another, is born only of confidence that the spirit to which ours is united is entitled, because of its faithfulness, its beauty and its delicacy, to this tender and worthy consecration, which should last all our lives. See: I am an excellent doctor for souls, and I swear to you, by the little head of my son, that what I am telling you is the key to happiness and that he who forgets my code will not be happy. I have seen much in the depths of others, and much in myself, as well. Learn from what I say. Do not believe, my beautiful Amelia, that the affection depicted in common novels— and there are few novels that are not common, penned as they are by writers who turn out novels precisely because they aren't capable of writing more enlightening things— is a true copy of life or reflects its precepts. A young woman who sees it written that the love of all the heroines in her books— or that of her friends, who have read them like her— begins suddenly, with a devastating electric shock, supposes, when she feels the first sweet loving feeling, that it is her turn in the human game and that her affection must have the same forms, rapidity and intensity as those light affections depicted in books written— believe me, Amelia— by people who are incapable of resolving the tremendous bitterness that stems from their conventional, unthinking manner of describing passions that don't exist or which exist in a way different from that which they describe. Do you see a tree? Do you see how long it takes for the thick branch to put forth a golden orange or a red pomegranate? Going deeper in life, you see that everything follows the same process. Love, like the trees, must go from seed to sapling to blossom and to fruit. In Cuba, people always begin with the fruit. Amelia mine, tell me what is in your heart. Tell me everything about the wolves who pass by your door and the winds that seek your fragrance. Accept my help so you will be happy; I cannot be happy myself, but I know how to bring happiness to others.

Don't think that my letter ends here. I've wanted to tell you this for some time, and now I've begun to tell it to you. I'll write you about myself another Thursday. Now, I have only to tell you that I'm going around like my own pilot, facing all the winds of life and bringing a noble and beautiful ship— which has made so many voyages already that it is taking on water— unscathed through difficulties. Ask Papa, who is a worthy sailor, to explain this to you. You don't know, Amelia mine, how much veneration and tender respect our father deserves. The man whom you see filled with peevishness and whims is a man of extraordinary virtue. Now that I have more experience in life, I have become aware of the full worth of his energy and all of the rare and sublime merits of his pure and frank character. Think about what I am telling you. They're not just details, made for small eyes. That old man is a magnificent person. Make his life sweeter. Smile at his peevishness. He has never been too old to love.

Now, farewell.

Write me without moderation and without weighing your words; I am not your censor or your examiner, but your brother. A sheet of paper covered with a scrawl that slopes off the page but which expresses the beating of your heart and speaks to me of what you feel without any misgivings or fear is more beautiful to me than a painstaking letter written in fear that it might displease me. Affection is the best and most eloquent of all grammar. Say tenderness! and you are a very eloquent woman.

Nobody has ever given you a better embrace than this one which I send you. Don't delay in writing.

Your brother,

J. Martí

To General Máximo Gómez

New York, October 20, 1884

General Máximo Gómez

Distinguished General and Friend,

When I left your house on Saturday morning, I was so distressed that I wanted to let two days go by so that the determination which that distress, together with others from the past, inspired in me would not be the result of a passing bewilderment or of excessive zeal in the defense of things which I would never wish to see attacked, but would rather be the product of mature reflection. It is very distressing to me to have to say these things to a man whom I believe to be sincere and good, and who has outstanding qualities for becoming truly great. But there is something that is more important than all of the personal liking I have for you, and even more than all apparent circumstantial reason. This is my determination not to do *anything*, out of blind love for an idea to which I have devoted my entire life, which would bring to my land a regime of personal despotism that would be more shameful and unfortunate than the political despotism to which it is now subjected, and that would be more serious and harder to uproot, because it would be justified by some virtues, embellished by the idea embodied in it and legitimized by success.

A nation is not founded as a military camp is set up, General. The preparatory work for a revolution is more delicate and complex than any other, but instead of a sincere desire to understand and conciliate all of the work, wishes and elements that are required for armed struggle (simply one form of the spirit of independence), one sees rather an intention— roughly expressed at every step or poorly disguised— of making all the resources of faith and of war which that spirit arouses serve the personal aims of the justly famed chiefs who present themselves to lead the war. In this situation, what guarantees can there be that civic freedoms—the sole object for which it is worth throwing a country into the struggle—will be any better respected in the future? What are we, General? The heroic, selfless servants of an idea which warms our hearts, the loyal friends of an unhappy nation, or the valiant and fortunate commanders who, with whip in hand and spurs on our boots, are preparing to bring war to a nation in order to take possession of it? Are you going to lose the fame won in an earlier exploit—fame for your courage, loyalty and wisdom—in another? If war— and its noble, legitimate prestige—is possible, it is because there already exists the spirit that demands it and makes it necessary, a spirit forged with much pain. That spirit must be protected, and the deepest respect must be paid to it in every public and private act; because, just as everyone who gives his life in the service of a great idea is admirable, he who makes use of a great idea to serve his personal hopes of glory or power is abominable, even though he may risk his life for those hopes. Everyone has the right to risk his life selflessly.

I am sure you are distressed, because I know that you always act in good faith and truly believe that, since you are inspired by pure motives, you are doing things in the only correct way. But the worst mistakes can be committed with the greatest sincerity, and it is absolutely necessary—in spite of every consideration of a secondary nature—for the unvarnished truth (which should play no favorites) to oppose all that is considered a threat and to replace it with serious things before you go so far along that path that there is no way to remedy the situation. General, you must master this difficulty, just as, on Saturday, I mastered the shock and disgust with which I heard an untimely outburst of yours and the curious conversation which General Maceo began provoked by it, in which he tried—an even greater insanity!—to convince me that we should consider Cuba's war as your exclusive property, in which nobody can think or do anything without committing a crime and which everyone should servilely and blindly leave in your hands if he wished to contribute to its success. No! By God, no! Seek to stifle thought even before it is expressed, as you would do in the future, leading an enthusiastic and grateful people, with all the trappings of victory? Our homeland belongs to no one—or, if it does, it will belong (and only in spirit) to whoever serves it with the greatest altruism and intelligence.

I have put my entire soul into a war undertaken in obedience to the mandates of the country, in consultation with the representatives of its interests, in union with the largest number of friendly elements that can be achieved; and I believed— because that is how I described it in a letter I wrote three years ago, to which I have your inspiring reply— that that was the war you have now offered to lead. I put my entire soul into it, because it will save my people, but I will never support the thing that I was given to understand in that conversation would be a personal adventure undertaken skillfully at an opportune time, in which the personal aims of the leaders could be confused with the glorious ideas which were making that war possible. I cannot defend a campaign undertaken as a private enterprise, without showing any more respect to the patriotic spirit which made it possible than expediency advised, combined with groveling at times to attract those persons or elements that might be useful in one way or another; a military career, no matter how brilliant and grandiose, that should be crowned with success (and the one who led it would win personal laurels); a campaign that, right from its first action, its first movements of preparation, would give no signs that it was being waged in the service of the country and not as a despotic invasion; an armed attempt that would not be publicly, explicitly, sincerely and solely motivated by the goal of placing civic freedoms in the hands of the country (which is already grateful to those who are helping it) at its conclusion; a war with shallow roots and fearful consequences, no matter what its magnitude and chances of success— and I realize that those chances would be great. No matter what my support may be worth— and I know that, since it comes from an indomitable determination to be absolutely honest, it is worth its weight in gold— I will never give it to you.

How could I undertake missions, attract support, make use of the support I already have, convince eminent men and overcome opposition, General, while these fears and doubts besiege my heart? Therefore, I am stopping all of the active work I had begun to take on.

Don't hold it against me, General, for having written to you, presenting these reasons. I consider you an honest man, and you deserve to think about what I have written. You may become very great— or you may not achieve that. To respect a people that loves and depends on us is the highest form of greatness. To make use of its griefs and enthusiasms for our own gain would be the worst ignominy. Ever since you were in Honduras, General, people have told me that you are surrounded by intrigues which are poisoning you, without your being aware of it, and that individuals are taking advantage of your goodness, your impressions and your habits to separate you from all whom you might meet who would join in your labors with affection and help you to free yourself of the obstacles that may beset your path and keep you from attaining the stature for which you are naturally endowed. But I confess that I have neither the desire nor the patience to go sniffing out and confounding intrigues. I am above all that. I serve only my duty, and with it, I will always be powerful enough.

Has anyone approached you, General, with warmer affection than that with which I have embraced you ever since the day I first saw you? Have you felt in many this unavoidable overflowing of the heart that would harm me so much in my life if I had to hide my purposes in order to further effeminate and petty ambitions for the present or hopes for the future? For, in spite of everything I have written— and carefully reread and confirmed— I believe that I still love you for your abundant merits, but not the war, which it now seems to me you may be representing mistakenly. That, no.

I still esteem and would serve you.

José Martí

To Fermín Valdés Domínguez

New York, February 28, 1887

Fermín,

My father has just died, and a great part of me with him. You can't imagine how much I loved him after I discovered, under his humble exterior, all the integrity and beauty of his soul. I had thought that my suffering couldn't be greater, but it is, for now I will never be able to love and boast about him as I wished, so that all might see and reward him in the last years of his life for that vigorous and proud virtue that I myself didn't fully appreciate until mine was put to the test. My grief is true and great, Fermín, but the courage and nobility you have just shown have managed to console it. We haven't written each other for some time, but I have just read your letters in *La Lucha* and the account of what is worth even more than they—the action of yours that led to them—and I cannot repress a desire to embrace you.

You have done, with singular dignity, what perhaps no one else would have decided to do. You have done it as truly great things are done, without pomp or hatred. Your moderation in justice will have earned you the respect of the very ones who wanted to offend you and will still the tongues of the envious, whom you must have met already, for nothing attracts them so surely as does character. You have served well the peace of our country, the only possible peace, without lies or dishonor, which must be based on the charity of the vanquished and the subduing and confounding of the wicked. You, calling without anger for the killers to confess to their crime, have sowed for the future with a surer hand than those who fan unfounded hopes or make threats that cannot be carried out, or for which they do not prepare with determination and wisdom. In one of the saddest, most eventful episodes in our history, you have preserved for us the incalculable strength of the victims. If we had

had the misfortune to have been at war, it could be said, Fermín, that you alone have defeated many battalions.

I don't want to talk about myself. What will become of me, now that I have no way of serving my homeland effectively? Acts such as yours are the only things that pull me out of this anxious agony for a while— this agony about which nothing should be said, because complaints dishonor the speaker. I know well that my land has all of the virtues required to make it respected and happy at last. It grows in the same thing that seems to dismay, strengthens its spirit with patience and common sense, and is gaining in goodness and energy. Everything will be possible there, because most Cubans are good people. And you, Fermín, are one of the best, for, at times and in situations that becloud men's vision and lead them to act without restraint, you have managed to be just without being vengeful. That is what I praise about you, and in acting thus you have served your homeland best. You must be happy that you have managed to control your wrath and, in a tragic and memorable time, satisfy the ghosts of your brothers.

All that remains of my soul is yours.

José Martí

To the Editor of the Evening Post: *A Vindication of Cuba*

To the Editor of the New York *Evening Post*[1]

Sir,

I beg to be allowed the privilege of referring in your columns to the injurious criticism of the Cubans printed in *The Manufacturer* of Philadelphia, and reproduced in your issue of yesterday.

This is not the occasion to discuss the question of the annexation of Cuba. It is probable that no self-respecting Cuban would like to see his country annexed to a nation where the leaders of opinion share towards him the prejudices excusable only to vulgar jingoism or rampant ignorance. No honest Cuban will stoop to be received as a moral pest for the sake of the usefulness of his land in a community where his ability is denied, his morality insulted and his character despised. There are some Cubans who, from honorable motives, from an ardent admiration for progress and liberty, from a prescience of their own powers under better political conditions, from an unhappy ignorance of the history and tendency of annexation, would like to see the island annexed to the United States. But those who have fought in war and learned in exile, who have built, by the work of hands and mind, a virtuous home in the heart of an unfriendly community; who by their successful efforts as scientists and merchants, as railroad builders and engineers, as teachers, artists, lawyers, journalists, orators and poets, as men of alert intelligence and uncommon activity are honored wherever their powers have been called into action and the people are just enough to understand them; those who have raised, with their less prepared elements, a town of working men where the United States had previously a few

[1] This letter was published in the New York *Evening Post*, March 25, 1889. It was written in English.

huts in a barren cliff; those, more numerous than the others, do not desire the annexation of Cuba to the United States. They do not need it. They admire this nation, the greatest ever built by liberty, but they dislike the evil conditions that, like worms in the heart, have begun in this mighty republic their work of destruction. They have made of the heroes of this country their own heroes, and look to the success of the American commonwealth as the crowning glory of mankind; but they cannot honestly believe that excessive individualism, reverence for wealth, and the protracted exultation of a terrible victory are preparing the United States to be the typical nation of liberty, where no opinion is to be based in greed, and no triumph or acquisition reached against charity and justice. We love the country of Lincoln as much as we fear the country of Cutting.

We are not the people of destitute vagrants or immoral pigmies that *The Manufacturer* is pleased to picture; nor the country of petty talkers, incapable of action, hostile to hard work, that, in a mass with the other countries of Spanish America, we are represented to be by arrogant travelers and writers. We have suffered impatiently under tyranny; we have fought like men, sometimes like giants, to be free men; we are passing that period of stormy repose, full of germs of revolt, that naturally follows a period of excessive and unsuccessful action; we have to fight like conquered men against an oppressor who denies us the means of living, and fosters—in the beautiful capital visited by the tourist and in the interior of the country, where the prey escaped his grasp—a reign of such corruption as may poison in our veins the strength to secure freedom; we deserve in our misfortune the respect of those who did not help us in our need.

But because, after the war, our government has systematically allowed the triumph of criminals, the occupation of the cities by the scum of the people, the ostentation of ill-gotten riches by the myriad Spanish officeholders and their Cuban accomplices, the conversion of the capital into a gambling den, where the hero and the philosopher walk hungry by the lordly thief of the metropolis; because the healthier farmer, ruined by a war seemingly useless, turns in silence to the plow that he knew well how to exchange for the *machete;* because thousands of exiles, profiting by a period of calm that no human power can quicken until it is naturally exhausted, are practicing in the battle of life in the free countries the art of governing themselves and of building a nation; because our half-breeds and city-bred young men are generally of delicate physique, of suave courtesy and ready words, hiding under the glove that polishes the poem the hand that fells the foe— are we to be considered, as *The Manufacturer* does consider us, an "effeminate" people. These city-bred young men and poorly built half breeds knew in one day how to rise against a cruel government, to pay their passages to the seat of war with the pawning of their watches and trinkets, to work their way in exile while the vessels were being kept from them by the country of the free in the interest of the foes of freedom, to obey as soldiers, sleep in the mud, eat roots, fight 10 years without salary, conquer foes with the branch of a tree, die— these men of 18, these heirs of wealthy estates, these dusky striplings— a death not to be spoken of without uncovering the head. They died like those other men of ours who, with a stroke of the *machete*, can send a head flying, or by a turn of the hands bring a bull to their feet. These "effeminate" Cubans had once courage enough, in the face of a hostile government, to carry on their left arms for a week the mourning-band for Lincoln.

The Cubans have, according to *The Manufacturer*, "a distaste for exertion"; they are "helpless," "idle." These "helpless," "idle" men came here 20 years ago empty-handed, with very few exceptions; fought against the climate; mastered the language; lived by their honest labor, some in affluence, a few in wealth, rarely in misery; they bought or built homes; they raised families and fortunes; they loved luxury and worked for it; they were not frequently seen in the dark roads of life; proud and self-sustaining, they never feared competition as to intelligence or diligence. Thousands have returned to die in their homes; thousands have remained where, during the hardships of life, they have triumphed, unaided by any help of kindred language, sympathy of race or community of religion. A handful of Cuban toilers built Key West. The Cubans have made their mark in Panama by their ability as mechanics in the higher trades, as clerks, physicians and contractors. A Cuban, Cisneros, has greatly advanced the development of railways and river navigation in Colombia. Márquez, another Cuban, with many of his countrymen, gained the respect of the Peruvians as a merchant of eminent capacity. Cubans are found everywhere, working as farmers, surveyors, engineers, mechanics, teachers, journalists. In Philadelphia *The Manufacturer* has a daily opportunity to see a hundred Cubans, some of them of heroic history and powerful build, who live by their work in easy comfort. In New York, the Cubans are directors in prominent banks, substantial merchants, popular brokers, clerks of recognized ability, physicians with large practices, engineers of worldwide repute, electricians, journalists, tradesmen, cigar makers. The poet of Niagara is a Cuban, our Heredia; a Cuban, Monocal, is the projector of the canal of Nicaragua. In Philadelphia itself, as in New York, the college prizes have been more than once awarded to Cubans. The women of these "helpless," "idle" people, with "a distaste for exertion," arrived here from a life of luxury in the heart of the winter; their husbands were in the war, ruined, dead, imprisoned in Spain; the "Señora" went to work; from a slave-owner she became a slave, took a seat behind the counter, sang in the churches, worked button-holes by the hundred, sewed for a living, curled feathers, gave her soul to duty, withered in work her body. This is the people of "defective morals."

We are "unfitted by nature and experience to discharge the obligations of citizenship in a great and free country." This cannot be justly said of a people who possess, besides the energy that built the first railroad in Spanish dominions and established against the opposition of the government all the agencies of civilization, a truly remarkable knowledge of the body politic, a tried readiness to adapt itself to its higher forms, and the power rare in tropical countries of nerving their thought and pruning their language. Their passion for liberty, the conscientious study of its best teachings, the nursing of individual character in exile and at home, the lessons of 10 years of war and its manifold consequences, and the practical exercise of the duties of citizenship in the free countries of the world, have combined, in spite of all antecedents, to develop in the Cuban a capacity for free government so natural to him that he established it, even to the excess of its practices, in the midst of the war, vied with his elders in the effort to respect the laws of liberty, and snatched the saber, without fear or consideration, from the hands of every military pretender, however glorious. There seems to be in the Cuban mind a happy faculty of uniting sense with earnestness and moderation with exuberance. Noble teachers have devoted themselves since the beginning of the century to explain by their words and exemplify by their lives the self-restraint and tolerance inseparable from liberty. Those who won the first seats 10 years ago at the European universities by singular merit have been proclaimed, at their appearance in the Spanish parliament, men of subtle thought and powerful speech. The political knowledge of the average Cuban compares well with that of the average American citizen. Absolute freedom from religious intolerance, the love of man for the work he creates by his industry, and theoretical and practical familiarity with the laws and processes of liberty, will enable the Cuban to rebuild his country from the ruins in which he will receive it from its oppressors. It is not to be expected, for the honor of mankind, that the nation that was rocked in freedom, and received for three centuries the best blood of liberty-loving men, will employ the power thus acquired in depriving a less fortunate neighbor of its liberty.

Finally, it is said that "our lack of manly force and of self-respect is demonstrated by the supineness with which we have so long submitted to Spanish oppression, and even our attempts at rebellion have been so pitifully ineffective that they have risen little above the dignity of farce." Never was ignorance of history and character more pitifully displayed than in this wanton assertion. We need to recollect, in order to answer without bitterness, that more than one American bled by our side, in a war that another American was to call a farce. A farce! The war that has been compared to an epic by foreign observers, the upheaval of a whole country, the voluntary abandonment of wealth, the abolition of slavery in our first moment of freedom, the burning of our cities by our own hands, the erection of villages and factories in the wild forests, the dressing of our ladies of rank in the textures of the woods, the keeping at bay, in 10 years of such a life, a powerful enemy, with a loss to him of 200,000 men, at the hands of a small army of patriots, with no help but Nature! We had no Hessians and no Frenchmen, no Lafayette or Steuben, no monarchical rivals to help us; we had but one neighbor who confessedly "stretched the limits of his power, and acted against the will of the people" to help the foes of those who were fighting for the same Charter of Liberties on which he built his independence.

We fell a victim to the very passions which could have caused the downfall of the 13 States, had they not been cemented by success, while we were enfeebled by procrastination; a procrastination brought about, not from cowardice, but from an abhorrence of blood, which allowed the enemy in the first months of the war to acquire unconquerable advantage, and from a childlike confidence in the certain help of the United States: "They cannot see us dying for liberty at their own doors without raising a hand or saying a word to give to the world a new free country!" They "stretched the limits of their powers in deference to Spain." They did not raise the hand. They did not say the word.

The struggle has not ceased. The exiles do not want to return. The new generation is worthy of its sires. Hundreds of men have died in darkness since the war in the misery of prisons. With life only will this fight for liberty cease among us. And it is the melancholy truth that our efforts would have been, in all probability, successfully renewed, were it not, in some of us, for the unmanly hopes of the annexationists of securing liberty without paying its price; and the just fears of others that our dead, our sacred memories, our ruins drenched in blood would be but the fertilizers of the soil for the benefit of a foreign plant, or the occasion for a sneer from *The Manufacturer* of Philadelphia.

With sincere thanks for the space you have kindly allowed me, I am, sir, yours very respectfully,

José Martí
120 Frost Street, New York
March 23, 1889

To mother

[On board the SS *Mascotte*] May 15, 1894

Dear Mother,

You are still suffering from your eye trouble, and I, from this silence of mine, which comes from my shyness in expressing great affection and from my way of complaining against the misfortune that takes you from me and as vengeance against this fatal necessity of saying and writing so much about public things, against this ever more stubborn and anxious passion of mine of withdrawing into myself.

But, as long as there is work to be done, an honest man has no right to rest. Each man should render the service he can, without anyone's chiding him for not doing so. From whom did I get my integrity and rebelliousness, from whom could I inherit them, but my father and mother?

Now Mother, I am going to Key West for a few days and, from there, will continue my work— purer than a newborn child, shining as a star, without any stains of ambition, intrigue or hatred. So, you see— how many times haven't I told you this?— why I can't write you.

To others, I can speak of other things. With you, I pour out my soul, even though you don't approve of what I do with all the affection I'd wish for and I can't write you in that unhappy land where you live without indiscretion or without lies. My pen runs on with my truth; I must either say what is in me or remain silent. Later, there is this ugly, irritating business of speaking about oneself. For the good of others, let me calmly call up all of the pity and order there is in me. And believe, because it is true, that your son couldn't be better employed in anything else. Moreover, nothing else, even selfishness, could have better put to rest my savage, interminable grief. It gnaws and gnaws at me, and I cannot remove it from my side.

I hear constantly about you, more than I would wish you to hear about me, because all that can reach you is anguish. Carmen doesn't learn— or is it that her goodness makes her suffer? Will I arrive in time to make the household a little happier?

My future is like that of white coal, which burns itself up to cast light on those around it. I feel that my struggles will never end. The private man is dead and beyond all resurrection, which would be that of the warmth of a happy home— an impossibility for me— wherein lies the only human happiness, or at least the root of all happiness. But the vigilant and compassionate man is still alive in me, like a skeleton that has emerged from its tomb, and I know that only conflicts and grief in men's battle await him and that it is absolutely necessary to enter it to console and improve them. I can be at peace only with those unhappy souls who attain power seldom and with too much anger. Death or isolation will be my only reward— and, if I live, the authority of my integrity in good people and work, from which I will always be able to save a crumb for my sister Carmen.

There I leave Carmita in Central Valley, a basket of hills where in summer, at least, you can live in happy poverty. I spent a few days there with Gómez's son, who is like a son to me, and I won't return there for some time. The mother and daughters arrived alone, in a bad snowstorm, but the apple and cherry trees have already blossomed, and they have their chickens and their acre of vegetable garden. Never before have I encountered anyone as meek and honest as Carmita. Now, I will see Manuel, who has stopped walking on air and is learning to be a cigar maker, to be trained in the brotherhood of man and the dignity of work. How are the gallant Oscar, whom I would like to have with me; the founding Mario, who should help me to create a pretty town in the countryside; and the patient Alfredo, the loyal manager? If I go on remembering, my soul will become anguished and be troubled and bloodied when it tackles the work it must do tonight. So, enough.

Yes, I would like everybody to write me and send the letters on the steamship to Tampa, where I can be reached care of Ramón Rivero y Rivero, Ibor Factory.

Write without embarrassment, as if you were seeing me every day. I see you constantly: my romantic Chata, my worthy Carmen, my sad Amelia and my wise Antonia; I never stop seeing you, even for an instant. Lightning once struck a man dumb; you don't want that to have happened to me, do you?

I cannot chide you, Mother. I love you and have made you suffer too much for that.

All the truth and sadness of your son.

José

To Federico Henríquez y Carvajal

Montecristi, March 25, 1895

Friend and Brother,

Such great responsibilities fall upon the shoulders of those men who do not withhold their slight strength from the world, and who live for furthering its decency and freedom, that any mode of expression is ineffective and childlike, as it were, and one can scarcely put into a slender phrase what one would say to a cherished friend with an embrace. These are my feelings now, on the threshold of a great duty, as I reply to your generous letter. It was of supreme benefit to me, and gave me the one strength that great undertakings require, and it is common knowledge that a warmhearted and honorable man looks to us for these things with enthusiasm. Rare as mountains are the men who know how to look down from them and feel with the heart of a nation, or of humanity. After clasping the hand of such a man, there remains the inner cleanliness that is left after winning a good fight in a just cause. Because you can thoroughly divine the real concern in my heart, I will purposely avoid its mention; I am writing to you with deep emotion in the silence of a home about to be abandoned this very day for the good of my country. The least I can do in gratitude for this virtue— since I am thus accepting my duty instead of shirking it— is to face death, whether it awaits us on land or sea, in the company of one who, as a result of my efforts and out of respect for his own, as well as for the passionate spirit common to our lands, is leaving his loving and happy home to set foot in our enemy-ridden country with a handful of brave men. I was beginning to die of shame— apart from my conviction that my presence in Cuba today is at least as useful as it could be abroad— at the thought that at so great a risk I might reach the conclusion that I was obliged to let him go alone, and that a nation might allow itself to be served, without a certain scorn and indifference, by one who preached the need of dying and then did not begin by risking his life. Wherever my first duty may lie, in Cuba or abroad, there I will be. It may even be possible or necessary, as up to now it would appear, for me to do both. Perhaps I can contribute to the basic need of shaping our renewed war so that, dispensing with useless of trifling details, its visible origins will contain all the principles necessary to the good name of the revolution, and the security of the republic. The difficulty of our wars of independence, and the reason for their slow and imperfect accomplishment, has resided less in the lack of mutual esteem on the part of their authors, and in the rivalry inherent in human nature, than in our lack of a form that should at once encompass the spirit of redemption and decency which, with an active number of objectives of a less pure character, promotes and maintains both the war and the methods and participants of the war. The other difficulty, which our proprietary and bookish nations have not yet overcome, is that of combining after emancipation methods of government which, without leaving the country's superior intellects discontented, would embrace— and permit their natural and increasing development— the more numerous and uncultured members of society whom an artificial government, however good and generous, might lead to anarchy or tyranny.

I promoted the war; with it my responsibility begins, not ends. For me, my country will never represent triumph, only agony and duty. Blood is at the boiling point. Now one must respect sacrifice and give it a humane and sympathetic meaning. The war must be made viable and invincible. If I am ordered to stay in it, as is my one desire, I shall stay; if, although my soul dies, I am ordered far from those who die as I would know how to die, then I shall have the courage for that also. Whoever thinks primarily of himself does not love his country; a nation's ills reside, no matter how subtly they are concealed at times, in the barriers erected or the haste imposed by the country's representatives in the natural course of events. From me, you may expect my absolute and constant submission. I will arouse the world; but my one desire would be to stay there close beside the last tree, the last fighter, and die quietly. For my hour has come. But I can still serve this unique heart of our republics. The free Antilles will preserve the independence of Our America, and the dubious and tarnished honor of English America, and perhaps may hasten and stabilize the equilibrium of the world. Look what we are doing—you with your youthful white hair; and I dragging myself along with a broken heart.

Regarding Santo Domingo, why need I make mention of it? How does it differ from Cuba? Although you are not a Cuban, is there a better Cuban than you? And Gómez, is he not a Cuban? And I, what am I, and who shall give me a country? Was it not my own soul, and my own pride, that enveloped me and vibrated around me at the sound of your voice on that valiant and memorable night at the *Sociedad de Amigos*? This experience is that one, and goes hand in hand with it. I obey, and will even say that I respect as a great privilege an American law, the happy necessity of departing, under the protection of Santo Domingo, for the Cuban war of liberation. Let us do upon the surface of the sea, in blood and affection, what the fire of the Andean mountain range is doing at the seabed.

I tear myself away from you and leave you a warm embrace and the plea that in my name, whose sole value is that it is today at the service of my country, Cuba may be grateful, today and tomorrow, for all the justice and charity it may receive. Whoever loves it, I will fervently claim as my brother. The only brothers I have are those who love Cuba.

Farewell to you and to my noble and indulgent friends. I owe you a pure and high-minded joy in this harsh and sordid world of men. Raise your voice high, for if I fall it will be for the independence of your country also.

Your,

José Martí

To mother

[Montecristi] March 25, 1895

Mother,

Today, March 25, on the eve of a long voyage, I think of you. I never cease to think of you. In the anger of your love, the sacrifice of my life hurts you; why was I born of you with a life that loves sacrifice? I cannot find the words. A man's duty is where he is most useful. But the memory of my mother is always with me, in my growing and necessary agony.

I embrace my sisters and their husbands. I hope that some day I may see all of you around me and proud of me. Then, yes, I will care for and pamper you with pride. Now, give me your blessing and believe that I will never do anything that is not honest and correct. Your blessing.

Your,

J. Martí

I have cause for being happier and more confident than you can imagine. Truth and tenderness are not useless. Do not suffer.

To José Martí y Zayas Bazán

[Montecristi] April 1, 1895

Son,

I am leaving for Cuba tonight, leaving without you, when you should be at my side. On leaving, I think of you. If I should die on the way, you will receive the watch chain that your father used to wear. Farewell. Be fair.

Your,

José Martí

To Carmen Miyares de Mantilla and her Children

Jurisdiction of Baracoa, April 16, 1895

Dear Carmita, My Girls, Manuel and Ernesto,

I am writing you from Cuba, in the shade of a hut made of royal palm fronds. The blisters I got from rowing the boat that brought us to land are already healing. There were six of us. We arrived at a beach covered with stones and thorns, and we are all right, in a camp surrounded by palm trees and banana plants, with the people on land and with our rifles by our sides. Along the way, I picked the first flower for the mother and ferns for María and Carmita, and I found a colorful stone for Ernesto. I gathered them as if I were going to see you, as if your house—your protective and welcoming house, which I always see before my eyes—were waiting for me, rather than a cave or a hillside.

My happiness is very great, Carmita. Without any illusions, excessive thinking about myself or selfish and puerile joy, I can say that I have finally attained the fullness of my being and that the honor I see in my fellow citizens, in the nature to which our courage entitles us, enraptures me. Only the light is comparable to my happiness. At all times, I see your pious and serene face, and I bring my lips close to the girls' foreheads at dawn and at sunset; when I see a new flower along the way; when I see a beautiful sight in these rivers and mountains; when, kneeling on the ground, I drink the clear water of a stream; and when I close my eyes, happy with a free day. You accompany and surround me; I feel you, silent and vigilant, around me. I lack only the girls. What do they lack? Can they be saved from their new afflictions? How will they have replaced my little help? My eyes have already written their names on many of Cuba's clouds and the leaves of its trees.

My happiness as a useful being increases my sorrow that they don't see me. Will they remember their friend thus, with such loyalty and vehemence?

Ah, María, if you could only see me going along these paths, happy and thinking of you with an affection more gentle than ever, wanting to pick you some of the purple and white star-like flowers that grow here in the mountains, but without any way to send them to you!

I have quite a load, my María, with my rifle over my shoulder; my *machete* and revolver at my belt; a bag with 100 cartridges slung over one shoulder and maps of Cuba in a large tube dangling from the other; my knapsack containing 50 pounds of medicine, clothes, my hammock, a blanket and books on my back; and your picture on my chest.

I'm running out of paper, and we can't send large packages. The sunlight is falling straight on the paper. Picture me alive and strong, with more love than ever for the girls who accompanied me in my solitude, for they are medicine for my bitterness. Don't fear for me. Our difficulties are great, but so are we, and we are bound to overcome them. Carmita will ask Gonzalo to let her read the personal parts of the letter I am sending him. Good Manuel, work. Carmita, write my mother. Little Carmita and María, prepare for school. High over the mountain, when I got here the night before last, I saw a palm tree and a star. How could I help thinking about Carmita and María? And about your mother's friendship, when I saw the clear sky of a Cuban night? Remember me with fondness.

Your,

Martí

To the New York Herald

This letter was handed to Eugene Bryson of the New York Herald *correspondent when he visited the Cuban revolutionaries in their camp in early May 1895. It is not clear whether this letter was ever published.*

Guantánamo, May 2, 1895

To the Editor,

The *New York Herald* is nobly offering the publicity of its daily newspaper to the Cuban revolution on behalf of the island's independence and the creation of a durable Republic. As representatives-elect of the revolution, empowered until such time as this revolution chooses authorities befitting its new form, it is our duty to express in concise terms to the people of the United States and to the world the reasons, composition and purposes of the revolution initiated by Cuba at the beginning of the century. It has been maintained in arms with recognized heroism from 1868 to 1878, and is being resumed today through the organized efforts of the country's sons both within the island and abroad. With the Cuban's expert bravery and mature character, we will establish an independent nation worthy and capable of the government which can release the stagnant wealth of the Cuban island (in the peace which can assure nothing less than man's satisfied respect) to the unobstructed labors of its inhabitants and to free access by the entire world.

With the joy of sacrifice and the solemn determination to die, Cuba has risen in arms not to interrupt— with a fanatical patriotism the inadequate ideal of political independence from Spain— the development of a people who might have reached maturity peacefully, without hindering the accelerated course of the world which, in these closing years of the century, is widening and renewing itself.

Rather we seek the emancipation from Spain of an intelligent and generous nation of international outlook and specific duties in America. Spain is inferior to Cuba in her aptitude for modern work and free government, and finds it necessary to shut off the island (so exuberant with native strength and the creative character) from the productivity of great nations. Spain wishes to maintain, by violently oppressing a useful American nation, the only market for Spanish industries and the revenue with which Cuba is paying Spain's debts upon the continent and maintaining in leisure and power the favored and unproductive classes who seek—not through their own manly efforts—the rapidly gained and plentiful fortunes which they continue to expect from Spain's conquests in America, fortunes obtained from the colony's venal occupations and iniquitous taxes.

Superficial thinking, or a certain kind of brutal disdain—dishonorable because of the ignorance it reveals of those who are shown to be incapable of respecting heroic virtue—can claim (with an incredible forgetfulness of Cuba's armed intellectual struggle for her freedom throughout this century) that the Cuban revolution is the insignificant longing of an exclusive class of poverty-stricken Cubans living abroad, or an uprising of the preponderance of Negroes in Cuba, or the country's sacrifice to an unsustainable dream of independence. The son of Cuba, who has been raised in war and emigration for a quarter of a century to such moral, industrial and political abundance, takes second place to the finest human product of any other nation. But that son suffers unspeakable bitterness to see his productive soil—and upon it his strangled human dignity—chained to the obligation of paying, with his free American hands, almost the entire proceeds of his productivity, and the daily and most painful proceeds of his honor, to the needs and vices of the monarchy. The Spanish government's bureaucratic composition and its continued protection of the worthless and perverse elements of society, through the gifts and land grants of America, prevent it from ever allowing the tormented island of Cuba (at the historic time when her land is being thrown open and the seas are embracing at her feet) to spread wide her ports and her gold-bearing entrails to a world that is surfeited with unused capital and idle masses. In the warmth of a firm republic, that world would find in the island the serenity of ownership and a friendly crossroads.

Cubans recognize the urgent duty imposed upon them by their geographical position in the world at the present time of universal gestation; and although childish observers or the vanity of the proud are unaware of it, they are fully capable, through the power of their intelligence and the impetus of their strength, to fulfill that duty. And they are the ones to fulfill it.

At the mouth of the ocean currents where three continents come together, at the instant when the active advance of humanity is about to stumble against the useless Spanish colony in Cuba, and at the gates of a nation dismayed by the plethora of products it might be able to buy but that it now has to buy from its oppressors, Cuba wants to be free. Cuba wants to be free so that man can achieve his full purpose there, so the world can go to work there, and so Cuba's hidden riches can be sold in the native markets of America where the interests of the Spanish master now prevent Cuba from buying. Cubans ask nothing from the world but a knowledge of and a respect for their sacrifices, and they are giving their blood to the universe. A superficial study of the national composition of Spain and of Cuba is enough to convince an honest mind of the need and justice of revolution, and of their incompatibility as nations because of their diverse origins and different degrees of development. An honest mind is convinced of the two nations' objectives which cause them to clash due to the violent subjection of the contemporary industrious American island to the backward European fatherland. It is evident in the modern loss of energy involved in the dependency of an agile and upright people in the world's most fraternal and hardworking age. It is evident in a throne that is obliged, because of the vice-ridden individual formation of its decadent majorities, to deny the natural marvel of Cuba and the energy in the Cuban character for working together in an effort to resolve Cuba's own superficial conflicts and those of every nationality in the world.

The harsh and jealous Spanish possessions allied 400 years ago against the harsh but effeminate Moor; unfortunately for Spain, like all conquests fatal to the conqueror, the monarchy became solidified and unified in the conquest of America's barren lands. The crown grew rich on their products, and with permanent possession of the Indies it quieted down, and under the kings employed the soldierly and adventurous population that composed Spain's nationality.

Laborious work on the land and in industries was handed over to the more learned, as a minor occupation, because the temptation of America attracted the most daring and capable men in the country, even from the lower and uncultured classes, and created— at first hopefully and then with satisfaction— a kind of vast and vagabond order of knighthood. The Spaniard, until recently a sober man, always found fighting and letters sufficient nourishment for his extravagant and exuberant life. America became so wide a haven of solid wealth or temporary gain that Spanish national life and personal character molded themselves to its productivity. There, Cuban riches were rediscovered (riches increased by means of commerce, Creole slavery and industriousness), the sources of which, with the loss of the continental colonies, seemed shut off to them. In the Spain of recent times, a tenacious imitation of luxurious modern life— lacking the industry and enterprise which in Europe's brilliant nations create and excuse it— has given the Spanish people more of the necessities of life, without a corresponding increase in the sources of production which in personal affairs continue (in very large part) to be the revenue from Cuba. This is Spain in relation to Cuba.

Meanwhile, what is Cuba?

Ever since the liberal turn of the century, under the guidance of her illustrious men in love with the New World's ideas and practices, Cuba— its insular mind endowed with a singular power of analysis— has been searching among the thoughtful nations and extracting from them an ideal superior to the bitter sweatshop conditions of slavery that so rapidly debased the natives. And when these yearnings for freedom bore fruit in the 1868 revolution, that nation of real men in their first act as a nation liberated the Negro slave who previously gave his master simultaneously an excessive pride and the joys of opulence. Women went off to the mountains dressed in bark cloth to accompany their husbands who were fighting for freedom. And the nation's illustrious men smiled as they burned down the buildings that housed the parchments and imperiousness. The pampered counselors roamed the woods for 10 long years with the Republic at their heels, at times with nothing to eat but wild roots and wild animals. The elegant youths, their rifles slung over their shoulders, sought a rostrum under the trees. The love-prone dandy, in a soul-felt burst of strength, learned to lop off the heads of tyranny with a single stroke of the *machete*. In the silence of the forest, the barefoot marquis buried with his own hands the body of the friend he carried upon his back to the grave. Imperfect as a giant child, the Republic was born out of the old nobility and the smooth-chinned democrats; battles were won where 300 men left 507 enemy dead; planted fields, factories and mills sprang up in the mountains made fertile by the revolution. And when the trend toward localization— brought about to please those inexperienced heroes— isolated and corrupted the war, and unsettled it to the point at which the Spaniard was able to gain ground, the courageous and intelligent Cuban people continued to scatter themselves over the capable countries of the world in the most diverse kinds of work. They came in the persons of many of their supporters to seek comfort in the joys of freedom as practiced by the nations of America, to the eclipse of their own. And in their wearisome life, the Cuban people replaced with the power and substance of work the timidity and distrust which is still noted as a detracting and depressing factor, and a result of slavery, in the elements of Cuban society that have been reared closer to the scaffold and to official vice. Those living in Cuba, the veterans and their children or imitators, were accumulating in painful and useless industriousness, under continuous and scurrilous criticism, the indignation now bursting forth with strength of character at the behest of the patricians of our freedom. From the traditions of her characteristically brilliant and successful men; from a reverence for the martyrs of independence; from long practice in war and exile; from the human power of self-denial and creation, and from the knowledge and exercise of a free and industrious life in the exemplary nations— the true Cuban, white or colored, is appearing in political life. He has a variety of learning and professions, an out-of-date sprightliness and inventiveness, the habit of tolerance and the ability to live with his fellow man, going beyond or at least equaling the sources of discord; for indeed the war and a united effort might have been strangled by a Republic constituted suddenly through artificial political relations between masters and slaves, without the sanction and slow testing of a gradual reality. Tempered in the fires of present-day life, this is what the Cuban people are like. They recognize their natural strength and are eager to share it. They speak the world's living languages and think with facility in the principal ones.

They excel because of their superior culture as second to none in the population centers where there is more opportunity for brilliance, and they have formed a firm, reasonable and enterprising character in their modest children. They have lifted themselves by their own bootstraps—in the face of a submissive and faithless colonial society—as a serene people offering themselves fearlessly to the scrutiny of fair-minded men, sure of their sympathy and approval. And will this Cuban national character, through the culpable acquiescence of free nations, live in bondage to the Spanish need for tribute in order to support the leisured classes in Spain who are escaping from the human community in wealth and idleness—leisured classes who in the 10 years of war were stained to the hilt, and can now be stained once more, with consent or aid from the mother republics, in the purest blood of the Cuban nation?

This character structure of the son of Cuba explains both his capacity for independence, which every honest country that knows him will respect, and such a fondness for his emancipation that it would be unjust to disdain or offend him. The Cuban character also explains the vague tendency of the weak or arrogant Cubans, or those unmindful of their country's energy, to support the island's emerging society and the social dominion with which they had wanted to rule over it, in a foreign power that might unwisely lend itself to intrude in the island's natural domestic struggles, a power favoring Cuba's oligarchic and useless class against its main productive population, the way the French empire favored Maximilian in Mexico. A sensible American republic will never contribute to thus perpetuate, under the false pretext of Cuba's incapacity, the spirit of mastery which political wisdom and humaneness advise uprooting in a people placed by Nature at the peaceful and prosperous crossroads of nations.

The United States, for example, would prefer to contribute to the stability of Cuba's freedom with sincere friendship for its independent people who love the States, and Cuba would make available to the States all its licentiousness, to be an accomplice of a worthless and pretentious oligarchy which had sought there nothing but a way to rapidly acquire local class power—truly infamous in the island—over the superior class, that of its productive fellow citizens. The United States is certainly not where men will dare to seek breeding grounds for oppression. The Cuban's unqualified talent for his calling and his government, and for the performing of duties assigned by his country in humanity's upward climb, took on new life and was to end in the definitive outbreak of war. The Cuban nation was bursting with discontent, bound to a master of incorrigible national composition, and is paying (with almost the entire proceeds from its scorned productivity in the endless struggle between Spanish interests— powerless to shut off the only market for Spain in the island— and the reprisals of the American Union) not only the current opprobrious obligations of the American Union's rapacious occupation because of the greed which is stagnating that union, but is also paying the debt contracted by Spain to drown it in blood during the ten years of the 1868 independence war. And Cuba is paying the debts of every one of the wars undertaken by Spain in America after the independence of Spain's own colonies and the United States, so that Spain may reestablish its European monarchic dominion in the free American republics. Even the expenses of the African colony must be met by Cuba. And to that confessed tax, much more bitter than the tax upon tea which caused Boston to rise in rebellion, is added the island's silent tax which its inhabitants— Cubans and Spaniards alike— are paying to those commissioned by law to mock them or make them comply. In Cuba not even the law is recognized without a tax, nor does blame fall upon the delinquent who is able to buy his redemption; and public immorality is so common that an intimate friendship with the thief, and daily connivance with him, come to resemble stainless acts to those who boast of being honest. Spanish vice is making the island decay. And the taxes from which the Spanish political class derives its main support weigh upon Cuba like the double hardship of expenditure and dishonor.

It is lawful to desire that Cuba employ in its own development, to the obvious advantage of the nations around it, the money it pays to maintain over itself the government that corrupts it. Cuba welcomes upon its own soil, with the forcible exclusion of its sons, the needy Spaniard who is fleeing his miserable nation by the boatload to dislodge the Cuban in Cuba from his workbench and from ownership of his land. When the Cuban war broke off in 1878 because of its own fatigue, the farsighted revolutionaries understood that the irremediable fabric of the Spanish nation, based upon its possession of the colonies, would prevent Spain from granting any political reforms foreign to its nature or hostile to its interests—reforms which a party of Cuban pacifists have been demanding for 17 years with no more success than the gaining of changes brought about by one of the island's advisory bodies which has neither authority nor sanction. Because this advisory body is composed principally of privileged Spanish authorities and an intimidated minority of Cuban nobility, it will never propose for the island any relief at all that is counter to Spanish interests or a threat to its own special privileges. The revolution had come with an elected, republican-based party, preparing in an orderly manner all the vital elements of Cuban independence, for the purpose of holding them at the point of action for the instant when, hopeless of any Spanish reforms, the definitive and immortal revolution would burst forth with a single voice, without reservation or retreat. Two generations: the veterans and their sons; two forces for independence: the combatants of the island and those from abroad to help them fight, joined forces for three years of organization in the enthusiasm of wisdom and the power of discipline. The entire island of Cuba, radically convinced of Spain's unwillingness to deprive itself of the colonial exploitation supporting it, and its reluctance to give the Cubans a better life, political and otherwise, rose in arms on February 24, 1895, not to lay its guns aside until the triumph of the Republic.

What obstacle could be encountered by this revolution born of the Cuban's conviction of his aptitude for work and government; born of the bloody payment of his finest sweat to the vice-ridden politicians and indolent nationals of the country which expels the sons of the soil in order to settle the privileged Spaniard upon their small piece of land? The revolution springs from the perennial memory, aroused by daily reasons for anger, of those extraordinary men who rescued their slaves from leg irons and arose from their rich man's armchairs to break the Spanish scepter with their bare hands. It came into being because of the Cuban's devout and ineffable yearning for the spiritual integration of the uncultured Creole whose natural luster perishes when not put to use, or whose disheveled family runs away to the hills out of fear of not having paid the tyrant his taxes. What obstacles could such a revolution encounter? The present composition of Cuba's forces demonstrates that the high-minded revolution— which will regard the timidity of the sluggish Cubans indulgently, and watch over the dignity of all the social forces— will easily defeat an enemy whose discontented and partially formed army fights unwillingly in war against freedom, and whose treasury can no longer bind the island as it did 25 years ago. For it cannot even shoulder its regular burdens, or approach the well-to-do Spaniard who denies to the war the fortune he put into safekeeping in the mother country, or, as in 1868, seized the property of Cubans who were wealthy then but are poor now. Cuba has both Spanish and Cuban populations. Out of the Spanish population, that element which, caught by its wealth in the sudden revolution of Yara, profited (for the now fewer masses of voluntaries) from the rancor of the more abject Spaniards against the Creole who considered them master, is already dead due to the indifference of its liberal and Creole-minded compatriots to the system of hatred and punishment.

And in those same masses that social anger, secret base of political ferocity, has diminished if not disappeared with the general suffering under the tyranny of Cubans and Spaniards alike. Out of that same class much has been drawn together in the heart of Cuba, with wife and children and a certain well-being. And if out of an unjust fear, those Cubans by adoption are still turning their eyes to the North, as if looking for protection from the reprisals of the Cuban Republic which will never occur, they will turn them, no longer ashamed and repentant, to the guns which they would have to hold against the breasts of their sons. In the presence of war, Cubans bow to the general law of human nature which leads generous men, cultured or uncultured, to the side of sacrifice— humanity's purest joy— and keeps the egoists— the world's obstacles— from the side of those who make the sacrifices. Political titles are new garments for this condition where men draw apart; and the success of religions and republics, carrying much religious fervor in their humane piety, points out that the stubborn driving force of the disconsolate, and the farsighted wisdom that makes use of this strength which might otherwise drift away, can always accomplish more than a shamefaced loathing for the sores of the poor, and the fondness of sedentary men for their house slippers and the sinecures of life. And the Cuban

Negro— who finds relief from social separation in his own culture and in his friendship for the fair-minded white man, and who does not divide white men and Negroes any more than the ancient nations of the world divided nobles and peasants— will rebel only against the one who supposes him capable of attempting a crime, because of the anger which would reveal his true inferiority, against the peace of his country.

On soil enriched by the sister death of servants and masters, the sublime emancipation of slaves by their Cuban masters erased all hatred for slavery. It is a singular honor for the Cuban nation, of which one must respectfully ask recognition, that without demagogic flattery or a hasty mixture of the different degrees of culture, she now shows the observer a freed man more cultured and devoid of rancor than that of any other nation on earth. Closer to freedom, the Negro peasant flies to his rifle, which in the 10 years of war he has never used in defiance of the law, and is known purely for the joyful love with which he greets— and the tenderness with which he regards— the man with the complexion of a master who walks at his side, or behind him, in defense of freedom. The only nations having anything to fear from justice are those refusing to practice it. The crime of slavery must be purged with at least the sufficiently mild penance of some social mortification. From the free Cuban countryside, at the edge of the grave where we bury white and Negro heroes together, we proclaim that among humankind one can hardly breathe fresher or more blameless air than that which in a spirit of reverence surrounds both Negroes and white men alike upon the road that leads from common worth to affection and peace.

With the power of this justice; with the force of indignation felt by the son of Cuba under the oppression and hardships with which Spain punished it in the war of independence and denied the most insignificant reforms in 17 years of a useless policy of waiting; with the responsibility of Cuba's duty in the work of alliance and action for which, at the meeting-point of oceans the nations of the globe, are preparing— from one end of their land to the other the Cubans, bearing no hatred for their oppressor and by the strict methods of an enlightened war, have again demanded of the ultimate fairness of guns the status of a Republic, one which will permit the son of Cuba to use his character and aptitudes and give him the right to open his sealed-off land to full commerce with those nations which Nature has placed at its doorstep, a right that is attracting the Cuban's general ability; for the Cuban stands second to none in the pride and order of liberty.

Fully aware of their obligations to America and to the world, the Cuban people today are bleeding from the Spanish bullet because of their task of opening to three continents the independent Republic which in a land of men will offer to mankind a friendly home and free trade.

We ask for no assistance here from Spanish America, because whatever nation refuses it to us will be endorsing its own dishonor. We silently show to the people of the United States, so they may do what they should, these legions of men who are fighting for what they fought for yesterday—legions marching unaided to the conquest of the freedom which is to open to the United States the island which Spanish interests are closing to it. Certain of the answer, we yet ask the world if it considers indifferent or impious the human spirit by which a generous nation is sacrificing itself to become accessible to that world.

In proof of the high purposes and cultured methods of Cuba's War for Independence, and in testimony of their singular gratitude to the *New York Herald*, the Delegate of the Cuban Revolutionary Party and the Commander-in-Chief of the Army of Liberation, duly empowered until the present date as representatives-elect of the revolution, do hereby affix their signatures.

The Delegate
José Martí

The Commander-in-Chief
Máximo Gómez

To Manuel Mercado

Dos Ríos Camp, May 18, 1895

Mr. Manuel Mercado

My dearest brother,

Now I can write, now I can tell you how tenderly and gratefully and respectfully I love you and that home which I consider my pride and responsibility. I am in daily danger of giving my life for my country and duty, for I understand that duty and have the courage to carry it out—the duty of preventing the United States from spreading through the Antilles as Cuba gains its independence, and from overpowering with that additional strength our lands of America. All I have done so far, and all I will do, is for this purpose. I have had to work quietly and somewhat indirectly, because to achieve certain objectives, they must be kept under cover; to proclaim them for what they are would raise such difficulties that the objectives could not be attained.

The same general and lesser duties of these nations—nations such as yours and mine that are most vitally concerned with preventing the opening in Cuba (by annexation on the part of the imperialist from there and the Spaniards) of the road that is to be closed, and is being closed with our blood, annexing our American nations to the brutal and turbulent North which despises them—prevented their apparent adherence and obvious assistance to this sacrifice made for their immediate benefit.

I have lived in the monster and I know its entrails; my sling is David's. At this very moment—well, some days ago—amid the cheers of victory with which the Cubans saluted our free departure from the mountains where the six men of our expedition walked for 14 days, a correspondent from the *Herald*, who tore me out of the hammock in my hut, told me about the annexationist movement. He claimed it was less to be feared because of the unrealistic approach of its aspirants, undisciplined or uncreative men of a legalistic turn of mind, who in the comfortable disguise of their complacency or their submission to Spain, halfheartedly ask it for Cuba's autonomy. They are satisfied merely that there be a master— Yankee or Spanish— to support them or reward their services as go-betweens with positions of power, enabling them to scorn the hardworking masses— the country's half-breeds, skilled and pathetic, the intelligent and creative hordes of Negroes and white men.

And that *Herald* correspondent, Eugene Bryson, told me more: about a Yankee syndicate, endorsed by the customs authorities who are too closely associated with the rapacious Spanish banks to be involved with those of the North, a syndicate fortunately unable, because of its sinewy and complex political structure, to undertake or support the idea as a government project. And Bryson continued talking, although the truth of his reports could be understood only by a person with firsthand knowledge of the determination with which we have mustered the revolution, of the disorganization, indifference, and poor pay of the untried Spanish army, and of Spain's inability to gather, in or out of Cuba, the resources to be used against the war, resources which it had obtained the time before from Cuba alone. Bryson recounted his conversation with Martínez Campos,[1] at the end of which Martínez Campos gave him to understand that, at the proper time, Spain would doubtless prefer to come to terms with the United States than hand the island to the Cubans. And Bryson had still more to tell me: about an acquaintance of ours whom the North is grooming as a candidate from the United States for the presidency of Mexico when the term of the president now in office expires.

I am doing my duty here. The Cuban war, a reality of higher priority than the vague and scattered desires of the Cuban and Spanish annexationists, whose alliance with the Spanish government would only give them relative power, has come to America in time to prevent Cuba's annexation to the United States, even against all

---

[1] Martínez Campos was the commander of Spanish armed forces during the first Cuban War of Independence (1868-78) and was recalled to Cuba when the revolution began in 1895.

those freely used forces. The United States will never accept from a country at war, nor can it incur, the hateful and absurd commitment of discouraging, on its account and with its weapons, an American war of independence, for the war will not accept annexation.

And Mexico, will it not find a wise, effective and immediate way of helping, in due time, its own defender? It will indeed, or I shall find one for it. This is a life-and-death matter, and there is no room for error. The prudent way is the only way worth considering. I would have found it and proposed it. But I must have more authority placed in me, or know who has it, before acting or advising. I have just arrived. The formation of our utilitarian yet simple government can still take two more months, if it is to be stable and realistic. Our spirit is one, the will of the country, and I know it. But these things are always a matter of communication, influence and accommodation. In my capacity as representative, I do not want to do anything that may appear to be a capricious extension of it. I arrived in a boat with General Máximo Gómez and four others. I was in charge of the lead oar during a storm and we landed at an unknown quarry on one of our beaches. For 14 days I carried my rifle and knapsack, marching through bramble patches and over hills. We gather people along the way. In the benevolence of men's souls I feel the root of my affection for their suffering, and my just desire to eliminate it. The countryside is unquestionably ours to the extent that in a single month I could hear but one blast of gunfire. And at the gates of the cities we either won a victory, or reviewed 3,000 troops in the face of an enthusiasm resembling religious fervor. We continued on our way to the center of the island where, in the presence of the revolution which I instigated, I laid aside the authority given me by the settlements abroad and acknowledged by the island, and which an assembly of delegates from the Cuban people— revolutionaries in arms— must replace in accord with the new conditions. The revolution desires complete freedom in the army, without the obstacles previously raised by a Chamber without real sanction, without the distrust of its republicanism by a suspicious faction of the young, and without the jealousy and fears, which could become too great a threat in the future, of a punctilious or prophetic leader. But at the same time, the revolution is eager for a concise and respectable republican representation—the same decent spirit of humanity, filled with a desire for individual dignity in representing the Republic, as that which encourages and maintains the revolutionaries in this war. As for me, I realize that a nation cannot be led counter to or without the spirit that motivates it; I know how human hearts are inspired, and how to make use of a confident and impassioned state of mind to keep enthusiasm at a constant pitch and ready for the attack. But with respect to forms, many ideas are possible, and in matters of men, there are men to carry them out. You know me. In my case, I defend only what I consider a guarantee of, or a service to, the revolution. I know how to disappear. But my thoughts will never disappear, nor will my obscurity leave me embittered. The moment we take shape, we will proceed; trust this to me and to others.

And now, having dealt with national interests, I will talk about myself, since only the emotion of this duty could raise from a much-desired death the man who, now that Nájera does not live where you can see him, knows him better and cherishes as his heart's delight that friendship with which you fill him with pride.

I know his silent gestures of annoyance, after my voyage. And however much we told him, from the bottom of our hearts, there was no response! What a fraud he is, and how callous that soul of his, that the honor and tribute of our affection has not moved him to write one more letter on the paper of the maps or newspapers that fill our day!

There are affections of such fragile honesty...[2]

[2] It is supposed that Martí stopped writing this letter to continue with it later, but he could never finish it.

PART 3

Verse

Ismaelillo

José Martí dedicated this book of poems to his son José Francisco, born in 1878. It was almost entirely written in Caracas, Venezuela, and published in New York, in 1881. It undoubtedly stands out as original among the emphatic and verbose Latin American literature of that time, for its freshness and wholesome candor, as well as for the atmosphere of candid tenderness that supports its lyricism.

Dedication

Son,

Alarmed by everything, I take refuge in you.

I have faith in human improvement, in life in the future, in the value of truth and in you.

If anyone should tell you that these pages are similar to others, tell them that I love you too much to profane you in that way. The things I depict for you here are just the way I saw them. You have appeared to me in those fancy trappings. When I have ceased to see you in one way, I've stopped depicting you. Those rivulets have passed through my heart.

May they reach yours!

Little Prince

This party is for
A little prince.
He has long hair,
Soft blond hair
That hangs over
His white shoulders.
His eyes appear
To be black stars
That move like the wind,
Shine, quiver and give off sparks.
He is my crown,
My pillow and my spur.
My hand, that bridles
Horses and hyenas,
Goes where e'er he takes it.
When he frowns, I tremble.
If he complains,
My face, like a woman's,
Turns white as snow,
Then red, as blood
Pours through my veins.
His pleasure causes
My blood to ebb and flow.
This party is for
A little prince.

Come, my gentleman;
Come this way.
Come, my tyrant,
Into this cave.
When he appears
Within my sight,
It seems a pale star
Casts its opal
Brilliance o'er all
In a dark cavern.

When he goes by
The shade acquires textures
Like the sun,
That wounds the blackest clouds.
Behold me, then, at arms
In the struggle.
The little prince
Wants me to fight again.
He is my crown,
My pillow and my spur.
And, just as the sun,
Breaking up the black clouds,
Turns shadows
Into bands of colors,
When he touches the thick wave,
He embroiders
My red and violet
Battle colors there.
So, my master wants
To return to life?
Come, my gentleman;
Come this way.
Come, my tyrant,
Into this cave.
Let me offer life
To him, to him.
This party is for
A little prince.

Fierce Horseflies

Come, fierce horseflies.
Come, jackals.
Move your proboscises and teeth.
Let the hordes attack
Like tigers do their prey.
Besiege me now and leap.
Here, green envy.
You, bite me
On both my lips.
Suck my blood and stain me.
Here, blindfolded,
Voracious jealousy!
And you, gold coin,
Dealers in virtue
Everywhere,
Deal in me!
Pleasure has killed Honor.
Come to me and kill.

Each with his weapon
Rises, does battle:
Pleasure, with his goblet;
The agile virgin,
With her friendly hands
Covered with myrrh.
Let the devil beat me
With his silver sword;
That blinding sword
Should not blind me.

Let the horde
Of attackers
Deafen me.
Let the plumed helmets
Shine like dazzling snow
On mountains of gold.
Let them launch hosts
Of steel-clad warriors
And banners, as the clouds
Loose drops of rain.
Let the green back
Of the land, broken
At the time of crisis,
Be covered with
Golden giants.
Let us fight, not by the light
Of the gentle sun
But by the fatal flash
Of weapons.
Let red lightning
Slash the fog.
Let the trees
Shake free their roots.
Let the mountains
Throw their foothills up
Like wings.
Let there be clamor
As if, at the same instant,
All souls would drop
Their bodily prisons
About their feet.
Let me gird myself
Against the sharp,
Threatening lances.
Let the blood flow down my skin
In thin threads
Like red asps.
Let the brown jackals

Sharpen their teeth in the mud.
Let the stubborn horsefly
File its flying sting.
Bite me on both my lips.
My talismans are coming;
Yes, they come.
Those giants
Have come like clouds,
And, light as clouds,
They'll fly away.

Toothless envy will go
With dry throat,
Hungry, through deserts
And calcined valleys,
The pruning seasons gnawing away
Its emaciated ranks.
The terrible devil
Will be garbed in gold,
With broken knife
In tired fist.
Tearful Beauty
Will go with cries of pain
To cloak her vain striving.
And, smiling,
I will bathe
My wounds
In the cool water
Of a friendly stream.

I watch those wary,
Dazzling carapaces
Disappear
In a radiant cloud.
The wings
Of the helmeted hosts
Stir and struggle,
Bearing all that golden cloud
Away.
Then a mysterious wind
Drags the waving pennants
Across the grass
Like colorful serpents.
The land suddenly splits
Into colossal crevices
And throws its green back
Upon the giants.
Horseflies, jackals,
Run and fly,
And the field is filled
With a fragrant vapor.
From the blind defeat
Frightful shouts evoking
Silenced captains
Can be heard
And the rough mane
Is stroked.
In the valley, the battle,
Like a buzzard, dies.
Meanwhile, smiling,
I stanch my wounds
In the cool water
Of a friendly stream.

I do not fear
Powerful armies,
Old temptations
Or voracious virgins.
The horsefly buzzes round me.
It turns; it halts and strikes.
Here, it raises up a shield.
There, it brandishes a club.
To left and right
The long sword breaks and scatters.
On its small shield
A hail of arrows falls.
It shakes them off
And then resumes attack.
Now they fly; yes, they fly:
Horseflies, giants,
With a crackling sound
Of iron that is rent.
Flashing sparks
Now fill the air.
Daggers and broadswords
Carpet the ground.
Horseflies, jackals:
Flying and hiding.
Like a bee, the horsefly buzzes.
It parts and moves the air.
It halts, hovers and leaves
The echo of a bird's wings.
It touches my hair,
Alights on my shoulder,
Crosses to my side
And dives into my lap.
Now, the enemy is routed;
Cowardly, it flees.
Sons, strong shields
Of exhausted sires.

Come, my knight,
My airborne knight.
Come, my naked,
Wingéd warrior.
Let us seek
That friendly stream
And bathe my wounds
In its cool water.
My little knight.
Flying warrior.

Free Verse

This book of poems was not published until 1913 by Gonzálo de Quesada Aróstegui. Written probably between 1878 and 1882, in these verses Martí succeeded in breaking the usual patterns of Cuban poetry with hendecasyllabic verses without consonance, showing him at the summit of his originality as a poet of original expression. Free Verse *emphasizes the renewing drive responsible for the ultimate triumph of Modernism.*

My Poetry

These are my poems. They are what they are. I have not borrowed them from anyone. As long as I could not lock up my visions whole, and in a form worthy of them, I allowed them to fly. Oh, how many golden friends have never returned! But poetry has its honesty, and I have always wanted to be honest. I also know how to trim my poems, but I do not wish to do so. Just as every man has his own physiognomy, every inspiration has its own language. I love the difficult sonorities, the sculptural line: vibrant as porcelain, swift as a bird, scalding and flowing as a tongue of lava. A poem should be like a shining sword that leaves the spectators with memories of a warrior bound for the heavens; when he sheathes his sword in the sun, it breaks into wings.

These poems—my warriors—are cut out of my very entrails. Not one of them has left my mind artfully or warmed over, but rather as tears leave the eyes and blood bubbles out of a wound.

I have not concocted my poems from any others, but tapped them from within myself. They are not written with academic ink, but with my own blood. That which I am giving you to see here, I have seen before, indeed I have, and I have seen much more that escaped before giving me time to set down their features. I myself am to blame for the strangeness, singularity, haste, rage, and piling up of my visions, for I have made them appear before me as I set them down. I found some garments in tatters, others whole, and made use of their colors. I know they are not fashionable. I love sincerity and the difficult sonorities even if they seem brutal.

I already know everything they have to say, and for myself consider it answered. I have wanted to be loyal, and if I have sinned I am not ashamed.

Iron

My bread is earned; make poetry,
Exert your hand in its gentle intercourse—
The hand which, like a fugitive lost
In the dark underbrush, or someone
Bearing a mammoth load unwillingly,
Not long ago was adding sums and juggling ciphers.
Bard, do you wish counsel? Then let
The beguiling harp slip from your pale and bleeding
Shoulder, stifle the sobs
That like an angry sea will flock to your throat,
And on the rich wood surface of a desk
Trim the little feather pens and toss
Your broken harp strings to the blowing winds.

Oh soul, good soul! Yours is a difficult task!
Kneel down, be still, submit, and lick
The sovereign's hands; extol, forgive
Shortcomings, or have them— which is the best way
To forgive them— and, timorous and meek,
Rejoice in wickedness, enshrine the vanities;
Then you shall see, my soul,
Your poor man's empty dish transformed
Into a dish of richest gold!
But be on guard, oh soul,
For men today use tarnished gold!
So pay no heed— the fops and scoundrels
Make their trinkets out of gold,
But not their guns; their guns are made of iron!

My sickness is severe; the city aggravates it;
The vast expanse of country eases it. Another vaster one
Would ease it better! Dark evenings
Draw me to them as if my native land
Were an extended darkness.

Oh friendly poetry,
I die of solitude, of love I die! Not
Of vulgar love affairs; those poison
And confuse. The fruit in woman
Is not beautiful, only the star.
The earth must be illumination, and every living thing
Shed starlight round it! And oh,
These model ladies, these cups
Of flesh, these female serfs before the master
Who gives them jewels and nourishes them as castaways!
I tell you, poetry, partaking of this flesh
Makes the teeth ache!
I die from an ineffable
Love, and from the pleasant
Need of taking— as a tender child
Is taken by caring hands— as much of sadness
And beauty as I can see.

From sleep that only replenishes the forces
Of the fortunate, increasing
The weariness and stubborn dispositions of the sad,
I leap to the sun as if inebriated. Pressing
May hands against my forehead, torrents of tears
Pour from my troubled eyes. I see
The sun so beautiful, my empty room, my useless virtue,
The strength which, like a ravenous herd
Of hairy animals, springs out of me to seek employment.
I touch the empty air, lean my unsteady
Body against the cold and naked wall,
And in my trembling skull
Thoughts float in agony
Like timbers from a shattered ship
Cast by an angry sea upon a burning beach!
None but the flowers of the paternal field
Are fragrant! Only one's native ceiba trees
Give shelter from the sun! One goes about
On foreign soil as in a drifting cloud; mere glances
Seem like insults; and the sun itself,
Instead of shedding pleasant warmth, blazes with rage!

Not with fond voices do echoes
People the winds of other lands, nor do pale
Well-loved spirits fly among the branches
Of dense woodlands!
Men live on living flesh and profaned
Fruits, alas! But exiles
Freed upon their very entrails!

Oppressors, banish those who reach
The honor of your hate; they are already dead!
Far better, oh barbarians, if when
You snatch them from their homes,
Your cruelest bailiff were to plunge his sharpest blade
Into the deepest portions of their honest hearts!
Pleasant it is to die, dreadful to live while dead.
But no! Not so! Happiness is a clement
Gift of fortune to the sad
Who knows not how to master it. Nature
Bestows misfortune upon her finest sons:
As iron fructifies the fields,
The forge shapes iron!

Yoke and Star

When I was born, without the sun, my mother said:
"Flower of my womb, noble Homagno,
Sum and reflection of me and of Creation,
Fish that becomes a bird, a charger, and a man,
Look at these two insignia of life I offer you
In pain; consider them and chose.
This is a yoke; he who accepts it enjoys,
Acts like a gentle ox, and when he lends his services
To gentlemen, sleeps on warm straw
And eats delicious, full-grained oats.
This one, oh mystery born of me
Like a mountain peak from a mountain—
This one, that lights and kills, is a star.
Because it sheds its brilliance, sinners
Flee from those who wear it, and in this life
All those who wear the light remain alone
Like monsters burdened by crimes.
But he who easily imitates an ox
Becomes one, and once again starts up the universal
Ladder like a submissive beast.
He who bravely girds himself with the star,
Since he creates, he grows!

When the living one
Empties his cup of liquor on the world;
When, to feed upon the bloody
Human feast, he gravely and contentedly tears out
His very heart, and casts his sacred word
To the North wind and the South,
The star envelops him with light as with a cloak,
The limpid air burns bright as at some festival,
And the living one who has no fear of living
Is heard to climb another step into the dark!"

Give me the yoke, oh Mother, so when I firmly
Stand upon it, the star that lights and kills
May better shine forth from my countenance.

Bristling Mane

My poetry destroyed— does it rise up
Like the bristling mane of a frightened
Horse that sees the claws and fangs
Of a dreaded wolf beside a dry tree trunk...?
Indeed it does! As when a dagger
Plunges into the neck of a steer,
It rises skyward in a slender thread of blood.
Only love engenders melodies.

Simple Verses

Martí spent the summer of 1890 in the cool of the Catskill Mountains, in upstate New York, to recover his health, very frail at the time. There he reminisced about his life, some episodes of which he reflects in his poetry. Here he brilliantly and synthetically expounds his principles and political beliefs. Published in 1891, Simple Verses *is one of the author's best known works, which includes the poem (I) that has become Cuba's most popular song,* Guantánamera *(Yo soy un hombre sincero/A sincere man am I).*

Prologue

My friends know how these verses came from my heart. It was in that winter of despair, when, due to ignorance or fanatical faith or fear or courtesy, the nations of Latin America met in Washington, under the fearful eagle. Who among us has forgotten that shield, a shield on which the eagle of Monterrey and Chapultepec, the eagle of López and Walker, clutched the flags of all the nations of America in its talons! Nor shall I forget the agony in which I lived, until I could confirm the energy and discretion of our people; nor the horror and shame in which I was kept by the legitimate fear that we Cubans might, with parricidal hands and solely to benefit a new concealed master, assist the senseless plan to separate Cuba from the greater Hispanic fatherland that claimed her for its own and could not be complete without her— such preoccupations sapped what strength was not consumed by unjust sorrows. The doctor sent me off to the mountains: there streams ran, clouds closed-in upon clouds, and I wrote poetry. At times, the sea roars in the dark of the night, and its waves break against the stones of a bloodied castle; and at other times, a bee is humming as it forages among the flowers.

Why publish something so simple, playfully written, and not my windswept *Free Verse*, my hirsute hendecasyllables, born of great fears or great hopes, of the indomitable love of liberty, or of the painful love of beauty, which flows as a rivulet of pure gold amid sand, turbid waters and roots, or as molten iron hissing and shooting off sparks, or as a burning fountain. Or my Cuban verse, so filled with anger that it is best left where it cannot be seen? And all those hidden sins of mine, and all those ingenuous and rebellious examples of literature from my pen? And why make the publication of these wildflowers the occasion for a course on my poetics, or explain why I repeat rhymes on purpose, or classify and group them so that they reach the sentiments by sight and sound, or dispense with them altogether, when a tumultuous idea does not require rhyme or tolerate too many hammer blows! These verses are published because the affection with which they were received by some good souls, during a night of poetry and friendship, has already made them public. And because I love simplicity, and believe in the necessity of putting feelings in plain and sincere form.

New York, 1891.
José Martí

I

A sincere man am I
From the land where palm trees grow,
And I want before I die
My soul's verses to bestow.

I'm a traveler to all parts,
And a newcomer to none;
I am art among the arts,
With the mountains I am one.

I know the strange names of willows,
And can tell flowers with skill:
I know of lies that can kill,
And I know of sublime sorrows.

I have seen through dead of night
Upon my head softly fall,
Rays formed of the purest light
From beauty celestial.

I have seen wings that were surging
From beautiful women's shoulders,
And seen butterflies emerging
From the refuse heap that molders.

I have known a man to live
With a dagger at his side,
And never once the name give
Of she by whose hand he died.

Twice, for an instant, did I
My soul's reflection descried,
Twice: when my poor father died,
And when she bade me goodbye.

I trembled once, when I flung
The vineyard gate, and to my dread,
The dastard hornet had stung
My little girl on the forehead.

Such great luck to me once came
As no man would dare to envy,
When in tears my jailer read me
The death warrant with my name.

I hear a sigh across the earth,
I hear a sigh over the deep:
It is no sigh reaching my hearth,
But my son waking from sleep.

If they say I have obtained
The pick of the jeweler's trove,
A good friend is all I've gained,
And I have put aside love.

I have seen an eagle gliding,
Though wounded, across the skies;
I know the cubby where lies
The snake of its venom dying.

I know that the world is weak
And must soon fall to the ground,
And, then, midst the quiet profound
The gentle brook will speak.

While trembling with joy and dread,
I have touched with hand so bold
A once-bright star that fell dead
From heaven at my threshold.

I have hid in my brave heart
The most terrible of pains,
The son of a land in chains
Lives for it and dies apart.

All is beautiful and right,
All is as music and reason;
And as diamonds 'ere their season,
All is coal before it's light.

I know when fools are laid to rest
Honor and tears will abound,
And that of all fruits, the best
Is left to rot in holy ground.

Without a word, I've understood
And put aside the pompous muse;
From a withered branch, I choose
To hang my doctoral hood.

X

My soul tremulous and lonely
At nightfall will grow forlorn:
There's a show, let us go see
The Spanish dancer perform.

It is well they've taken down
The flag that stood at the entrance;
For I don't think I could go hence
If that banner were still flown.

The Spanish dancer enters then,
Looking so proud and so pale:
"From Galicia does she hail?"
No, they are wrong: she's from heaven.

She wears the matador's tricorne
And also his crimson cape.
A gilliflower to drape
And with a great hat adorn!

On passing her eyebrows show,
Eyebrows of a traitorous Moor:
And the Moor's proud look she wore,
And her ear was white as snow.

The music starts, the lights dim,
In shawl and gown, there advances
The Virgin of the Assumption
Dancing Andalucian dances.

Her head raised in challenge, she
The cape o'er her shoulders will spread:
With her arched arms framing her head,
She taps her foot ardently.

Her studied taps tear the batten,
As if each heel were a blade,
And the stage had been inlaid
With the broken hearts of men.

The festive feeling is burning
In the fire of her eyes,
The red-speckled shawl now flies
In the air as she is turning.

With a sudden leap she starts,
Rebounds, then turns, and bows down:
Wide her cashmere shawl she parts
To offer us her white gown.

All her body yields and sways;
Her open mouth is enticing;
A rose is her mouth: while dancing
She's tapping her heels always.

Then turns she feebly to wind
The long and red-speckled shawl:
And shutting her eyes to all,
In a sigh leaves all behind.

The Spanish dancer has done well;
Red and white was her long shawl:
The tremulous, lonely soul
Withdraws again to its cell!

XXIII

From this world I will depart,
And the natural door will try:
Green leaves will cover the cart
On which I'm taken to die.

Don't in darkness let me lie
With traitors to come undone:
I am good and as the good die,
I will die face to the sun!

XXXIX

I have a white rose to tend
In July as in January;
I give it to the true friend
Who offers his frank hand to me.
And to the cruel one whose blows
Break the heart by which I live,
Thistle nor thorn do I give:
For him, too, I have a white rose.

XLV

I dream of marble cloisters
Where in silence blessed
The standing heroes rest:
At night, by the soul's light,
I speak to them: at night!
They are on file: I pass
Among their ranks: I kiss
Their hands of stone: they open
Their eyes of stone: they move
Their lips of stone: they shake
Their beards of stone: they grasp
Their swords of stone: and weep:
The swords spin in their sheaths!:
Silent, I kiss their hands.

I speak to them at night!
They are on file: I pass
Among the ranks: and weeping too,
Embrace a statue: "Oh, statue,
It's said that your sons drink
The blood of their own veins
In their masters' poisoned cups!
That they speak the foul tongue
Of ruffians! and with them
Eat the bread of opprobrium
At the bloodstained table!
And lose in useless words
Their last fire! It's said,
Oh statue, sleeping statue,
That your race is dead!"

The hero I embraced
Flings himself at me:
He grabs me by the collar:
Sweeps the earth with my head:
And raising his sunlike arm,
The statue speaks: the white hands
Reach for their belts:
And from their pedestals
The men of marble leap!

XLVI

Your sorrows, my heart, you should hide
Where no man can e'er discover,
So that you may spare my pride,
Don't trouble with them another.

I love you, Verse, my friend true,
Because when in pieces torn
My heart's too burdened, you've borne
All my sorrows upon you.

For me you suffer and bear
Upon your amorous lap
The painful love I leave there,
Every anguish, every slap.

As I love, in peace with all,
And do good works, as my goal,
You thrash your waves, rise and fall,
With whatever weighs my soul.

That I may cross with fierce stride,
Pure and without hate, this vale,
You drag yourself, hard and pale,
The loving friend at my side.

And so my life its way will wend
To the sky serene and pure,
While you my sorrows endure
And with divine patience tend.

Because I know this cruel habit
Of throwing myself on you,
Upsets your harmony true
And tries your gentle spirit.

Because on your breast
I've shed all of my sorrows and torments,
And have whipped your quiet currents,
Which are here white and there red,

And then pale as death become,
At once roaring and attacking,
And then beneath the weight cracking
Of pain it can't overcome.

Should I the advice have taken
Of a heart so misbegotten,
Would have me leave you forgotten,
Who never me has forsaken?

Verse, they tell us of One Greater
To whom the dying appealed;
Verse, as one our fates are sealed:
We are damned or saved together!

José Martí: Selected Bibliography

FIRST EDITIONS

Martí, José. *Abdala*. In *Patria libre*. October 23, 1869.
_____. *Adúltera; drama inédito*. Havana, 1935.
_____. Ral, Adelaida (pseud.). *Amistad funesta*, New York, 1885.
_____. *Amor con amor se paga; Proverbio en un acto*. Mexico, 1876.
_____. *Flores del destierro (versos inéditos)*. Edited by Gonzalo de Quesada y Miranda. Havana, 1933.
_____. *Ismaelillo*. New York, 1882.
_____. *Ismaelillo, Versos sencillos, Versos libres*. Havana, 1913, V. XI. of *Obras del Maestro*.
_____. *Versos sencillos*. New York, 1891.

POETRY

Martí, José. *Poesías completas*. Edited by Rafael Esténger. Madrid, 1953.
_____. *Poesías de José Martí*. Prologue, edition and notes by Juan Marinello. Havana, 1928.
_____. *Versos de amor*. (inéditos). Collected and edited by Gonzalo de Quesada y Miranda. Havana, 1930.
_____. *Versos sencillos*. Prologue by Gabriela Mistral. Havana, 1939.
_____. *Poesía completa*. A critical edition. Editorial Letras Cubanas. Havana, 1985. 2 vols.

PROSE

Martí, José. *Amistad funesta* (novela). Edited by Gonzalo de Quesada y Aróstegui. Leipzig, 1911. Vol. X of *Obras del Maestro*.
______. *Epistolario*. Editorial de Ciencas Sociales. Havana, 1993. 5 vols.
______. *Artículos desconocidos*. Prologue by Félix Lizaso. Havana, 1930.

______. *Cartas a Manuel A. Mercado.* Mexico, 1946.

______. *Epistolario de José Martí.* Edition, introduction and notes by Félix Lizaso. Havana, 1930–1931. 3 vols.

______. *Nuevas cartas de Nueva York.* Edited by E. Mejía Sánchez. Mexico, 1980.

______. *Obras escogidas.* Selection, prologue and notes by Rafael Esténger. Madrid, 1973.

TRANSLATIONS BY MARTI

Antigüedades clásicas I. Antigüedades griegas. By J. H. Mahafy. New York, 1883.

Antigüedades clásicas II. Antigüedades romanas. By A. S. Wilkings. New York, 1883.

Mis hijos (*Mes fils*) by Victor Hugo. *Revista Universal.* Mexico, March 12, 1875.

Misterio . . . (*Called Back*). By Hugh Conway. New York, 1886.

Nociones de lógica. By William Stanley Jevons. New York, 1886.

Ramona, novela americana. By Helen Hunt Jackson. New York, 1888.

"La Rima". Original sonnet by Augusto de Armas, translated into prose by José Martí. *Ahora.* Havana, October 17, 1934.

"El Tejedor". Original poem by Enrique Heine. *Ahora.* Havana, January 27, 1935.

MAGAZINES EDITED BY MARTI

La edad de oro: Publicación mensual de recreo e instrucción dedicada a los niños de América. New York, V. I, 1–4. July–October 1889. Director: José Martí. Editor: Da Costa Gómez.

COLLECTED WORKS (COMPLETE)

Martí, José. *Diario de Campaña.* Editorial de Ciencas Sociales. Havana, 1985.

_____. *Nuestra América.* Edición crítica. Centro de Estudios Martianos y Casa de las Américas. Havana, 1991.

_____. *Obras del Maestro.* Ed. Gonzalo de Quesada y Aróstegui.

Havana, 1900–1933. 16 volumes.
_____. *Obras completas de Martí.* Ed. N. Carbonell. Havana, 1918–1920. 8 volumes.
_____. *Obras completas de José Martí.* Prólogo: Armando Godoy and Ventura García Calderón. París, 1925.
_____. *Obras completas.* Prólogo: Alberto Ghiraldo. Madrid, 1925. 8 volumes.
_____. *Obras completas de José Martí.* Paris, 1926. 2 volumes.
_____. *Obras completas.* Ed. Gonzalo de Quesada y Miranda. Havana, 1936–1953. 74 volumes.
_____. *Obras completas.* Prológo y biografía: M. Isidro Méndez. Editorial Lex. Havana, 1946. 2 volumes.
_____. *Obras completas.* Havana, 1963–1973. 28 volumes.
_____. *Obras completas.* Edición critica. Centro de Estudios Martianos. Havana, 1983– . 3 volumes.

TRANSLATIONS

Martí, José. *The America of José Martí: Selected Writings.* Ed. Juan de Onís. The Noonday Press. New York, 1953.
_____. *Martí on the U.S.A.* Selected and translated with an introduction by Luis A. Baralt. Southern Illinois University Press. Carbondale, 1966.
_____. *Inside the Monster, by José Martí. Writings on the United States and American Imperialism.* Translated by Elinor Randall, with additional translations by Luis A. Baralt, Juan de Onís and Roslyn Held Foner. Edition, introduction and notes by Philip S. Foner. Monthly Review Press. New York, 1975.
_____. *Our America: Writings on Latin America and the Struggle for Cuban Independence.* Edition and Introduction by Philip S. Foner. Monthly Review Press. New York, 1977.
_____. *On Education: Articles on Educational Theory and Pedagogy and Writings for Children from The Age of Gold by José Martí.* Translated by Elinor Randall. Introduction and notes by Philip S. Foner. Monthly Review Press. New York, 1979.
_____. *Major Poems.* A Bilingual edition. Translated by Elinor Randall. Edition and Introduction by Philip S. Foner. Holmes and Meier Publishers. New York, 1982.

_____. *On Art and Literature: Critical Writings.* Edition and Introduction by Philip S. Foner. Monthly Review Press. New York, 1982.

JOURNALS DEVOTED TO MARTI

Anuario del Centro de Estudios Martianos. Havana, 1978–.
Anuario Martiano. Havana, 1969–1978.
Archivo José Martí. Havana, 1940–1953. 6 volumes.

BIBLIOGRAPHIES

Blanch y Blanco, Celestino. *Bibliografía Martiana* (1954–1963). Havana, 1965.

González, Manuel Pedro. *Fuentes para el estudio de José Martí*. Havana, 1950.

Peraza Sarausa, Fermín. *Bibliografía martiana* (1940–1952). Havana, 1954.

Ripoll, Carlos. *Archivo José Martí*. New York, 1971.

_____. *Indice universal de la obra de José Martí*. New York, 1971.

REBEL LIVES

A new series from Ocean Press

SLOVO

The Unfinished Autobiography of ANC Leader Joe Slovo

A revealing and highly entertaining autobiography of one of the key figures of South Africa's African National Congress. As an immigrant, a Jew, a communist, a guerrilla fighter and political strategist — and white — few public figures in South Africa were as demonized by the apartheid government as Joe Slovo.

Introduction by Nelson Mandela.

ISBN 1-875284-95-8

I WAS NEVER ALONE

A Prison Diary from El Salvador

by Nidia Díaz

Nidia Díaz (born María Marta Valladares) gives a dramatic and inspiring personal account of her experience as a guerrilla commander during El Salvador's civil war. Seriously wounded, she was captured in combat in 1985 by Cuban-exile CIA agent Félix Rodríguez. More than a moving testimony of a political prisoner, this book shows how an individual can survive extreme brutality and isolation. Nidia Díaz was the FMLN's Vice-Presidential candidate in 1999.

ISBN 1-876175-17-6

CHE — A MEMOIR BY FIDEL CASTRO

Preface by Jesús Montané

Edited by David Deutschmann

For the first time Fidel Castro writes with candor and affection of his relationship with Ernesto Che Guevara, documenting his extraordinary bond with Cuba from the revolution's early days to the final guerrilla expeditions to Africa and Bolivia. Castro vividly portrays Che — the man, the revolutionary and the thinker — and describes in detail his last days with Che in Cuba, giving a remarkably frank assessment of the Bolivian mission.

ISBN 1-875284-15-X

REBEL LIVES

A new series from Ocean Press

MY EARLY YEARS

by Fidel Castro

Introductory essay by Gabriel García Márquez

In the twilight of his life, Fidel Castro, one of the century's most controversial figures, reflects on his childhood, youth and student activism. In an unprecedented and remarkably candid manner, the Cuban leader describes his family background, his childhood and education at elite Catholic schools, and the religious and moral influences that led to his involvement in politics as a youth.

ISBN 1-876175-07-9

PRIEST AND PARTISAN

A South African Journey of Father Michael Lapsley

by Michael Worsnip

The story of Father Michael Lapsley, an anti-apartheid priest who became the target of a South African letter bomb attack in 1990 in which he lost both hands and an eye.

Foreword by Nelson Mandela

ISBN 1-875284-96-6

CHE IN AFRICA

Che Guevara's Congo Diary

by William Gálvez

Che Guevara disappeared from Cuba in 1965 to lead a guerrilla mission to Africa in support of liberation movements. Considerable speculation has always surrounded Guevara's departure from Cuba and why he went to fight in Africa. *Che in Africa* is the previously untold story of Che Guevara's "lost year" in Africa.

ISBN 1-876175-08-7

40 YEARS OF THE CUBAN REVOLUTION

A new series from Ocean Press

CUBA AND THE UNITED STATES
A Chronological History
by Jane Franklin

Based on exceptionally wide research, this updated and expanded chronology by U.S. historian Jane Franklin relates day by day, year by year, the developments involving the two neighboring countries from the 1959 Cuban revolution through 1995. An introductory section chronicles the history of Cuba from the time of the arrival of Christopher Columbus.

ISBN 1-875284-92-3

CUBAN REVOLUTION READER
A Documentary History
Edited by Julio García Luis

An outstanding new anthology documenting the past four decades of Cuban history and its tumultuous revolution. This Reader presents a comprehensive overview of the key moments in the Cuban Revolution: including events on the island and Cuba's impact abroad in Latin America, Central America and Africa. Most of the materials are published in English for the first time and contributors include Fidel Castro, Che Guevara, Carlos Rafael Rodriguez and Raul Castro. It provides an unprecedented documentary history of the Cuban Revolution in the years 1959-98, edited by one of Cuba's most prominent journalists and historians.

ISBN 1-876175-10-9

A NEW SOCIETY
Che Guevara on the Cuba Years 1959-65
Edited by David Deutschmann

This book is the product of Guevara's experience as the President of the National Bank, the Minister of Industry and as a central figure in the Cuban revolutionary government in the years 1959-65.

40 YEARS OF THE CUBAN REVOLUTION

A new series from Ocean Press

FIDEL CASTRO READER

Edited by Mirta Muñiz and Pedro Alvarez Tabío

The voice of one of the 20th century's most controversial political figures — as well as one of the world's greatest orators — is captured in this new selection of Castro's key speeches over the past four decades.

Through his mastery of the spoken word, Fidel Castro reveals the unfolding process of the Cuban revolution, its extraordinary challenges and numerous crises, its chaos and achievements.

ISBN 1-876175-11-7

CHE GUEVARA READER

Writings on Guerrilla Strategy, Politics and Revolution

Edited by David Deutschmann

This book presents the most comprehensive selection of Guevara's writings ever to be published in English.

This wide-ranging selection of Guevara's speeches and writings provides an opportunity to assess Guevara's contribution to the Cuban revolution in its early years. As the most authoritative collection to date of the work of Guevara, the book is an unprecedented source of primary material on Cuba and Latin America in the 1950s and 1960s. It includes an extensive chronology, glossary and a complete bibliography of Guevara's writings.

ISBN 1-875284-93-1

PSYWAR ON CUBA

The Declassified History of U.S. Anti-Castro Propaganda

Edited by Jon Elliston

Newly declassified CIA and U.S. Government documents are reproduced here, with extensive commentary providing the history of Washington's 40-year campaign of psychological warfare and propaganda to destabilize Cuba and undermine its revolution.

ISBN 1-876175-09-5

BOOKS ABOUT LATIN AMERICA TODAY
from Ocean Press

LATIN AMERICA: From Colonization to Globalization
Noam Chomsky in Conversation with Heinz Dieterich
In a series of new interviews by Mexican-based academic Heinz Dieterich, Noam Chomsky addresses some of the major political issues confronting Latin America today. This book will be indispensable for those interested in Latin America and the politics of the region.
ISBN 1-876175-13-3

AFROCUBA
An Anthology of Cuban Writing on Race, Politics and Culture
edited by Pedro Pérez Sarduy and Jean Stubbs
What is it like to be Black in Cuba? Does racism exist in a revolutionary society that claims to have abolished it? How does the legacy of slavery and segregation live on in today's Cuba? *AfroCuba* looks at the Black experience in Cuba through the eyes of the island's writers, scholars and artists. The collection mixes poetry, fiction, political analysis and anthropology, producing a multi-faceted insight into Cuba's rich ethnic and cultural reality.
ISBN 1-875284-41-9

CUBA: TALKING ABOUT REVOLUTION
Conversations with Juan Antonio Blanco by Medea Benjamin
A frank discussion on the current situation in Cuba, this book presents an all-too-rare opportunity to hear the voice of one of the island's leading intellectuals. Blanco discusses the fall of the Soviet Union and its impact on Cuba. This expanded edition features a new chapter by Juan Antonio Blanco, "Cuba: 'socialist museum' or social laboratory?"
ISBN 1-875284-97-7

Ocean Press, GPO Box 3279, Melbourne 3001, Australia
● Fax: 61-3-9372 1765 ● E-mail: ocean_press@msn.com.au
Ocean Press, PO Box 834, Hoboken, NJ 07030 USA
● Fax: 1-201-617 0203